Educate Toward Recovery:

Turning the Tables on Autism

A Teaching Manual for the

Verbal Behavior Approach to ABA.

By

Robert Schramm, MA, BCBA

www.pro-aba.com

Although this book is intended for parents and therapists of children with autism spectrum disorder, the authors and publisher must emphasize that the information in the field of Behaviorism is ever growing and changing. While the opinions and techniques contained herein are the cumulative effect of the author's efforts, the author, publisher or producer can accept no responsibility for the implementation of the contents of the work. Consumers are advised to consult with the professional guidance of a trained and certified behavior analyst before beginning any therapy/education program that includes these techniques.

For more information on the author or the institute

Knospe-ABA please visit the website, *www.knospe-aba.com.*

A German version of "Educate Toward Recovery" called

"Motivation und Verstärkung" is available at *www.pro-aba.com.*

Spanish and Italian versions of "Educate Toward Recovery"

are available at www.lulu.com/knospe-aba

ISBN 978-1-84799-146-1

www.pro-ABA.com

Dedication:

There are two very important groups of people, without whom this book would not be possible. The first is the ABA/VB teachers, researchers, and scientists who have helped clear the path that I now navigate. There are far too many to mention them all, but a few that are especially noteworthy are: Vincent J. Carbone, ED.D, James Partington, Ph.D., Mark Sundberg, Ph.D., Patrick McGreevey, Ph.D., Jack Michael, Ph.D., and, of course, B.F. Skinner, Ph.D. Without their hard work and scientific study it would be impossible for my teaching to be as successful and rewarding as it is.

Just as important are the parents of children with autism who have allowed us to take part in the efforts of their family. As the parent of a child in need, you have entered into a foreign place with the bravery and humility to ask for help. Nadine and I will always carry in our hearts the joy your families have brought us.

Acknowledgments:

I thank, Elizabeth Giangrego, Eugene Catrambone, and J. Michaels for their editorial assistance and advice, as well as, Kevin Corcoran for his support with the cover design. In addition, I thank my wife Nadine. Without her love and support, this book and our institute, Knospe-ABA would not have been possible.

A Note to Behavior Analysts

The purpose of this book is to introduce the important sciences of Applied Behavior Analysis and Verbal Behavior to parents, teachers, and therapists of children with autism who are facing important educational issues without formal training. This book is not intended for working behavior analysts. As a Board Certified Behavior Analyst who is extremely successful teaching the use of behavioral principles to non-behaviorists, I have found that the biggest roadblock in our ability to share the important aspects of our science with the parents who need it most is our insistence on detailing interactions beyond the practical. This sort of detailed analysis is crucial to offering the very best education possible to an individual child. However, this book is designed to explain to non-behaviorists supporting the education of children with autism why they need these sources of information and how they can obtain them.

This book shows how behavioral theory can be applied by parents, teachers and therapists to help children with autism learn. I purposely offer simplified definitions of complicated concepts and avoid weighing down the text with long explanations of origin and support. In addition, I use terms such as, "willingness," "desire," "attempt," "understand," and "control," when explaining the reasons for our techniques. Although some of these terms have no real behavioral basis, I find that they help to translate scientific behavior speak into everyday language. Parents and teachers who are inundated with the detailed and specific breakdowns of behavior that ABA professionals use to analyze and develop programs for their children are often intimidated by or turned off to our science. What the science of ABA has lacked is a practical guide for parents and other educators to adapt ABA principles and procedures to their daily lives. With this book I recognize that it is our inability to effectively teach our science to those who need it that hinders the education of far too many children. If we want our science to help parents become better teachers to their children with autism, we need to be better teachers when it comes to teaching parents the science of behaviorism. I hope that with this book I am planting seeds of behavioral understanding and appreciation in grounds that previously might not have been exposed to its benefit. In addition to helping families realize the potential in their children, I fully expect this explanation of behavioral usefulness to take root for the betterment of the behavioral sciences, autism intervention, and education in general.

Contents

Introduction

Because the word "expert" conjures a picture of someone who has all the answers and nothing left to learn, I have never been very fond of the title "autism expert." Perhaps the only one who is "expert" in autism is the person who is considered to have autism.

Autism is a label designed to describe a series of specific behaviors exhibited by a group of individuals. Whether we choose to perceive people labeled "autistic" as being other-than-normal or just one part of the normal range of human variance is often a deciding factor on whether we choose to treat or educate them. Since I am not convinced that autism is a separate type of existence, I am not sure that I, or anyone else, can be considered an expert on it. At best I consider myself a behavior analyst, informed autism consultant, and child advocate. Regardless of the number of people with autism I have helped, I have never tried to become an autism expert. I have merely tried to become as well informed as I can on each particular child and apply the best teaching methods I know to his specific needs. In doing so, I hope that I have been able to give every child the benefit of being understood in a way that I would like the world to understand me.

If I use "expert" in quotes, it is merely an acknowledgement of the reality that as professionals, we may know a great deal about the concept of autism, but unless we live with it, the best we can do is identify the signs and symptoms and offer evidence-based strategies to help affected people live fuller lives. Additionally, parents are the only people qualified to ever be considered expert on an individual child. So, please do not take what might appear at first to be a blatant disregard for the professionals who have worked extremely hard to be considered autism experts as anything more than it is. It is merely based on my belief that autism is not a disease that requires a cure but a descriptive label for someone who has proven extremely difficult to teach. It is this teaching difficulty from which I try to help a child recover. "Recovery" is the term for a child who was once labeled as autistic by the medical community and is now no longer deemed autistic because of a lack of those same diagnosable behaviors. This does not mean that this child is somehow a better or more complete person than he was before the label was removed. It also does not mean that the cause of the autism has been mysteriously eradicated. It merely means that as a team of caring supporters, we have found a way to educate this child to the point that the doctors have stopped calling him names.

Although it has never been my stated purpose, the fact is that through the teaching methods described in this book some children can recover from autism. Others will make fair to incredible progress while never reaching that best possible outcome. This is why the stated goal of my institute Knospe-ABA has always been to help children be more successful in life. In my mind that means teaching toward recovery regardless of whether or not we ultimately arrive there. And this is why I chose to title this book "Educate Toward Recovery: Turning the Tables on Autism."

Autism can be both a mysterious and potentially devastating disorder. For many families, the grim diagnosis begins a journey down a winding road marked by fear and unanswered questions. This situation is made worse by the worldwide lack of autism awareness. Although a diligent person with average resources can obtain information with relative ease from any supposed expert, good advice is often more difficult to locate. My goal for this book is to provide an unassuming, learned, and caring source of current and useful information for parents and autism professionals. As a teacher, child advocate, and Board Certified Behavior Analyst, I have worked with children diagnosed with autism and related disorders in the United States and Europe. In doing so, I have met a never-ending stream of parents recently given the diagnosis of autism and virtually no recommendation or reassurance for their family's new future. Left to sift through the countless theories about therapy models while enduring the almost fantasy-based promises of magical overnight cures; these parents are the ones with whom my heart remains. Although this book will be extremely valuable to any professional working with a child with autism, it has been written with the needs of the parent in mind.

I want this book to provide practical ideas and advice for you, the parent of a child in need. I expect it will become the building blocks for you to aide your child along the road to a life full of promise and hope. Some of these building blocks will help to clarify the uncommon jargon of the autism community, while others will clarify what autism is and more importantly what it means to your family. It is also important that you learn of the qualified assistance that is available to you and how with a little of this help you can drastically improve your family's quality of life. Most importantly, you must realize that there is one constant variable in the life of each child with autism. That variable is you, the child's parent, or caregiver. It is only you that will be able to see all of the ways that autism has affected your child and family. So then you must find the confidence and patience to provide everything necessary for your child with autism's development. You will need to be careful to avoid the many pitfalls along the way. Most of these pitfalls are born out of the questionable and often debilitating advice from "experts" that have simply given up trying to find a better way. Since receiving your child's diagnosis, you have been engaged in a journey whose ultimate end can only come in knowing that you are the one true expert when it comes to your child with autism. Please consider this book to be your guide on this journey. Contained in its pages are my views and recommendations on the sciences of Applied Behavior Analysis and Verbal Behavior (ABA/VB).

These recommendations have been formulated from the practical experience of my work with many children on all points of the autism spectrum. I will explain in simple terms why understanding the principles of ABA/VB is the best way to systematically address the numerous challenges that autism can foster. I use real-world examples of how parents can benefit from looking at the result of every interaction a child encounters, not as a learning opportunity that is either seized or lost, but rather a learning experience that is either beneficial or harmful to his development.

Regardless of the outcome, interactions are never neutral. They will always have an impact on your child's ability to connect with others. When you can apply the lessons of this book to your daily interactions with your child, you will learn to better understand him. Simultaneously you will begin to unlock for him the mysteries of the social world. Perhaps the most refreshing aspect of this book is that it is <u>not</u> a scientific dissertation on autism therapy. I am not a researcher or a scientist. Almost all of the material covered herein is not the result of my groundbreaking theories and testing. It is, in fact, my interpretation of and perspective on the irreplaceable hard work of others. This work has been done and continues to be done throughout the world. The list of brilliant and caring people behind the principles and procedures of this book is impressive. It is only to these people with names like, Skinner, Michael, Spradlin, Sundberg, Ray, Ruebner, Braam, McGreevey, Partington, and Carbone, who deserve credit for the material within the 300 pages of this manual. What I am is a student, practitioner, and teacher. I have studied most, if not all, of the widely recognized and publicized therapies for autism. I have practically applied many of these methods with children and adults with and without autism to varying degrees of effectiveness. I have developed my personal philosophy and approach based on these countless hours of scientific study and experience, helping children with autism spectrum disorder to live fuller and more successful lives. With the help of my wife and team at Knospe-ABA, I have focused on teaching these techniques to the people who need them the most: you the parent or supporter of a child in need.

Although this book is based on the experiences and opinions of an individual, Applied Behavior Analysis (ABA) and Verbal Behavior (VB) are not. ABA is evidence-based teaching that has been proven scientifically to be effective. This evidence has been published, reviewed, and in most cases replicated independently. For these reasons ABA has become the most commonly accepted path for families of children with autism to follow throughout much of the world. In addition, ABA is currently the only autism therapy recommended for long-term benefit by the United States Surgeon General. As a treatment for autism, Chapter Three of the Surgeon General's report on Mental Health, 1999, states, "Thirty years of research demonstrated the efficacy of applied behavioral methods in reducing inappropriate behavior and in increasing communication, learning, and appropriate social behavior." In my study and experience, Verbal Behavior (VB) has, without question, proven itself the most behaviorally advanced and effective approach to ABA. It has moved ABA beyond the rote, repetitive, table learning of its past and developed it into a natural, relationship building, holistic learning program. A good ABA/VB program is designed to teach your child the reasons behind the give and take that is so important in connecting with the social world. It is connecting your child with this natural societal reinforcement that will motivate him to make beneficial relationship and learning choices beyond the teaching setting.

This book is meant to bring the awareness of these methods out of the classrooms of the university and into the living rooms of the families who need it most. It discusses the benefits of scientific principles that I have studied and personally found effective. I will demonstrate through the rest of this book why battling against autism's often debilitating effects with the science of ABA/VB is the best option available to give your child his most reasonable chance at a full recovery. Whether your child is recently diagnosed with a special need, or has been in an older ABA program for years, learning about the Verbal Behavior approach to ABA is imperative. However, this book is meant only to point to and describe the path ahead. It is not meant to walk you down it. To fully benefit from the principles of ABA/VB, I would strongly recommend that you continue to read more about these sciences and locate a Board Certified Behavior Analyst (BCBA) to help you. For more information on the scientific reasons behind why ABA/VB is the best path you should choose for your child with autism, I recommend Catherine Maurice's book "Behavioral Interventions for Young Children with Autism" (published in 1996), Mary L Barbara's book "The Verbal Behavior Approach" (published in 2007) and that you become acquainted with scientific journals such as The Journal of Experimental Analysis of Behavior, The Analysis of Verbal Behavior, The Journal of Applied Behavior Analysis or the many other professional journals dealing with the field of autism education and therapy. You will also find a useful list of recommended reading at the end of this book.

ABA can now be studied in one of the almost one hundred accredited post-graduate, Master's, or Doctorate programs currently available in seven different countries. These programs, as well as the internationally accepted codes of conduct for behavior analysis and the names of certified behavior analysts in your country, are available on the Behavior Analysts Certification Board's website at *www.BACB.com*. This book is meant as a supplement to those programs and publications for parents who want a clear and pointed look at how ABA/VB can help their children gain important behavior, social, language, and general learning skills.

The life you can give to your child identified with Autism Spectrum Disorder has changed dramatically in just the last few years. The techniques and methods discussed in this book are the catalyst of this positive change. I truly hope you enjoy this book and find it the start of a long but rewarding journey toward recovery. Please, feel free to contact me at *knospeaba_robert@yahoo.com* with any thoughts or stories you would like to share about your experiences.

ABA/VB Terms in Plain English

Applied Behavior Analysis (ABA): A scientifically validated approach to teaching.

Antecedent: Anything present in the environment prior to the behavior of interest.

Augmentative Communication: Any communication performed through assisted means.

Aversive: Anything that causes irritation, discomfort, or pain.

Behavior: Any measurable change in a person that somehow affects the environment.

Competing Behavior: Any behavior that a person cannot demonstrate at the same time he is demonstrating the behavior of interest.

Consequence: Anything that occurs after and may exert control over the behavior of interest.

Declarative Language: Social language that does not require a response.

Differential Reinforcement: The process of giving different amounts of reinforcement to different types or levels of behavior.

Discrete Trial Teaching (DTT): A 3-part system that uses a discriminative stimulus (S^D) and a reinforcing stimulus (S^R) to evoke a target response.

Demand/Direction/Instruction/S^D: any requirement placed on the child.

Escape Extinction: Not allowing a child to escape a learning task or situation without first meeting with the demands of that task or situation.

Establishing Operation (EO): An environmental set of conditions that temporarily alters the value of a reinforcer causing an increased frequency of behavior related to that reinforcement.

Echoic: The repetition of a modeled vocal sound or word.

Errorless Learning: Pairing new demands with the lowest prompt necessary that actually evokes a target response in order to create a pattern of reinforcement for that target response.

Extinction: Not reinforcing a behavior that had previously been reinforced.

Extinction Burst: The period of time a behavior in extinction actually <u>increases</u> before beginning to <u>decrease.</u>

Fading: The act of systematically removing a prompt from an S^D.

Imperative Language: Instructional language that expects a response.

Intensive Trial Teaching (ITT): Teaching to planned targets when there is <u>not</u> a naturally occurring EO (motivation).

Intraverbal: Any words, spoken or signed, in response to the different spoken or signed words of others.

Mand: A request.

Manding: The act of requesting.

Motor Imitation: The copying or mimicking of a modeled body movement.

Natural Environment Teaching (NET): Teaching to planned targets where there is a naturally occurring EO (motivation).

Negative Punishment: Anything <u>removed</u> from the environment after a behavior that <u>decreases</u> the likelihood of that behavior recurring under similar circumstances.

Negative Reinforcement: Anything <u>removed</u> from the environment after a behavior that <u>increases</u> the likelihood of that behavior recurring under similar circumstances.

"On-the-Move" Teaching (OTM): Teaching to unplanned targets when there is a naturally occurring EO (motivation).

Perseveration: An unusually strong attraction to an item or activity.

Positive Punishment: Anything <u>added</u> to the environment after a behavior that <u>decreases</u> the likelihood of that behavior recurring under similar circumstances.

Positive Reinforcement: Anything <u>added</u> to the environment after a behavior that <u>increases</u> the likelihood of that behavior recurring under similar circumstances.

Prompt: Anything added to an S^D that assists in evoking a target response.

Prompt Fading: The act of systematically removing a prompt from an S^D.

Punisher: Anything that acts as punishment.

Punishment: Anything that occurs after a behavior that <u>decreases</u> the likelihood of that behavior recurring under similar circumstances.

Receptive (Language): Following instructions that do not involve speech.

Reinforcer: Anything that acts as reinforcement.

Reinforcement: Anything that occurs after a behavior that <u>increases</u> the likelihood of that behavior occurring again under similar circumstances.

Response: Any behavior occurring after an S^D.

Receptive by Feature, Function or Class (RFFC): The skill of being able to identify an object by its features, functions, or class, through receptive means.

S^D (Discriminative Stimulus): Any antecedent that has established a history of <u>evoking</u> a specific behavior.

Spontaneous Language: Any language that is initiated by the individual without request.

S^R (Reinforcing Stimulus): Any consequence that has established a history of <u>reinforcing</u> a specific behavior.

Sign Language (Sign): An augmentative communication system based on the exchange of mutually understood body movements.

Stimming: The act of engaging in stereotypical, repetitive movements that is self-reinforcing.

Tact: A label.

Tacting: The act of labeling.

Target Response: The behavior you are intending to evoke.

Trial: A single teaching attempt.

Textual: The skill of reading a word or words.

Verbal Behavior: Any behavior that is specifically reinforced by another person.

Verbal Imitation: The repetition of a modeled vocal sound, word, or words.

Writing: The skill of handwriting or typing words.

Chapter 1

The Road to a Better Way

Life is a journey. It is a constant search for a better way. We search for a better way to teach our children, make and keep friends, earn money, organize our files, and keep control of our hectic lives. As we experience successes, we become increasingly better about repeating the behavior that leads us to these desired outcomes. Conversely, we become better about avoiding the behavior that has been unsuccessful at achieving our goals. This is the basic concept of Behaviorism.

Once you receive a diagnosis of autism for your child, you begin a new journey. This journey is a search for a better way to help your child learn the skills necessary to live a happier more fulfilling life. The problem with this journey is that for those living in remote parts of the world without a connection to others in similar circumstances, this road is mostly barren and lonely with few markers to point the way. Conversely, the road for those connected to the larger autism community is cluttered with signs pointing in almost every direction. Under these two circumstances it is impossible for parents to guide their children's growth and development without experiencing confusion, fear, and guilt. Regardless, of how you have approached your child's life challenges, you will always wonder if you could have done more. This is a natural

There is absolutely nothing within a parent's control that can cause a child to develop autism.

byproduct of parenting. There is absolutely nothing within a parent's control that can cause a child to develop autism. There is no evidence from any reputable source that states otherwise.

I supported the education of children with disabilities as an Inclusion Specialist in California in the late 1990s. I had studied advanced teaching methodologies for six years and was now deemed a master of special education. What I found was that even with all of this preparation and specialized training, I remained completely ill-equipped to make any headway on the effects that autism has on those inflicted. I knew that there was something incredibly special about these children, but I could not seem to help them be more successful in any truly meaningful way. Wanting to be a beacon of hope for these parents, my futile attempts and failures hurt me deeply. I wanted to help children to grow, learn, and succeed. I wanted to find a better way and all I could think was, "I just don't know what else to do."

Traditional teaching methods do not work well for children labeled with Autism Spectrum Disorder.

Unfortunately, I was not alone in this situation. Many dedicated and loving teachers have been given the responsibility to educate children with the diagnosis of autism with no more insight to teaching these children than I had. The problem is traditional teaching methods do not work well for children labeled with Autism Spectrum Disorder. Most instructional approaches try to explain behavior with terms regarding feelings, cognition, and intent. These terms do little more than sooth a teacher's frustrations or help him to rationalize a child's failures. Even though it feels comforting to have a name for your child's problems like sensory integration issues, attention deficit disorder, apraxia, oppositional defiance disorder or even autism, these diagnoses are nothing more than descriptions that label and categorize children. Knowing the name of a set of behaviors your child demonstrates does nothing to help you understand how he can be educated toward recovery from that label. The same is true for statements regarding feelings or cognition. Saying a child is bored, uninterested, tired, lazy, unsure, silly, immature, or unmotivated are also descriptions of behavior that serve as little more than roadblocks to effective teaching.

Unlike many other disabilities, the symptoms of autism are normally not apparent at birth. Autism can sneak up and steal a seemingly perfect child away from his family in a matter of days. This usually occurs sometime in the first three years of life. It is difficult for anyone to understand how a once-thriving child can inexplicably fade away before his very eyes. Parents can see that the child they were just beginning to experience is still there, but for some unexplained reason, the child appears to be hidden behind the disorder unable to interact in typical ways. Most of the parents I have met of children with autism are the most dedicated and caring individuals on the planet. They will stop short of nothing on their search for a better way to help their children. But, for most, that better way has been near impossible to find. To make matters worse, the guidance a parent would typically count on from local services is not always up to date and often lacks sufficient support or direction.

Children with autism can and do learn from their environment and through the science of Applied Behavior Analysis (ABA) with Verbal Behavior (VB), we can learn to change their environment in ways that teach them how to be more successful in life. Natural things such as hunger, thirst, or cold motivate us all. Parents never have to worry about teaching children to desire items that automatically benefit or reward them. These things are natural and innate. However, most of our daily behaviors occur because of conditioned motivators. These are items we learn to desire through positive experience. Some of these motivations might be for money, material items, convenience, and social acceptance. These are conditioned motivators that we as parents are charged with passing on to our children. Typically, conditioned motivators are relatively easy to teach. For these answers we usually only need to look to our own experiences. How did I learn this skill that my child is missing? What would my parents have done in this situation? What would motivate me? In most cases, this type of self-questioning is all one would need to find strategies sufficient to help us pass along to our children the skills our parents passed along to us. Unfortunately, it is often the use of teaching strategies that were effective in supporting our typical needs that acts as a barrier to our ability to help children who are born with a pre-disposition to autistic behavior.

Children with autism learn from their environment and through ABA/VB, we can learn to change their environment in ways that teach them how to be more successful in life.

Children with autism are motivated by objects and situations that most typical people perceive as mundane, boring, or monotonous. The behavior choices children with autism make may seem odd or unpredictable to us. Their interests may be narrow and repetitive. Thus, normal parenting and teaching strategies are ineffective at reaching these children. Parents, as well as most teachers, are not equipped with the knowledge and skills necessary to make a difference in the motivations of these children. When dealing with a child with autism typical "common sense" practices that most every parent or teacher would use will often carry the opposite of their desired effect.

I was profoundly affected by an amazing child with autism while working for a school district in California. Aaron was an extremely bright but troubled seven-year-old with autism. I was charged with the task of helping Aaron succeed in a regular first-grade classroom. Like many other parents of children labeled with autism, Aaron's parents refused to see their child excluded from the instructional opportunities of general education. They were unwilling to watch Aaron be left behind to suffer in an alternative classroom. They wanted Aaron to be in a class that came complete with intellectual challenge, high expectations, and positive peer role models. Aaron's parents understood that these would be the essential factors in helping their son to succeed despite his social and behavioral deficits. Like others fighting an often antiquated or overburdened school system for an appropriate education for their children, Aaron's parents often felt marginalized or ignored. Too frequently, "experts" consider parents like Aaron's unrealistic or in a state of denial about their child's potential. They are often told that their child may never speak or live independently, and in some cases are told to prepare for the inevitable decision to have their child institutionalized. Even I, a teacher and advocate for children with autism, have been advised against giving parents false hope that their non-vocal child will someday talk. With these hopeless assertions, I adamantly disagree.

There is no such thing as false hope. There is only hope or lack of hope.

First, there is no such thing as false hope. There is only hope or lack of hope. Given this choice while I am responsible for the welfare of a child, I will choose hope every time. Secondly, I have learned from experience that we cannot presume to know anything absolutely. When given the appropriate supports and instruction, children can make significant progress. If a child has a tongue and can make varying sounds, there is a very strong opportunity for him to learn to talk. The reason many of these children have not learned to talk in the past has little to do with their ability. It usually has more to do with professionals who choose to spend their time discouraging hope and lowering parent expectations rather than searching to find a better way. With a constant barrage of discouragement and a lack of measurable results, over time, even the most steadfast and determined parents will eventually be worn down. However, armed with the proven methodologies and teaching strategies to invoke change, these same parents can motivate others to raise expectations and improve their child's prospects for a more productive life.

Whenever Aaron was engaged in anything that he found interesting or fun, he was as sweet and bright as any boy I have ever seen. The problem arose for the school when Aaron was asked to perform tasks in which he had no interest. When pushed, this little boy was capable of turning into a Tasmanian devil. He could effortlessly wreak havoc on any plans designed to move him toward any goal that he had no interest in achieving. I used every trick and technique I had learned to help Aaron, including seeking help from every type of "expert" I could contact. I read every behavior manual I could get my hands on. Unfortunately, no technique or strategy was so fool proof that it did not prove me the fool. Aaron found his way around any plan hatched toward helping him to learn anything he was not inherently motivated to learn. Eventually I came to the same conclusion as the rest of the school and district that Aaron could not succeed in general education and needed to be removed to a specialized classroom. I remember this failure as a crushing blow to my confidence. After all, how special of an inclusion specialist could I have been when I was telling a family that their child could no longer be included? I recently heard a joke that I thought was funny but in many ways, also sadly true. The question is, "What is the definition of a specialist?" The answer is, "Someone who knows almost everything about almost nothing."

When I meet a child with needs similar to Aaron's, I consider what could have been. What if I had met Aaron a few years later? Better yet, what if someone had taught me about ABA/VB a few years earlier? I have long since lost touch with Aaron and his family and I still wonder how he is progressing. As I said, it was my inability to help him succeed that affected me more than anything.

So often in life it is our greatest failures that bear the fruit of our ultimate success. It was my inability to offer Aaron help for his future that opened the door to mine. He was the conduit to me discovering the science of ABA and I will never forget him or the desire he filled me with to find a better way. To improve my teaching I began taking classes and trainings designed to help educate children with autism. I studied the Picture Exchange Communication System (PECS) and began to implement it with my students with some success. I studied the Treatment and Education of Autistic and

Armed with the proven methodologies and teaching strategies to invoke change, parents can motivate others to raise expectations and improve their child's prospects.

Related Communication Handicapped Children (TEACCH) program and began to implement it with my students with some success. I studied the play therapy of Stanley I. Greenspan, MD, called Floortime (*www.floortime.org*) and began to implement it with my students with some success. However, the few instances of limited success I was seeing led me to believe that I was merely learning how to use tools to make a wall or a door. I knew that this was not going to be enough for me or for the children I wanted to help. If I truly wanted to be a master of my craft, I would need someone to teach me how to build an entire house. To make a difference for these children, I would need to learn how to become a carpenter.

Eventually my search led to the science of Applied Behavior Analysis and eventually to the Verbal Behavior approach to ABA. For many years, the science of ABA was known in the autism world as either Behavior Modification or the Lovaas method. However, it is more appropriate to say that Dr. Lovaas and others like him were the designers of the first implementations of ABA used to help people labeled with autism. The principles Dr. Lovaas based his program on were developed by B.F. Skinner and can be found in his book called "The Behavior of Organisms" (published in 1938). Although Dr. Lovaas did so much to help others see ABA as a method of helping to teach children with autism, the understanding of how to implement behavior principles at that time would generally be considered crude and inappropriate by today's standards. However, time and research have led to vast improvements to these early procedural methods of ABA. Although there is still an unfortunate stigma in much of the world attached to ABA because of the procedures used by many Behavior Modification professionals in the 1970s and even the early 1980s, the science of ABA has progressed steadily over the years. As older techniques and strategies were tested and improved upon, our ability to understand how autism affects children and how we can best affect autism has increased. As the science of ABA developed, so did its effectiveness. The ABA used today only loosely resembles the ABA used in the early days of autism intervention. The programmed teaching has been replaced with individualization and spontaneity. Generally, the use of aversive techniques has been replaced with positive reinforcement procedures. Rather than opting for more sterile teaching environments void of distraction, we now recommend more natural environment teaching. Regardless of these and other changes made in technique, Skinner's principles remain intact, as the foundation for all that is Applied Behavior Analysis.

Parents who were exposed to the early methods of ABA often had an extremely difficult choice to make. Although the evidence demonstrating the effectiveness of ABA in teaching children behavior and general learning skills has increased each year, parents had to deal with the use of procedures that were often times difficult to accept. Parents were told that there was a way that they could help their children to learn more effectively, but the methods being used to accomplish this were often distasteful. As it was for many years, ABA was a great benefit to some families while many others decided that the outcome was not worth the process.

In the past decade there has been a change that allows us to say that ABA is now the right choice for almost all families of children with autism and its related disorders. This change was the development of the Verbal Behavior (VB) approach to ABA.

Thanks to the development of Verbal Behavior, ABA is now the right choice for almost all families of children with autism.

VB is both a philosophy of ABA and a series of evidence based teaching techniques that focus the principles of ABA on the acquisition of language skills. The people developing VB, Jack Michael, Mark Sundberg, Joe Spradlin and others (many of who were teaching and learning at the University of Western Michigan in Kalamazoo) including Dave Ray, Tom Rueber, Steve Braam, Cassie Braam and James Partington, had founded a series of new techniques to apply Dr. Skinner's book of 1958, "Verbal Behavior" to the needs of children with language delays. It was from the procedural differences of the Verbal Behavior approach to autism intervention that the true potential of ABA began to be realized.

In the relatively short period from the late 1990s into the 2000s, Verbal Behavior has become the autism therapy of choice in the United States. Thanks to ABA, and in a large part to the advancements of the Verbal Behavior approach to ABA, more children are making important progress and recovering from the effects of autism every year. One of the main reasons for this success is the inclusion of parents as the most important teachers of their children. For too many years, parents were pushed to the sidelines expected to watch as their children became increasingly delayed and controlling. Why is it necessary to rely solely on the school system that in many cases has little understanding of how to help children with autism to make meaningful progress and only enough

From the late 1990's into the 2000's, Verbal Behavior has become the autism therapy of choice in the USA.

money to pay for the minimum quality service? Why should a family pay $20,000 to $40,000 a year or more for large privately owned ABA services who require the use of their own therapists up to 40 hours a week to teach a child? Instead, parents could now be taught the principles of ABA and procedures of Verbal Behavior for themselves. Once they know these methods, they can begin grasping the opportunities presented during every daily interaction they have with their child.

To help their children make significant progress, parents need to exploit the potentially thousands of daily opportunities to interact with their children to teach acceptable social and communication skills. Parents can then hire their own therapists at negotiable rates. Many times parents can count on family members, or neighbors who will volunteer their time to help. University students studying Education or Psychology often work at no charge in exchange for receiving experience or credit from their instructors. The parents and their consultants can train these in-home helpers and therapists how to work with their child in the most effective and affordable ways. One of the best examples of this scenario comes from a family who had two children with autism. The mom's name is Juliet Burk and the use of the word *"had"* is correct because as of July of 2004, Juliet's second son Ethan, is considered recovered from autism. Juliet and her in-home team of supporters had in about four years time lifted the label of autism from the younger of her two sons.

> *I have two (autistic) spectrum kids. One is completely recovered*
> *and wouldn't believe you if you told him he was ever autistic in*
> *any way. It's gone. No signs. NONE! I have another who got a*
> *lot better. He still has struggles, but he has a life, and joy... I*
> *never had anybody promise me recovery. I've never heard of*
> *anyone promising that. Everyone has always rather cautiously*
> *warned me that, "peculiarities will persist." But, dedicated*
> *teachers, our angels, always fed me with hope based on*
> *progress. (Juliet Burk)*

If your child's therapists or teachers are not using some form of ABA to educate your child with autism, they are likely working unaware of the large body of evidence supporting its use. In addition, if they are using ABA with your child but not incorporating Verbal Behavior, they have fallen behind the available research and, for most children, are no longer offering optimal levels of intervention service.

The path to better teaching has not come easily. It was developed out of the successes and failures of many brilliant and caring people like yourself. Regardless of where you or your child is now, never forget that life is a journey and nobody knows all the answers. Although I hope it is helpful to you in meaningful ways, this book should only be considered one small part of your never-ending search for a better way.

Summary of Chapter 1

There is absolutely nothing within a parent's control that can cause a child to become autistic. There is no evidence from any reputable source that states otherwise (page 13).

Traditional teaching methods do not work well for children labeled with Autism Spectrum Disorder (page 14).

Children with autism can and do learn from their environment and through the science of Applied Behavior Analysis (ABA) with Verbal Behavior (VB), we can learn to change their environment in ways that teach them how to be more successful in life (page 15).

Armed with the proven methodologies and teaching strategies to invoke change, parents can motivate others to raise expectations and improve their child's prospects for a more productive life (page 16).

In the last decade there has been a change that allows us to say that ABA is now the right choice for almost all families of children with autism and its related disorders. This change was the development of the Verbal Behavior (VB) approach to ABA (page 19).

If your child's therapists or teachers are not using some form of ABA to educate your child with autism, they are likely working unaware of the large body of evidence supporting its use. In addition, if they are using ABA with your child but not incorporating Verbal Behavior, they have fallen behind the available research and, for most children, are no longer offering optimal levels of intervention service (page 20).

Chapter 2

Understanding the Label of

Autism

This chapter is designed to explain how and why a child is labeled with autism. It does not contain the many theories behind the root causes of autism, nor will it discuss different autistic labels. I purposely avoid these topics as they only serve to distract you from your main goal, educating your child. Knowing that there are potentially both genetic links and environmental factors involved will not give you any insight into how to best prepare your child for his future.

Autism has been a mysterious disorder since before there was a name for it. The longer our society studies autism the more effective we are at identifying those affected by the criteria that are considered autistic. Although more people are diagnosed with autism every year, the criterion of autism has not changed. What has likely changed is our interpretation of the criteria and/or the number of people who fall within its limits. A child is diagnosed with autism when he exhibits at least six specific types of behavior in three deficit categories. These three categories are social interaction, communication, and behavior and interests. Deficits include a lack of appropriate eye contact, failure to develop appropriate peer relationships, a lack of spontaneous attempts to

A child is diagnosed with autism when he exhibits at least six specific types of behavior in three deficit categories.

share enjoyment, and a lack of varied spontaneous fantasy play. Signs may also include a delay or total lack of spoken language, the use of stereotyped or repetitive use of language, preoccupation with one or more abnormal patterns of interest, and stereotyped repetitive motor movements. Please realize that this is only a partial list. You will find a complete list of behaviors associated with autism in the Diagnostic and Statistical Manual, IV-TR, revised in 2000 by the American Psychiatric Association. If your child demonstrates a minimum of these behavioral deficits in specific categories, he is likely diagnosed with autism. In addition, these delays must present themselves before your child is age three and are not attributable to another problem such as Rett's disorder. If your child demonstrates enough of this behavior but has learned to talk at an early age, you will probably find him diagnosed with Asperger's syndrome.

Currently, no existing blood or genetic test can identify your child as "having autism."

Currently, no existing blood or genetic test can identify your child as "having autism." The autistic label relates solely to a demonstration of specific types of behavior. Without the benefit of a physical test, how does one really know if a child has autism? Additionally, how can one ever say that a child is cured? The answer to these questions is simple: If Autism Spectrum Disorder is diagnosed by a series of marks on a checklist of demonstrated behavior choices, then it only makes sense that when a child no longer exhibits this behavior, he will no longer be recognized as having autism. Does that mean he is cured? Does that mean he is recovered? Does that mean that he never truly had autism to begin with? These questions are often asked about children who have graduated out of the diagnosis of autism and moved on to happier, more successful lives. To me these questions are an unimportant waste of time and energy. What matters is that we started with a child who was labeled with autism and unable to perform many of the rewarding communication, play, and behavior skills that aid all of us in our successes and happiness. And now, that same child is not labeled by the medical community and can perform most, if not all, of these rewarding skills. To me these results are all that should count.

When you think of your child with autism, picture him dug in at the beach and surrounded by a giant wall of sand. This sand wall is uneven, has many cracks, and is tall enough in most areas that your child cannot see over it or reach beyond it into the outside world. By most accounts of adults with autism who can express their feelings in books or lectures on the topic, this inner world is viewed as a sanctuary from the confusing and unpredictable world. Nevertheless, there is some form of barrier between your child and the rest of the world.

If we try to picture each area of this sand wall as a different skill that your child needs to demonstrate, then he needs to climb over the top of this wall to interact with the outside world. The very low areas of the wall represent the skills that your child has acquired with little or no outside help. Depending on how autism affects your child, the lower parts of the wall could represent skills such as pulling you toward something that he desires. In many cases, a child will cry, have tantrums, strike out or self-inflict trauma as a tool to gain your attention or force you to leave him alone. A highly motivated child with different abilities will occasionally surmount intermediate areas of his wall. Some of these skills may include pointing or infrequently using one-word requests. Finally, there are other sections of this sand wall that are far too high for your child to climb without your help. The benefit of this analogy is that it demonstrates how ABA and VB work in unison to help your child consistently conquer increasingly difficult parts of his wall and connect with the outside world.

Understanding Applied Behavior Analysis is the equivalent to understanding how to systematically and consistently use reinforcement.

Understanding Applied Behavior Analysis is the equivalent to understanding how to systematically and consistently use reinforcement. Understanding Verbal Behavior is akin to knowing how to capture or create motivation. For your child to surmount the more difficult areas of his wall, he will need to be motivated to do so. The technical term for this motivation is ***establishing operation*** (EO). An establishing operation is anything that temporarily alters the value of a reinforcing consequence. In other words, an EO is a condition that makes something temporarily more or less valuable to your child than it would be otherwise. For instance, water is generally much more valuable on a hot sunny day than it is on a day that is cool and breezy. Nothing has changed about the water itself, but the value of the water in relation to you has changed through the establishing operation of warmth or more specifically dehydration. As you can imagine motivation is a major factor in the education of children with autism and the better you learn to manipulate environmental conditions to create motivation (EO), the better teacher you will be. Motivation is the one thing that well-meaning but often poorly informed professionals might tell you that your child is lacking. I cannot count the number of times I have heard teachers and therapists proclaim, "I know your child can do the skill, but he

Understanding Verbal Behavior is akin to knowing how to capture or create motivation.

Every unstructured minute in your child's waking life is a minute that the effects of autism are free to pull your child farther away from you.

Children with autism have higher levels of motivation than most typical children. However, their motivation is often significantly different.

just doesn't want to." Or they might say, "It doesn't matter what I do. She just doesn't seem to care," or "I can't find any way to motivate him." The reason these statements and others like them are flawed is that they assume the child is fully capable but choosing not to follow our directions. This type of thinking is counterproductive. It allows the teacher or therapist to blame the child rather than the autism as the source of the problem. In addition, it invites concentration on the child rather than the teaching methods as the path or obstruction to the solution. This misdirected focus results in ineffective instruction and can lead to a dysfunctional learning relationship between child and adult.

For many parents, living with a child diagnosed with autism becomes a constant struggle. They feel as if they are battling against their child to get him to behave more appropriately. I counsel parents caught in this seemingly endless string of power struggles to avoid thinking in terms of "us" against "him." Instead, your struggle is an intense tug-o-war with you and your team of supporters on one side and the effects of autism on the other. Your child is the rope in the middle of this battle that will only go in the direction of the strongest pull. Autism is a fiercely strong and competitive adversary that does not rest. Every unstructured minute in your child's waking life is a minute that the effects of autism are free to pull your child farther away from you.

To beat autism you must find a way to keep a constant grip on the rope while leveraging the help of an extremely important ally, your child's environment. Currently, your child's environment is the strongest partner autism has to keep a constant pull on your child. It is filled with things that may be used to distract you from your goals. However, autism's partner can be won over and used as a friend in your fight. It is only with the irreplaceable help of a specially structured environment that you can begin to understand and use your child's motivation. This motivation will be the reason that your child chooses to help you to pull against the effects of autism. It is only through a deliberate manipulation of the environment that you can guarantee your child will consistently assist you in your attempts to teach him. Chapters 5 and 6 detail the process by which you can win over your child's environment and use it to help you teach.

Children with autism are motivated. In many cases, they have higher levels of motivation than typical children. However, their motivation is often significantly different. How can someone say that a hungry child who will choose to go five hours without eating because he refuses to put away his Legos first is not motivated? How can a person say a child is not motivated who does not know how to follow a simple direction? Yet that child can find his favorite computer software from Mom's best hiding place, plug in the computer, turn it on, and use a mouse to find the program with his favorite dancing characters? And how can anyone say a child who will refuse to eat any foods that are not the color red is not motivated? Children and adults with autism may be the most highly motivated people I know. As a society, we tend not to view it as such, because this motivation is usually for objectives that we do not understand.

The goal of any good ABA/VB program is to identify the child's naturally occurring motivation, capture it, and use it to help him learn. In doing so, we can begin to add new, more typical or appropriate desires to his list of motivating items while making his less appropriate motivators less important to him.

The goal of any good ABA/VB program is to identify the child's naturally occurring motivation, capture it, and use it to help him learn.

In keeping with our earlier sand wall analogy, you can look at motivation as water. If we can fill the inside of the child's world with enough water that he can float up closer to the top of the sand wall surrounding him, he will eventually be near enough to make the climb. This motivation will provide the desire and ability your child will need to get over that wall and demonstrate the skill you are trying to teach.

In the same way that you can consider Verbal Behavior a tool to help you motivate a child to try a new or different behavior for the first time, Applied Behavior Analysis can be thought of as a reason for the child to want to use this new or different behavior again. ABA is the study of interactions and the application of that study to help people be more successful in meaningful ways. Reinforcement is the major principle that has been driving ABA and its successes over the years. This principle states that anything that happens after a behavior and increases the likelihood of that behavior recurring is a reinforcer for that behavior.

Anything that happens after a behavior and increases the likelihood of that behavior recurring is a reinforcer for that behavior.

Everything that we do is a behavior including complex learning skills. If we look at your child's ability to leave his own world and get over the wall as a behavior, then we can see reinforcement as the experience we want present when he succeeds. If we can ensure that he has effective positive experiences (reinforcement) every time he uses a specific behavior to get over the wall, then he will have every motivation to want to climb over that wall again. Reinforcement of that specific behavior **creates** a motivation for your child to try his best the next time an opportunity for this specific behavior occurs.

Motivation is the reason your child will attempt a skill this time. Reinforcement is the reason he will have more internal motivation and require less external motivation the next time. Using motivation and reinforcement in unison will create an ever-increasing desire to accomplish any skill to which these two principles are consistently applied. This last statement is extremely important as it clearly states why Applied Behavior Analysis and Verbal Behavior help a child desire the learning process. If your child is consistently given motivation to attempt a new skill and finds that the successful completion of that skill is consistently met with a positive experience, your child will have an ever-increasing desire to accomplish that skill again. If you can begin applying these two principles of reinforcement (ABA) and motivation (VB) to every skill you want your child to learn, then he will begin to desire learning every skill you want to teach him.

Using motivation and reinforcement in unison will create an ever-increasing desire to accomplish any skill to which these two principles are consistently applied.

Another reason this sand wall analogy is apropos is that the walls that surround your child are not completely solid. Being made of sand presents both a problem and blessing to your child's education. It is a problem because there are usually cracks in the wall that allow your child to get to his reinforcement whether he uses the skills you are trying to teach him or not. If left unfilled, these cracks will let the motivation that you carefully pour in seep out. Thus, your child will have little motivation to succeed. Fortunately, by being made of sand, covering the cracks in this wall and filling your child with the necessary motivation to splash over the top will allow the reinforcement waiting on the other side to drag back in and erode the top of the wall away. This leaves that section of the wall a little less daunting to overcome and that skill a little easier to demonstrate the next time. A good ABA/VB program uses the principle of motivation to push your child toward new and challenging skills while using reinforcement to increase future desire and lessen the skill's difficulty level. Each time your child successfully achieves a skill the corresponding section of his wall becomes easier to surmount in the future. An added bonus of these reinforced successes is that the sand eroding away from the top of the wall tends to fill in the troublesome cracks below. Thus, your child becomes increasingly easier to motivate and future skills become easier to achieve.

Although it sounds as if I am describing autism, in actuality I am describing how each of us learns. We are all born surrounded by our own uneven barrier of skills we have yet to learn. To become fully functioning social beings each of us must erode the existence of these walls regardless of their topography. Some of us are better at overcoming this barrier than others. Some have higher walls in some areas and lower walls in others. Some have sections of our wall that we never surmount while others seem to be able to do anything they set their mind to accomplishing. Your child with autism is no different from any other child. He only has more difficulty surmounting the sections of his wall that society deems mandatory. This inability to overcome the parts of his wall that represent those six or more areas of the three major deficits of social interaction, communication, and behavior and interest is the criteria for his diagnosis. Whether we discover a single gene or set of environmental causes that is responsible for autism, teaching a child to overcome his learning barriers will most likely remain the best, if not only, path to recovery. Knowing a child is predisposed to developing "autistic" behavior has the potential to keep his learning barriers from becoming learning delays, provided the child is appropriately educated before these delays develop. Regardless of individual opinions on the cause and effect of autism, this sand wall analogy provides a useful way to understand the task ahead of you.

It is not autism but the environment's natural responses to the unpredictable motivations of a child with a predisposition to autism that amplifies the behavior that brings a child his diagnosis. Thus, it is only a better understanding and manipulation of the environment's responses to the motivations of a child with autism that can help him develop the behavior needed to recover.

Autism is a spectrum disorder that affects an ever-increasing percentage of the population. It affects the ability of a child to interact appropriately in many social and learning categories. If left uneducated, many children will continue to be pulled by the controlling effects of autism until they are incapable of managing even simple human interactions. If left untrained, parents and teachers will often inadvertently motivate and reinforce increasingly more problematic behavior. However, if you can develop a better understanding of your child, then study and apply the principles and techniques of ABA/VB, you can help your child reduce or replace his diagnosable behavior. At the same time, you will help your child become increasingly more successful in life.

Only a better understanding and manipulation of the environment's responses to the motivations of a child with autism can help that child develop the behavior needed to recover.

Summary of Chapter 2

A child is diagnosed with autism when he exhibits at least six specific types of behavior in three deficit categories. These three categories are social interaction, communication, and behavior and interests (page 23).

Currently, no existing blood or genetic test can identify your child as "having autism." The autistic label relates solely to a demonstration of specific types of behavior (page 24).

Understanding Applied Behavior Analysis is the equivalent to understanding how to systematically and consistently use reinforcement. Understanding Verbal Behavior is akin to knowing how to capture or create motivation (page 25).

Autism is a fiercely strong and competitive adversary that does not rest. Every unstructured minute in your child's waking life is a minute that the effects of autism are free to pull your child farther away from you (page 26).

Children with autism are motivated. In many cases, they have higher levels of motivation than typical children. However, their motivation is often significantly different (page 26).

The goal of any good ABA/VB program is to identify the child's naturally occurring motivation, capture it, and use it to help him learn. In doing so, we can begin to add new, more typical or appropriate desires to his list of motivating items while making his less appropriate motivators less important to him (page 27).

ABA is the study of interactions and the application of that study to help people be more successful in meaningful ways. Reinforcement is the major principle that has been driving ABA and its successes over the years. This principle states that anything that happens after a behavior and increases the likelihood of that behavior recurring is a reinforcer for that behavior (page 27).

Motivation is the reason your child will attempt a skill this time. Reinforcement is the reason he will have more internal motivation and require less external motivation the next time. Using motivation and reinforcement in unison will create an ever-increasing desire to accomplish any skill to which these two principles are consistently applied (page 28).

It is not autism but the environment's natural responses to the unpredictable motivations of a child with a predisposition to autism that amplifies the behavior that brings a child his diagnosis. Thus, it is only a better understanding and manipulation of the environment's responses to the motivations of a child with autism that can help him develop the behavior needed to recover (page 29).

Chapter 3

The Language of ABA

An individualized ABA program can be thought of as a specific language and a way of interacting and relating that has rules and restrictions. When followed closely, these rules provide order, clarity, and comfort for a child with autism. When these rules are followed haphazardly, your interaction can make an already confusing world even more difficult to understand.

According to many adults with autism who have written of their experiences, living with autism means not being able to understand the abstract; having difficulty handling change and disorder; not being able to feel comfortable in your own body, or finding your place in the social world. Thus, the mind creates an inner world that exists as a place of calmness, serenity, and order. Everything in a child's inner world makes sense to the child because he has total control. The child can choose to focus on items that exist in everyday life which always behave or react the way they are expected according to a set of consistent rules. When your child looks into a mirror, it will always reflect his image. When he looks at a crystal from the proper angle, he will see how the light is refracted into a consistent even predictable pattern. A specific compact disc always plays the same songs and a specific video always plays the same story. Also, when your child puts objects in a specific order the objects remain in that order--that is until someone else becomes involved. People are a

An individualized ABA program can be thought of as a specific language and a way of interacting and relating that has rules and restrictions.

consistent source of chaos and confusion in the world. People have moods, ideas, opinions, feelings, behavior, language, and emotional baggage that they carry with them from one interaction to the next. People are the world's most unpredictable and controlling components. The confusion a person can add to the peaceful and ordered inner world of the child with autism is often immediate and intense. Children with autism choose solitude because they do not understand the unpredictable nature of others and they lack the tools to successfully interact in situations that they cannot in some way control.

Based on the limited interests of many children with autism there is seldom enough motivation and reinforcement available to encourage consistent participation in anything more than instrumental social interactions. Without this motivation and reinforcement, children with autism become delayed in their understanding of the relational benefit of other people. A child with autism avoids social interaction because social interaction does not make sense to him. The lack of order and varying rules of interaction make it too complex a task. The rules for interacting with mom usually differ from the rules for interacting with dad. Then, if there are siblings involved, there can be three or more people in the child's environment that function under different sets of complex and ever-changing rules. This situation causes the child with autism to feel a lack of control over his environment. This lack of control causes fear and uncertainty that will often lead a child to begin fighting for control by any means possible. Some advanced learners with autism have the ability to use language extremely well. Unfortunately, instead of participating with others in conversation many only learn to use language in ineffective ways. They may, for example, ask repetitive off-topic questions. Or, they may change the topic to an area in which they are well versed or have more interest. These choices of behavior are likely a means for gaining control. Many adults with autism have noted that when others control the topic of conversation the person with autism feels excluded or unable to contribute. In order to feel comfortable and involved, some people with autism need to find ways to monopolize the choice of topics so that they can ensure they will always feel like a part of the interaction. One form of controlling the conversation is to ask questions of another person that lead to highly predictable answers. If all else fails, the ultimate way to regain control is to escape the social interaction completely. At this point the person with autism might choose to leave the interaction behind and withdraw into a comfort zone

Children with autism choose solitude because they do not understand the unpredictable nature of others and they lack the tools to successfully interact in situations that they cannot in some way control.

that makes sense. It could be a shimmering beam of light, a pattern of numbers, or a favorite vocal sound.

An individualized ABA program can be thought of as a specialized language. Specific behaviors are consistently met with specific consequences. Because your consequences are predictable and ordered, they make sense to your child. If you are using ABA effectively, your child will begin to better understand you. You will become a calming influence in your child's life and he will have fewer reasons to withdraw and more incentive to interact.

Most children and adults with autism love the computer because a computer uses a language of ordered actions and reactions. The computer is the purest form of ABA ever invented. When sitting at the computer, your child is faced with a choice of buttons on a screen. If he pushes this button, the lights flash a certain way. If he pushes another, he will hear music. If he tries a third, the computer will turn off. This is true every single time he sees those three buttons. There is nothing random or confusing about using a computer. If your child moves the mouse in just the right way and the arrow lands on top of the right button, the same thing will happen every time offering a sense of control. Children with autism tend to love computers because computer software operates consistently and predictably. The computer does not decide to play music when the child has asked it to show flashing lights. A computer does not tell the child when it is time to be turned off. The computer reacts with perfect behavioral consistency.

If you are using ABA effectively, your child will begin to better understand you. You will become a calming influence in your child's life and he will have fewer reasons to withdraw and more incentive to interact.

The best way to begin speaking to your child in a way that he understands is to become clear, concise, and consistent in actions and words, similar to a computer. The more often a parent can present his child with a set of options and offer consequences to the child's choices in predictable ways, the less confusing the parent will seem to the child. The more often a parent can offer consistent directions and consequences for a child's responses the more likely it is that a child will have a feeling of order and control when he is with that parent. Then it will become less likely that the child will feel the need to steal control in inappropriate ways. Of course, because of your ability to quickly analyze situations and tailor instruction to the child's responses and needs, you can be a much greater influence on your child than a computer can.

When you, the parent of a child in need, can become trained in the principles and strategies of ABA/VB you will unlock your ability to teach. You can begin to make gradual changes to your child's environment that encourages his behavior choices in more complex and meaningful ways. Conversely, without a firm understanding of ABA your interactions with your child will be less systematic and more random which will cause you to be more confusing to your child. As you become more confusing, your child will likely choose to spend more time withdrawn in his own world, finding the order and control that he desires. In effect, he will slip deeper into the grasp of autism. Once you and your family have learned how to speak and interact effectively through the principles and procedures of ABA, your child will begin to believe that it is possible to understand and communicate. These people that have been so important, but at times so frustrating over the years, will finally be accessible. He will be more likely to seek interaction. In doing so, he will become more comfortable in the larger social world. When your family communicates according the principles of ABA, the natural language of autism, your child will become comfortable to a point that your individuality and spontaneity will not be looked at as a form of confusion from which he needs to seek protection. It can instead become a form of surprise, excitement, and joy. Once you begin using ABA with your child, you can begin to turn the tables on autism. All of the things you currently view as problems caused by autism will begin to look like gifts of teaching opportunity. Things such as perseveration, self-stimulation, echoic language, and extinction bursts can become the tools you use to teach. Understanding your child's ABA language creates the best opportunity for intimate regular interactions building toward teaching him the language of the social world. The best way to teach a child with autism to understand people is by having the people he is trying to interact with understand ABA.

I have never met a child with autism who was not capable of manipulating the principles of behavior in the most amazing and complex ways to achieve his desires. I know parents who have demonstrated the most bazaar behavior. This type of unusual behavior could only have been taught to them through the language of ABA. For example, I know a mother who has to spend about 30 minutes every night preparing her child with autism for bed. The routine is exactly the same every single night and goes something like this: This mom has to pick up her child and carry him to his bed on her shoulders. She needs to put on only his light-blue pajamas on his bottom and the bright orange shirt with long sleeves on his top. Then she needs to tuck him into bed and sing

The best way to teach a child with autism to understand people is by having the people he is trying to interact with understand ABA.

a song. Just before the song is done he asks her for a glass of water, and she goes into the bathroom to get him one. Although the glass is always the same, and always full, the child drinks exactly half of the glass and tells mom to go back in the bathroom and fill it up again. When she returns, she needs to put the glass on the nightstand and read him the last few pages of "The Little Engine That Could." In addition to reading to him, she has to allow him to hold the book and turn the pages. After he shuts the book, mom needs to say "ALLLLLLLLLL DOOOOOONE!" Then she can kiss him goodnight, walk outside, and shut the door. After the door shuts, she waits for him to call out to her. She opens the door, looks inside, and he says goodnight. Then and only then, he will finally go to sleep.

What is wrong with this picture? Why do parents surrender to this type of control? Many will say it is because they have no choice. They have grown to believe that there is no other way. Whether or not this seems odd to you, this is a fairly typical example of how parents who do not understand the language of ABA are being trained by their kids. If this type of situation is occurring in your home, your child has taught you how to behave. Do you allow your child to choose his own clothing even when it means wearing the same shirt three days in a row? Has your child trained you to still allow him to sleep between you and your spouse every single night at the age of 12? Have you been trained to know exactly what, when, and how you are allowed to feed your child? Has your child figured out how to train you to follow him around and pick up everything that he drops? Has your child convinced you that there is only one correct way to drive home from school or walk to the park? Are you convinced that the only time you can talk on the phone or use your computer occurs when he is asleep?

Each of these behavior choices you might be making was in some way imbedded into you by your child's natural ability to use the principles of ABA. ABA is an understanding of the way that antecedents and consequences can affect behavior. If you start to put the wrong pajama bottoms on your child, he will likely provide some sort of consequence for that behavior. If he screams and throws himself against the wall, you have just been given a clear and concise message about whether that was a good choice you were making. If you decide to ignore that message and continue with the "wrong" pajamas, then he might provide a consequence for your choice by hitting himself in the head. Obviously you do not want your child hurt. So, to protect him from himself, you might change your behavior and put the same old light-blue pajama bottoms on him again. Your behavior is then reinforced with a smiling, quiet, cooperative child. After multiple trials of this procedure, you will find yourself picking out the "right" pajama bottoms in the first place. Do you see how your child is affecting your actions through the principles of behavior? If you cannot respond through the language of ABA, there is a good chance that you will end up with some form of a nighttime routine of your own. Conversely, if you understand ABA you will be able to respond to your child in his physical language of actions and reactions. You will make sense to him and you will be more predictable. When you are clear, concise, and consistent with your child, he will be able to better predict your actions. He will feel more of a sense of comfort and control in his environment. With this need for control and comfort met, he will no longer have to push for them in problematic ways before going to sleep.

It is only when your child seeks out your interaction on a consistent basis that you can truly teach him in meaningful ways.

Your child with autism understands and uses the principles of ABA. When you respond in kind, you will feel more comfortable with each other as he learns to be more at ease in the social world. Children who are at ease and in control are happier and more willing to seek out interaction with others. It is only when your child seeks out your interaction on a consistent basis that you can truly teach him in meaningful ways.

Remember, the concept presented in this chapter is not specific to the scientifically proven principles and procedures of ABA/VB. There are currently several hundred individual studies that indicate the effectiveness of applied behavioral techniques. These studies can be found in the scientific journals detailed at the back of this book. This chapter is not meant to provide proof of ABA's effectiveness. It instead offers what my experience has shown to be a useful non-behavioral explanation as to *why* ABA is so powerful in the world of autism intervention. Do the examples I use mirror what you already know about your child? Do you see how your child has used ABA to manipulate your environment and affect your behavior choices? Do you see how autism is in control of you? If so, keep reading and I will show you how to use the science of ABA/VB to turn the table on your child's autistic behavior.

Summary of Chapter 3

An individualized ABA program can be thought of as a specific language and a way of interacting and relating that has rules and restrictions. When followed closely, these rules provide order, clarity, and comfort for a child with autism. When these rules are followed haphazardly, your interaction can make an already confusing world even more difficult to understand (page 33).

Children with autism choose solitude because they do not understand the unpredictable nature of others and they lack the tools to successfully interact in situations that they cannot in some way control. (page 34).

An individualized ABA program can be thought of as a specialized language. Specific behaviors are consistently met with specific consequences. Because your consequences are predictable and ordered, they make sense to your child. If you are using ABA effectively, your child will begin to better understand you. You will become a calming influence in your child's life and he will have fewer reasons to withdraw and more incentive to interact (page 35).

The best way to teach a child with autism to understand people is by having the people he is trying to interact with understand ABA (page 36).

Your child with autism understands and uses the principles of ABA. When you respond in kind, you will feel more comfortable with each other as he learns to be more at ease in the social world. Children who are at ease and in control are happier and more willing to seek out interaction with others. It is only when your child seeks out your interaction on a consistent basis that you can truly teach him in meaningful ways (page 38).

Chapter 4

Understanding the Purpose of Behavior

I often ask parents who are new to learning about ABA/VB what they consider to be the most difficult challenge involved with teaching their child to learn new skills. Problematic behavior choices always top the list. Regardless of how a child is currently affected by autism, there will always be behavior choices that a parent, teacher, or therapist would rather not see again. Experience has shown me that it is imperative for parents to understand the process of positively affecting their child's individual behavior choices prior to any attempts at teaching advanced learning skills. Upon closer inspection, most would agree that general learning skills are nothing more than complex behavior choices. If you have not been instructed in ways to positively affect the individual behavior choices of your child, then you will also be unable to positively affect his skill acquisition. To know best how to help your child avoid ineffective or problematic behavior choices, you need to understand the purpose that each choice serves.

The only way to positively affect your child's behavior choices is to analyze the purpose behind the choice.

The only way to positively affect your child's behavior choices is to analyze the purpose behind the choice. If you cannot pinpoint the purpose of

The best way for someone to analyze the purpose of a behavior is to do a functional analysis of the behavior.

Knowing the purpose of an inappropriate behavior allows you make that behavior unsuccessful at achieving that goal while making other more appropriate behaviors rewarding.

your child's behavior you will not predictably know how to affect it. Parents often tell me that their children will frequently make behavior choices for no apparent reason. Yet, upon further investigation with a properly trained eye, this is never the case. Every behavior has a purpose. If you cannot decipher what that purpose is, you have not been provided with the proper training necessary to identify it. Behavior analysts believe that all behavior occurs for one of four possible purposes: To gain something from another person (socially mediated positive behavior), remove something from another person (socially mediated negative behavior), to gain something that is in itself desired (automatic positive behavior), or to remove something that is in itself undesired (automatic negative behavior).

The best way for someone to analyze the purpose of a behavior is to do a functional analysis of the behavior. A functional analysis allows you to decide if a behavior is being maintained by attention, escape, or self-stimulation. The key to knowing how to reduce or eliminate an inappropriate behavior is to identify correctly which of the purposes a behavior serves. Once you know the goal of the inappropriate behavior, you can intentionally begin to make that behavior unsuccessful at achieving that goal. At the same time you can begin to make more appropriate behavior choices rewarding by insuring their use achieves the desired goal. These two activities performed concurrently over time will allow you to help your child make appropriate and ultimately more beneficial behavior choices on a consistent basis.

To effectively address and affect behavior in positive ways, you must be able to decide what behavior is and is not appropriate on a moment's notice. Many inappropriate behavior choices are obvious. Aggressive behavior-- hitting, spitting, scratching, biting--or self-injurious behavior such as head banging, or biting oneself is usually easily recognized. However, other inappropriate behavior is not as easily noted. Is crying an inappropriate behavior? Is laughing an inappropriate behavior? Is asking to go to the bathroom an inappropriate behavior? The answer to all of these questions depends on the situation. When a child is happy, laughing is appropriate. When a child is sad, crying is appropriate. And yes, when a child needs to go to the bathroom, there is nothing inappropriate about asking. However, when your child uses one of these three behavior choices as a means toward achieving an inappropriate goal or to obtain control in a given situation, then that behavior should be considered inappropriate. So, what should you do if your child asks to go to the bathroom while you are teaching another skill? In most cases, the best approach is to acknowledge but decline the request and continue with your teaching. Once your child has stopped trying to avoid the task and is now performing it correctly you can pause and ask if he still needs to go to the bathroom. If he does, be sure to resume the same skill upon his return. This demonstrates to your child that although you respected his request, it was not useful for avoiding a specific demand or a difficult teaching task. If you do allow your child to ask for things after you have given a direction two specific problems will begin to emerge: he will begin to see that you do not always expect your directions to be followed and he will begin requesting more items during teaching as a form of escape.

One simple way to decide if a behavior is inappropriate is to think about whether you would like to see that behavior repeated in similar situations. Sometimes you need to look further down the road. For example, would that type of behavior be accepted in a school classroom or in the local community pool? This is an important question to ponder. Although when at home you may not mind your child running around naked, climbing up on tables, or turning the lights on and off this behavior would clearly be deemed unacceptable in any classroom or community environment. You need to remember that your ultimate goal is to see your child successful in life. Raising the behavioral expectations of your home environment is an important early step in making this goal a reality. When you willingly allow your child with autism to make any behavior choice at home that would not be allowed in a classroom, you effectively set him up to fail in the school environment.

When you willingly allow your child with autism to make any behavior choice at home that would not be allowed in a classroom, you effectively set him up to fail in the school environment.

Another way that you can decipher if a behavior choice your child is using is inappropriate is to pay attention to your feelings. Whenever you are feeling pressured, rushed, angry, confused, or out of control your child is likely engaged in some form of inappropriate behavior. Things happen quickly when you are interacting with your child. To consistently affect your child's behavior choices in positive ways, you need immediately to differentiate between acceptable and unacceptable forms of behavior and apply the best consequence to each choice. To know how to react to each and every behavior in a clear, concise, and consistent way, you need to understand what your child is trying to accomplish with the behavior.

The best way for a parent, teacher or therapist to analyze the intent or purpose of a behavior is by quickly asking three questions:

1. What was the exact behavior I did not like?

2. What was happening in the environment just *before* the behavior?

3. What changed in the environment directly *after* the behavior?

The first question is designed to ensure that you are pinpointing the appropriate important behavior that you would like to change. It is difficult to measure a change in the behavior of being bad. In addition, "causing trouble," "not trying hard," or "acting autistic" are not good behaviors to try to address. It is much easier to work on a specific behavior such as, "walking away from mom," "not responding to his name when called," or "throwing the soup bowl on the floor during lunch."

The second question is designed to see if there is an antecedent to the behavior that can be considered a cause. For example, if every time you put a specific sweater on your child he bites himself, finding a way to eliminate that behavior should be an easy task. The second question can also give you an idea about the purpose of the behavior. For example, dad talking on the phone just before the child threw the soup bowl on the floor might lead you to think that the behavior could have been an attempt to gain dad's attention. If the child was involved in repetitive hand flapping just before he did not respond to his name, this might indicate that the behavior purpose came from self-stimulation. In addition, if mom had just picked up the child's toothbrush before the child walked away, it might lead you to think that the behavior was used for escape.

The third question is sometimes the most difficult but often the most important question to answer correctly. What is the consequence that is reinforcing the behavior in question? Identifying exactly what changed in the child's environment after a behavior occurs can often help you determine what is reinforcing (increasing the future use of) the behavior. Once the possible reinforcement is identified, you can begin to make informed choices designed to eliminate that reinforcement. For example, if after throwing the bowl on the floor dad got off the phone and reprimanded the child it would lend further evidence that the behavior was an attempt at gaining dad's attention. It would also lead you to believe that in the future when the behavior occurs dad should remain on the phone and not allow the behavior to be successful in winning his

The best way for a parent, teacher, or therapist to analyze the intent of a behavior is to quickly answer three questions about the behavior.

attention. If after the child walked away from his mom she decided to put the toothbrush away, this would give further evidence that the desired goal of that behavior was escape.

After you have asked and answered these three questions, you should have a better idea as to which of the above mentioned purposes a behavior is serving for your child. The next step is to plan an intervention that will stop reinforcing the inappropriate behavior and, instead, begin reinforcing other more desirable behavior choices.

Here are some examples of what you could do for the three main purposes of behavior.

Attention. If throwing the soup bowl on the floor was used to get dad's attention, then dad should not give any attention the next time the bowl hits the floor. Instead, he should plan to give as much attention as possible when the child is eating appropriately.

Plan an intervention that will stop reinforcing the inappropriate behavior and, instead, begin reinforcing other more desirable behavior choices.

Avoidance/Escape. If throwing the soup bowl on the floor was used to avoid or escape an instruction (for example, "Say bread,") then the purpose of the behavior is likely avoidance/escape. In this case, dad must not reinforce that behavior by continuing to present the same or a similar instruction. Then, when the child has complied, dad can reinforce compliance by lessening future demands for a period of time.

Self-Stimulation. Behavior in which a child engages whether he is with others or alone is, generally, for the purpose of self-stimulation. These behavior choices are reinforced naturally and may be difficult to affect, as you are not needed to reinforce them. If the reason the child is throwing the soup bowl on the floor is that he likes the sound it makes, you need to look for options on limiting that naturally occurring reinforcement. A few choices might include buying a floor mat, not giving the child access to the bowl, or using a paper or plastic bowl. Consider any available option to remove the sound that reinforces the behavior. In addition, giving the child an opportunity to experience the specific or similar preferred sound at an appropriate time would likely decrease the need to experience it at the dinner table.

Control. In the science of behaviorism "control" is <u>not</u> a separate possible function of behavior and by listing it here I am not attempting to indicate that it is. However, when escape, attention, or self-stimulation behavior is used solely to obtain or maintain the dominant position in an interaction or relationship, there are other considerations that will benefit your attempts to affect these more complex behaviors. My conceptual support for addressing socially mediated "control" behavior is detailed in Chapter 7. For now, this serves as an example of what you could do when you assess that your child's behavior choice has been made because of its ability to maintain his dominance in a your relationship or take a leadership role in the current interaction. When you have assessed that the child wants to gain power and control by using a specific behavior choice, you cannot allow the inappropriate behavior to be successful toward pushing your buttons, making you angry, or altering your approach in any way. Getting you to change your behavior by affecting your emotions or reactions is the reinforcer that is maintaining this type of behavior. Instead, search for and develop opportunities for the child to request independence or earn your willing participation in his activities appropriately and then reinforce these choices. For example, if you decide that the child is throwing the soup bowl on the floor because he is retaliating over not getting his way, the behavior is likely an attempt at gaining control of the current interaction and dominance in the relationship. By not reacting to the bowl hitting the floor you do not give it any power. Therefore, you leave the child no reason to repeat the behavior in similar situations. Once the child engages in appropriate control choices, dad should then find a way to give some control back to the child. For example, dad could give the child a choice of activities or participate in a child led activity.

Once you have asked yourself these three questions and made a decision on the possible purpose of the behavior, you will have an idea of what you can do to affect the behavior choice in positive ways. However, the only way to know if your plan is sound is to put it into practice and collect data to see if the behavior is occurring less over time. Your child may not immediately cease the behavior when confronted with an intervention. Even if he does, an immediate result is not a true test of whether a behavior plan is going to be successful. Stopping a behavior for the moment is nice, but it is not an indication that the child is learning not to use that behavior again in the future. The only way to determine a true reduction in the use of a behavior is to keep data. After a reasonable amount of time, objectively collected data will show

The only way to know if your behavior plan is sound is to put it into practice and collect data to see if the behavior is occurring less over time.

whether the behavior begins to occur less frequently. Only this will reliably determine if an intervention is having its desired effect. Usually one to two weeks is enough time to determine if a plan is working. If the behavior maintains or increases beyond a week or two, you need to stop the plan, rethink the possible purposes, and move on to a different tactic.

When you have a specific inappropriate behavior that you cannot seem to reduce, or when you are dealing with aggressive behavior that endangers your child or others, you should immediately call for professional help. Your best choice is usually a board certified behavior analyst (BCBA) who can complete a detailed functional analysis of the behavior to experimentally identify its purpose and design a safe and effective treatment plan.

Summary of Chapter 4

The only way to positively affect your child's behavior choices is to analyze the purpose behind the choice. If you cannot pinpoint the purpose of your child's behavior you will not predictably know how to affect it (page 41).

Once you know the goal of the inappropriate behavior, you can intentionally begin to make that behavior unsuccessful at achieving that goal. At the same time you can begin to make more appropriate behavior choices rewarding by insuring their use achieves the desired goal (page 42).

When you willingly allow your child with autism to make any behavior choice at home that would not be allowed in a classroom, you effectively set him up to fail in the school environment (page 43).

The best way for a parent to analyze the intent or purpose of a behavior is by quickly asking three questions (page 44):

1. What was the exact behavior I did not like?

2. What was happening in the environment just *before* the behavior?

3. What changed in the environment directly *after* the behavior?

Once you have asked yourself these three questions and made a decision on the possible purpose of the behavior, you will have an idea of what you can do to affect the behavior choice in positive ways. However, the only way to know if your plan is sound is to put it into practice and collect data to see if the behavior is occurring less over time (page 46).

When you have a specific inappropriate behavior that you cannot seem to reduce, or when you are dealing with aggressive behavior that endangers your child or others, you should immediately call for professional help. Your best choice is usually a board certified behavior analyst (BCBA) who can complete a detailed functional analysis of the behavior to more scientifically identify its purpose and design a safe and effective treatment plan (page 47).

Chapter 5

Increasing Positive Behavior Choices

with Instructional Control

Can a child with autism jump? Can he wave? Clap his hands? Can he make sounds? Can he say some words? The answer to all of these questions is, "usually." So why is it that a child might be able to do many of these things when *he* wants to but never when *you* ask? This question has baffled parents and professionals for years. The answer can be summed up with two important words: "instructional control." If you want your child to perform any of these naturally-occurring skills on request, you will need to have a good learning relationship with him. To build that relationship, instructional control must be earned.

When evaluating a child's capabilities with standardized intelligence tests, a professional usually observes your child and makes a few notes. He will then begin to issue directions such as asking your child to jump. Then he watches to see if your child jumps. Next he might ask your child to clap his hands and watch to see if your child claps his hands. After that, he might ask your child to repeat a specific sound.

Generally, even children with autism who have not had the benefit of good ABA/VB intervention can perform each of these skills under their own initiative. However, without ABA/VB many do not understand the request or are unwilling to perform specific skills upon request. When your child does not perform these skills during testing, the examiner will place a little minus sign on the test after each of these operations. Eventually, your child is not only diagnosed as autistic but also as developmentally disabled or mentally retarded.

Most children with autism do not lose their intelligence or personality, but these qualities have instead become disconnected.

Most children with autism do not lose their intelligence or personality, but these qualities have instead become disconnected. What your child does not have is the ability to demonstrate these traits consistently and in traditional ways. Just because your child does not jump when asked to do so, does not necessarily mean that he cannot jump. It also does not mean that he cannot learn to jump on request. Similarly, your child may make sounds when alone in his room but refuse to make sounds when you ask him to. This does not mean that he is unable to learn to talk. It does mean that your child likely has little or no meaningful reason to follow your directions or put in the consistent effort needed to gain these skills. Compounding this problem is the fact that many children with autism tend to be extremely intelligent in spite of their inability to perform on IQ and other standardized tests. A majority of the children labeled autistic with whom I have worked are usually the most intelligent people in the room. Unfortunately, this frequently means that they are too intelligent for their own good. Many children who develop autism are smart enough to realize from the earliest stages of cognition that others are unable to consistently force them to do anything that they do not want to do. This early realization working in tandem with perceptual and/or sensory issues gives a child with autism the ability to avoid learning the important attention, focus, and interaction skills that provide a basis for everything else we learn. I have become increasingly convinced that it is society's inability to effectively understand and manipulate this superior intelligence that amplifies autism's deficits. As teachers and guides, our job is to provide your child *reasons* for better attention, focus, and interaction. The scientific study of behavior has shown that the reasons your child needs to build better attention, focus, and interaction skills must come in the form of reinforcement and/or motivation and can only be earned through good instructional control.

Children with autism tend to be extremely intelligent in spite of their inability to perform on IQ and other standardized tests.

According to the Website behavioranalysts.com "instructional control is the likelihood that your instructions will evoke a correct response from your child/student (your instructions control the responses of your child). If you do not have instructional control, you might describe your child as noncompliant or nonresponsive." The Website also goes on to state that, "Instructional control involves two critical components: You must be associated with the delivery of reinforcement and you must develop a history of reinforcing compliance to your instruction."

In a learning situation the decision of who has control over the interaction at any given time must belong to the teacher for that situation consistently to be effective. Earning instructional control means that you have gained your child's willingness to let you make decisions about how the two of you will proceed in your interactions. This willingness is earned by creating a motivation in your child to be involved in adult-led activities. The best way to gain this motivation is by actively pursuing the following behavior goal. The overall goal of any child's behavior plan should be to show the child that the fastest and easiest way to get what he wants is to follow directions while using appropriate language and behavior skills.

Achieving this goal is a prerequisite to motivated learning and the most important aspect of any autism intervention or learning relationship. Without having met this goal, you do not have instructional control and you are powerless to consistently help guide your child. Without your guidance your child's skill acquisition relies on his own interests and remains completely under his control. Until you are able to help your child overcome a single-minded focus on his own desires to participate in your choice of learning activities, you will not be able to help him in meaningful ways.

Regardless of what other therapists and therapies have promised, recovery from the diagnosis of autism is not a realistic possibility without successfully earning and maintaining instructional control. My first introduction to the concept of instructional control came from a Verbal Behavior workshop in California with Dr. James Partington, PhD, BCBA. In that workshop, Dr. Partington described how he was able to gain instructional control with a certain little girl. This girl was so lost to aggressive and self-injurious behavior that most therapists, including qualified behavior analysts, had given up on her. Dr. Partington described how, through the careful use of preferred toys and food items followed by the introduction of heavily reinforced easy-to-follow instructional activities, he was able to reverse the child's aversion to people.

The overall goal of any child's behavior plan should be to show the child that the fastest and easiest way to get what he wants is to follow directions while using appropriate language and behavior skills.

Recovery from the diagnosis of autism is not a realistic possibility without successfully earning and maintaining instructional control.

Instead he established himself as a source of pleasure and became a generalized reinforcer to the child.

A similar philosophy on instructional control was introduced at the Carbone Clinic workshop "Teaching Verbal Behavior: Hands on Training for Tutors and Therapists" presented in 2003 by Cherish Twigg, MS, BCBA and Holly Kibbe, MS, BCBA in New York. In both cases, it was evident that a relationship needed to be developed that allowed for the child to see the adult, not as a barrier to preferred items, but as a source of good things. Therefore, the first thing an adult needs to do with any child is "to pair." Pairing is a behavioral principle that states when two items or activities are consistently experienced together the perceived value of one will influence the perceived value of the other.

Pairing: When two items or activities are consistently experienced together the perceived value of one will influence the perceived value of the other.

Money is a great example of how this principle works. As adults most of us have a strong desire to possess money. It is what causes many to spend more of their waking hours at work rather than play. For some people the value of money has grown to the point that, when all else fails, they will steal or even kill for the ability to acquire enough. This strong motivation to possess money was not innate. Nobody was born with a desire to earn money. In fact, for most of us thousand dollar notes could have floated around in our environment completely untouched throughout much of our childhood. It was not until the possession of money had been adequately paired with the acquisition of other highly valued items in our environment that our perceived value of money developed. Through the process of pairing, money itself became a generalized reinforcer for our behavioral choices. In fact, in our society money has been so comprehensively paired with reinforcement that in many cases money itself has more value than the items it can buy. Money in the bank now carries with it the value of safety, security, wealth, option, and opportunity. A person's feelings of self worth are often based on how much money is available to him. Feelings such as these could only have been attributed to the possession of money through the behavioral principle of pairing.

The Goal of Pairing is to establish yourself as a reinforcer for your child's behavior choices allowing you to become a generalized reinforcer for good behavior.

As regards your child's education, the goal of pairing is to establish yourself as a reinforcer for your child's behavior choices. In other words you want to become someone whom your child will make positive choices to please. This is done by consistently and comprehensively pairing yourself with your child's favorite things. Pairing in this fashion causes the value of these reinforcing objects to be transferred to your child's perceived value of you. Once your interaction is well paired with fun activities, your child will begin to see your interaction as a fun activity worth making behavioral adjustments to maintain. In essence, you can condition yourself as a generalized reinforcer for your child's positive behavior choices. Becoming a generalized reinforcer means that your child will prefer your presence in his environment. He will desire to keep your interaction and will begin to make choices designed to maintain it. Most typical children see their parents as generalized reinforcers. This is part of what allows them to be typical. Unfortunately, without comprehensive pairing, most children with autism do not.

The traditional approach to instructional control suggests that once you have sufficiently paired yourself with positive reinforcement and fun, the next step in good teaching is to begin including easy "instructional control activities" into your pairing interactions. It is through the repeated reinforcement of easily followed instructions that you can teach a child that following directions is easy and fun. When I began my work as a behavior analyst, I was guided by this popular approach to instructional control. Although, everything about pairing and instructional control activities is absolutely true, using these techniques is not universally effective in creating a willing learner. In many cases pairing with a child and then introducing easy instructional control activities would develop the trust necessary to show that following directions was beneficial. Unfortunately, many children with autism are more determined to maintain the upper hand in their environment. For these more controlling children who refuse to relinquish their, "I say it, mom and dad does it" lifestyle, there remain far too many intricate ways to evade directions and avoid learning. It is with these children that even many of the best VB consultants will still use a physical manipulation of the child to maintain a teaching connection. Most of the top autism consultants in the world still recommend traditional ABA compliance procedures as behavioral tools when a child's willing participation has waned. To avoid your child's use of escape behavior, ABA and many VB consultants will recommend a process called escape extinction. *Escape extinction* is the process of not letting a child's use of escape behavior lead to actual escape of the task or teaching setting. In other words it is the refusal to let the child escape teaching. Often a gentle physical prompt such as a pulling on the arm or pushing down on the shoulder is used to force a child back into a learning activity and keep the escape behavior from being successful. If a physical prompt is not

Escape extinction is the process of not letting a child's use of escape behavior lead to actual escape of the task or teaching setting.

needed, a direct verbal demand might be used such as "Come here," "Hands still," "Sit down," or "Fold your hands" to return the child back to a useful learning posture. The amount of escape extinction needed is dictated by your child's behavior, your consultant's recommendation, or your ability to make learning fun.

Although the power of motivating a child through the process of pairing oneself with fun activities was immediately apparent, I began to realize that the benefit of pairing was instantly diluted anytime I resorted to the use of escape extinction. Once direct pressure to a child is applied, the child's motivation to escape that pressure increases. Thus, my attempts to pull a child toward learning had one of two possible results. Either the child would begin using his energy to fight against this pull in increasingly severe ways or he would succumb to it and participate. However, this unmotivated participation would only last if he began enjoying the interaction or found another opportunity to escape. Either case was less than satisfactory to me. As someone who is ever conscious of the criticism that ABA does not teach better ways to live, but rather trains a child to follow directions, I had to find a way to reconcile this part of my teaching.

Captive learning through the use of escape extinction should be used only as a last resort.

One of the main reasons that the Verbal Behavior approach surpasses traditional ABA as a method of teaching toward recovery is that VB teaching procedures are designed to increase the reinforcing value of teaching. As a result VB teaching procedures reduce the relative value of escape. However, because of incomplete methods of earning instructional control, even qualified and experienced VB consultants are often unable to limit their use of escape extinction with some children. When working with the most difficult children, consultants often find themselves going against the verbal behavior principles by spending an inordinate amount of time keeping a child involved in captive learning. In most cases captive learning through escape extinction should be used as a last resort and then only with a plan in place to reduce its need in the future.

I knew that if I truly wanted to teach toward recovery, the child would need to actively choose to seek out and maintain my teaching. For this to occur, my teaching procedures would have to leave room for the child to escape teaching when he so desired. However, the value of the result of his escape had to be meaningfully lower than the reinforcing value of my teaching setting. Motivated learning could only be maintained to the level it was needed if the child was responsible for developing positive learning behaviors of his own free will. I realized that whenever possible instructional control could not and should not be forced on a child. Instead, each child's motivated participation in learning was something that I would have to earn.

I began to pioneer my own guidelines to instructional control designed to minimize the problems many of our families were having because of the use of escape extinction procedures. The first step was to realize that pairing is not a prerequisite to instructional control. In fact, pairing is better understood as one of the important ingredients that, in concert with other elements, is necessary to earn and then maintain instructional control. I began to apply my study and experience to the development of a simple series of comprehensive steps that allowed families to achieve instructional control without the use of escape extinction. These seven steps, when collectively applied, are the full realization of the procedures of Verbal Behavior. They allow you to manipulate your child's environment so that it creates a quicker and easier path to instructional control. Regardless of whether you choose to call it instructional control, compliance training, a master/apprentice relationship, or mutual respect, these seven steps enable you to enlist the environment as an ally in your battle against autism. Once you systematically apply these seven steps to your child's environment, you will no longer need to actively control your child through escape extinction. Your child's natural desires will become his motivation to participate in joint activities, follow your instructions, and share in the responsibility of maintaining your social interactions. He will begin making the choice to actively engage in increasingly more difficult tasks because you have earned his desire to maintain your interaction. It is only when your child is making the *independent choice* to maintain and prolong your interactions that you can begin teaching beyond the limits of what he was formerly willing to learn.

It is only when your child is making the independent choice to maintain and prolong interactions that you can begin teaching beyond the limits of what he was formerly willing to learn.

All seven steps must be in place if you are to successfully develop the best possible learning relationship with your child. The failure to adhere to even one step upsets the entire balance and your child will consistently be able to find a way to avoid the benefits of your teaching. In addition to the process of *gaining* instructional control, incorporating these steps into your family lifestyle will ensure that you *maintain* a positive learning relationship. The more capable parents, teachers, and therapists become in following these seven steps, the better and faster their children begin to choose positive learning behavior on a

All seven steps of instructional control must be in place if you are to successfully develop the best possible learning relationship with your child.

regular basis. Experience has also shown that each subsequent person to earn instructional control with a child will help make the process quicker and easier for the next. Thus, when you and your spouse can earn instructional control, it will be easier for grandma and grandpa. In turn, grandma's and grandpa's successes will make it even easier for your child's school therapist and teacher to earn instructional control with your child.

As previously stated, understanding ABA/VB is like becoming a carpenter able to build a complete and unique structure. In keeping with this analogy, the process of earning instructional control with your child is akin to pouring a solid foundation. The quality and complexity of everything you will build relies on the strength of this foundation. Some parents say, "My child doesn't respect my authority." The best way to earn your child's respect is to earn his instructional control. These seven steps will become your foundation to effective teaching.

Seven Steps to Instructional Control

Step 1: Show your child that you are the one in control of the items he wants to hold or play with and that you will decide when and for how long he can have them.

Anything your child prefers to do or play with is potential reinforcement for his positive behavior choices. Your control over these items is essential in the early stages of earning instructional control. Your child should not be deprived of prized objects. Rather, he should be expected to earn time with them by following simple instructions and behaving appropriately.

You designed your child's environment. You made the choices of what to buy for him to play with, wear, sleep on, or eat. As the parent you are responsible for deciding when or if you put something into or take something out of your child's environment. This is true whether you choose to use it for teaching or not.

The first step of instructional control involves making decisions about what items your child is allowed to have in his environment and what he can do to cause you to introduce or remove those items. To restrict reinforcement, begin by removing preferred items from your child's room and the remainder of the house. Put these objects in a place where they can be seen but not accessed by your child. At the very least, make sure that your child knows where they are now being kept. A clear container should suffice for younger children. A locked room or a locked cabinet in the child's room may be needed for older children. At this point, do not try to remove an item while it is being used even if it means waiting until your child is sleeping or out of the house.

Restriction of reinforcement becomes more important once you begin working with your child. Whenever you see him put down a reinforcing item you must immediately put it away. If he walks over and begins to play with, hold, or look at something that you have not thought to restrict, take note of that item and when he is finished remove it from the environment. This way you can reintroduce it as a possible reinforcer. If your child has favorite activities, consider ways that you can control these as well. Mini-trampolines can be hung against the wall, window shades can be closed, and swings can be lifted up and out of reach when not in use. Once you have taken control over access to preferred items and activities in the environment, you can instantly begin using your discretion on the introduction and removal of these items based on instructional control steps 2 through 7.

Some more advanced learners with autism might not need comprehensive restriction of reinforcement as you begin a program. Taking control of their favorite items may be enough to keep them interested in your teaching. However, this can lead to problems when your teaching becomes more difficult. As the difficulty level of your teaching increases, so will the value of lesser reinforcers. As the value of these unrestricted reinforcers increase, so does the likelihood that your child will begin escaping to these items. If this occurs, increase the number of items and activities that are kept under your control. In most cases it is better to over-restrict reinforcement in the beginning. Thus you are the person who can generously give reinforcing items to your child on a minute-by-minute basis. Conversely, when you fail to control your child's preferred items and activities, you become the person who forcefully removes these things from him on a minute-by-minute basis. The sooner your child understands that you are willing and capable of restricting all forms of reinforcement, the sooner he will decide that following your lead is always in his best interest.

Step 2: Show your child that you are fun. Make each interaction you have with him an enjoyable experience so that he will want to follow your directions to earn more time, sharing these experiences with you.

In the best ABA/VB Programs approximately 75% of every interaction you have with your child should be reserved for the process of pairing yourself with fun activities and known reinforcement. Pairing activities should be led by your child's motivation and should include only non-verbal and declarative language. *Declarative language* is language that asks for nothing of your child. It only serves to share your thoughts and feelings. This is important language for your child to learn and should be modeled throughout your interactions. You should practice sharing your thoughts and ideas with your child in silly and exciting ways without requiring anything in return.

Do not mistake the idea of reserving 75% of your interaction for pairing to mean that you should pair with your child for fifteen minutes and then teach for five. Instead, if it takes your child about 15 seconds to answer three instructions, you should then spend about 45 seconds, reinforcing and sharing in fun activity with him before introducing your next set of instructions.

Declarative language asks nothing of your child and only serves to share your thoughts and feelings.

To pair yourself with reinforcement, follow your child's interests and offer him access to play with anything he is interested in as long as you are allowed to play along with him. Make his playtime more fun because *you* are a part of it. If your child wants music, you should be the one to provide the music. In addition, you could hold him, bounce and dance with him while he is listening. It is perfectly okay to turn off the music when he chooses to leave the area or begins to play or behave inappropriately. However, it is important, especially in the early stages of gaining instructional control, to demonstrate that you will immediately turn the music back on as soon as he returns or ceases the inappropriate activity. Another wonderful opportunity for pairing yourself with reinforcement arises when your child is playing on a swing. You can easily make this activity more enjoyable by playing with and tickling him while he swings. Try pushing him high in the air or spinning him around. Pretend that he is about to hit you and then move out of the way at the last second. Observe what makes him smile so that swinging with you is more fun than swinging alone. Pairing procedures should be based around your child's most reinforcing items and activities. Learn to maximize their reinforcing value. You should work to increase his level of enjoyment beyond what he would be capable of on his own. Be careful not to take any fun out of the item. This is sometimes more difficult than you think. If playing with your child is not something you are particularly good at, practice! Good pairing is essential to good teaching.

Step 3: Show your child that you can be trusted. Always say what you mean and mean what you say. If you instruct your child to do something, do not allow him access to reinforcement until he has complied with your request. This step allows for prompting him to completion if necessary.

To understand this step you need to consider the difference between teaching time and free time. When establishing instructional control with your child, you must actively decide when it is time for him to learn and when he has free time. Make it clear that this decision is made by you and that it does not rest with your child.

Respect a child's free time. Children should be allowed to do what makes them happy as long as they are not breaking any house rules or demonstrating unsafe or hurtful behavior. If your child demonstrates a desire to play with a toy during free time he should be allowed unless you are planning to use it for teaching soon. How your child demonstrates this desire depends on his current level of ability. It could include pointing to or looking at an item. It might include using signs, single word requests, or involve full sentences. Understanding and teaching to the many levels of requesting will be discussed in Chapter 13.

If your child engages in a stereotypical self-stimulating behavior during his free time, it means that he does not have the access to or knowledge of a more reinforcing activity at that time. If you are capable of offering him something he would prefer, you should. However, if you do not have the time or if you cannot help him find something he enjoys better, do not force him to cease an activity that makes him happy during his free time. This will only damage the relationship you are trying to build with Step 2 (pairing) and will likely increase his desire to participate in that self-stimulatory activity in the future. Your child's "need" to engage in self-stimulating behavior will diminish and eventually disappear in direct proportion to your successful efforts to introduce or create a desire to participate in newer more reinforcing skills and activities.

Regardless of how your child currently chooses to spend his free time, the more free time you allow him, the less time he will have to engage in learning activities with you. Structure your day so that your child has as little free time as possible. If you have maintained good control over his reinforcement and are pairing yourself and learning with fun during 75% of your interaction time, your child will actually prefer to participate in your teaching activities rather than be alone.

You should only be using imperative language during the 25% of your interaction with your child in which you are not engaged in pairing. *Imperative Language* is any form of language that expects something in return. However, when you do use imperatives, it is important that you expect, wait for, and then reinforce only appropriate responses to those imperatives. During teaching time, do not reward your child for avoiding learning. When you present a direction or instruction (formally known as a discriminative stimulus or S^D) you should expect your child to choose to satisfy that imperative. A *Discriminative stimulus (S^D)* is a signal that reinforcement is now available. When you use reinforcement in comprehensive ways, your instructions become signposts that alert your child that specific choices will lead to positive outcomes and others will not. Until he decides to respond to your S^D (pronounced SD) appropriately, you must not allow him to experience any additional reinforcement. The choice you are trying to teach will only be in your child's best interest if you stop allowing reinforcement to follow when he ignores you, refuses you, or acts inappropriately. When a positive learning behavior is in your child's best interest he will begin to choose it sooner and more often.

It is important to remain flexible in your teaching expectations as there are often many potentially appropriate responses to any one imperative. For instance, if you are trying to teach your child the difference between hard and soft and you ask him, "What kind of ball is this?" Even though you are expecting the word, "hard" you need to be flexible enough to accept the answers "small," "round" or even "golf ball," when these answers also apply. A great way to remain flexible but get your teaching goal met is to accept the answer by saying something like, "Yes, you're right, it is small and round but what else is it?" (prompting the answer "hard" if need be).

Imperatives or S^Ds should be presented to your child throughout the day in all environments. Sometimes your child will be interested in watching a video and you can teach him while sitting at a small table in front of the television. Other times he will be interested in jumping on the trampoline and you can teach on the floor using the trampoline as a reinforcer. If he wants to eat chips, you can teach in the kitchen reinforcing his positive behavior choices with his favorite chips. The location in which you teach him is not important. In fact,

Imperative language expects something in return from your child.

A Discriminative stimulus (S^D) is a signal that reinforcement is now available.

you should purposefully teach him in every situation you experience throughout the day. It is more important that your child is participating in your learning by choice, and that there are many opportunities to teach each target skill throughout the day.

The type of reinforcement you use to build skills should also depend on what your child is motivated to have or do at that very moment. Remember, that reinforcement is not the act of giving a child an object he likes after completing something you wanted. Rather, it is creating a circumstance that makes the child more likely to repeat a desired behavior. Because of your careful control of the child's environment (Step 1), as well as your playfulness, you should have become your child's strongest consistent reinforcer (Step 2). In addition, you will continue to use objects as reinforcers by allowing access to these favorite items only after a job well done. Be aware; the objects that reinforce your child's behavior often will not be what you have planned. Reinforcement is only reinforcement if it works to increase behavior. Do not get trapped in patterns of using specific objects or food items as reinforcers in specific teaching settings. Reinforcement should come from the observation of what your child is demonstrating he might like at that moment. Try not to consider reinforcement a thing. It is better thought of as a free flow of positive items and experiences moving in both directions between you and your child.

Reinforcement time should be thought of as a free flow of positive items and experiences moving in both directions between you and your child.

I remember the first day I began working with a little boy named Justin. I had asked his family what Justin's favorite items were to play with so that we could begin locating reinforcers for his positive behavior choices. When I arrived at the house I found a table full of his favorite toys including music CDs, cars, mini streetlights, talking teddy bears, and the like. However, as soon as his family and I began pairing with Justin we found that the only thing he really wanted to do was to push a computer table chair around the house. No matter how much mom and dad tried to coax him into playing with the other items, the chair was what he wanted to have. I quickly decided to begin using the chair as the item mom and dad were to pair themselves with and it eventually became one of his strongest teaching settings. After a very short time of pairing with Justin's favorite activities, mom and dad became as reinforcing to him as pushing the chair. Then, as reinforcers in their own right, they eventually were able to transfer the fun of their interaction to more appropriate play items. This reduced and ultimately eliminated the computer chair as a preferred activity for Justin. It was only his parent's willingness to observe what Justin wanted to do and use it as a source of reinforcement that allowed them quickly to begin productive teaching and to develop an influence over his preferred activities.

To say what you mean and mean what you say, you must consider your choice of words carefully. If you ask your child a question, he should be allowed to answer. Additionally, you should respect his decision even if it gets in the way of teaching. This means you have to think about the possible responses *before* you ask the question. For example, you have asked your child if he wants to work with you and he answers "No." Your child has not made an inappropriate response. In fact, you offered your child an option to work or not to work. He has opted not to work. You must realize that it was your decision to ask a question rather than give an instruction that caused the problem. You can avoid unnecessarily confusing your child by using more specific language. Say what you mean and mean what you say. Tell your child exactly what you want him to do by direct instruction. When you say to your child, "sit down," "come to me," or "do this," you should always expect your child to respond with an appropriate choice. If you have a ball that your child wants to play with and you direct him to sit down, you should not give him that ball until he is seated. If he does not take his seat, withhold the ball and all other forms of reinforcement until he makes a better choice. Conversely, if you ask your child if he wants to come and sit down, you should respect his choice not to come and the ball and other reinforcement should remain available to him.

Remember that Step 1 requires comprehensive restriction of reinforcement. If you are holding the ball that your child wants and there is nothing else available that your child enjoys, he will eventually choose to sit independently to gain access to the ball. However, when your child does not sit on his own you may choose to use a prompt to help speed up the process. Be sure to stop any prompts that your child resists. If he is resisting the prompt he has not made the choice to participate and you need to wait. If he lets you prompt him to completion, you should then reinforce appropriately. Often when I begin teaching instructional control techniques to a family I find that the parents desire to teach will not allow a child room to decide that he wants to learn. For example, when a parent attempts to get a child to participate in a known skill such as, sitting up straight, the child is then expected to choose to sit in a more appropriate position. Often this is not going to be a child's first response as following parent directions has normally been paired with a loss of control. So the child may not choose to sit appropriately. In these instances it is better to patiently wait with an unlimited supply of reinforcing items at your fingertips and give the child time to see that there is little else of interest to do. Then when the child comes back to try to tempt mom and dad to interact with him, the instruction "sit up straight" should be repeated and if necessary a gentle physical prompt to help the child sit can be used. If the child fights against the prompt my advice is to let go and once again wait for his interest to bring him back. However, I often find parents want their child to participate so badly that they will use a forced physical prompt when the child begins to pull away.

Forced Physical prompting causes the child to follow an instruction against his will. Parents will often follow this forced prompt with some forced reinforcement such as pushing a treat into the child's mouth or pushing the ball he wanted into his chest. Forcing your child to participate in this way usually garners one or all three of the following reactions. The child will likely refuse the reinforcement, immediately try to reverse the behavior that was just forced upon him, and/or he will lash out in some form of aggressive behavior. These are the only choices a child being overpowered has left to exert his control. If this type of behavior then meets with positive outcomes for the child, he will begin using it more often. Conversely, if the parents show more initial patience and are willing to wait until the child has decided that participating is in his best interest, the parents will find the child willingly accepting their prompt and happily accepting their attempts at reinforcement. Additionally, the child will also stay in the activity longer while giving a more consistent effort.

Be sure to find a way to offer more reinforcement when your child does a skill without your help and less when you have to prompt the correct response. For example, when you ask your child to sit and he takes a while to come to you and only complies with the help of your prompting, you might ask him to do a quick skill before giving him the ball he wants. However, if he comes to you and sits immediately and without a prompt, you might then choose to pick him up and tickle him while giving him the ball. The need for prompts or repeated repetition of the S^D may indicate that either the value of your interaction is not strong enough or you are in some way reinforcing his escape and avoidance behaviors. It is possible that he was never really that interested in the ball to begin with. Perhaps, the fact that you kept rapidly repeating your instruction was reinforcing to your child's ignoring behavior. To counteract the need for excessive prompts, you must increase your efforts to find and capture your child's motivation *before* giving him an instruction and reevaluate how you respond to him while he is refusing you. These are topics that will be discussed further in Chapter 6.

Once you have given your child a specific instruction, do not allow him to use requests as a form of escape. You do not want to teach your child that asking for something will get him out of the work he is doing now. Even natural requests for food or drink can be acknowledged but refused until he has finished the instruction or set of tasks you have asked him to do. You can then reinforce his appropriate participation in the task as well as his positive requesting behavior with the item for which he asked. This item could then serve as motivation and reinforcement for continued teaching. However, be careful not to let requests for items lead to a discontinuation of teaching. This will only encourage your child to begin using requests as a form of escape. Every parent wants their child to be able to ask to go to the bathroom at appropriate times. However, it is not functional or productive if he is asking to go when he wants to escape difficult learning tasks.

Step 4: Show your child that following your directions is beneficial and the best way for him to obtain what he wants. Give your child easy directions as often as possible and then reinforce his decisions to participate by following them with good experiences.

Once you have established control over your child's reinforcers, you can begin using them to support his appropriate behavior choices. To follow this step effectively you need to be aware of Premack's Principle. In the case of teaching your child, this principle means that he must follow a direction and/or demonstrate an appropriate behavior before you allow him to have something he wants. Premack's principle is better known as Grandma's Rule: "Before you get your desert, you first have to eat your dinner." The best way to ensure that your child adheres to this rule is for you to make a request or issue an instruction to your child before giving him anything that he might want from you. Your direction can be anything related or useful such as asking, "Throw that in the garbage for me first" or "Sit down and I'll get it for you." The more opportunities your child is reinforced with something he wants after first following a direction or demonstrating an appropriate behavior, the quicker he will learn that following rules and directions is the best way to get to what he desires.

Resist the temptation to ask your child if he wants something before you give him a requirement to meet in order to get it. Even though it is appropriate to ask your child to do something before you fulfill his request, you want to stay away from "if ____, then _____" statements. These statements are shortcuts to getting what you want from your child but they are fraught with limitations and potential problems. It is always better to surprise your child with an item or action that you think he wants *after* he has made a positive choice. The use of "if, then" statements does not translate into better choice making for your child. Instead it invites him to begin negotiating with you. He may choose to participate with you only when he considers the item you are offering as "good enough" to participate. "If, then" statements once again take the control of the interaction out of your hands and gives it back to your child. The last thing you want is for your child to be making decisions on the amount of effort he will give, based on the quality of the reinforcement you have told him will come. In practice the difference may seem subtle; however, it is extremely important. You want your child to make positive learning choices because in general they have proven to be in his best interest. This is the case with all of us but will only happen when reinforcement is pervasive but unpredictable. Restaurant servers usually work for gratuity. The amount a patron tips is often predicated on the quality of the service. Your ability to effect service depends on the server knowing that you have complete control over the amount you will give and he can only affect that amount by the quality of his service. Your choice to announce your tip at the beginning of the meal only lessens the motivation of the server to give you his very best throughout the evening. The same is true with your teaching relationship with your child. Which do you think he will prefer? Being consistently told that if he does something, he will get something in return or, instead, just knowing that when he makes positive choices of any kind, he can normally count on you to be there for him with things that make him happy.

To quickly get through the early phases of earning instructional control, provide your child with hundreds of opportunities a day to make an appropriate choice based on a direction. Then you need immediately to reinforce this positive choice. Once you have taken control over his reinforcement, it will be easy to provide him with opportunities to follow directions. Since you have access to his favorite items under your control, your child must come to you to obtain what he wants. When he does, you only need to ask him to do something first. It could be as simple as asking him to return the last item he was playing with, touch his nose, turn off the television, or repeat his request using more appropriate language. Start with simple tasks. Be careful giving directions for which you cannot prompt an answer. Physical responses such as motor imitations are normally easy to prompt. S^Ds (instructions) that require vocal responses should only be attempted after you have become comfortable with your child's skill level and willingness to participate. If your child refuses to or is unable to speak, you cannot prompt him to do so. This leaves you no choice but to wait or give in.

In addition to giving easy promptable S^Ds, the process of following directions should always be fun. To ensure this, instructional control directions should usually end with your child receiving some form of playful social reinforcement as well, such as tickles, statements of praise, or high-fives. The best ways to reinforce behavior including the important issues surrounding verbal praise is more specifically detailed in Chapter 8.

Step 5: Provide consistent reinforcement. In the early stages of earning instructional control with your child, reinforce after each positive response. Eventually change to an ever-increasing variable ratio of reinforcement.

Consistent reinforcement is important because your child must understand that certain behavior choices result in his coming in contact with something he values. All human behavior is predicated on this relationship to positive reward. Generally, we all choose the behavior we do based on the likelihood that it will lead us to some form of desired reinforcement. Even if that benefit is merely a sense of pride in one's accomplishments, reinforcement is at the root of everything we do. This understanding of good choices leading to good things will only occur if *every* good choice is met with a positive result. Because many of these choices are based on the S^Ds you have given him, he will begin to see that following these instructions is a necessary prerequisite to gaining life's rewards. The connection of clear instructions, leading to good choice making, leading to effective reinforcement is not lost on a child who is very good at getting what he wants. As your child learns that it is in his best interest to attend to your directions and give good responses, he will start to apply the necessary effort to focus on what you want from him. Ultimately, he will begin to come to you looking for a learning opportunity because he knows this is the first step to getting to his favorite things. This awareness of the importance of others is one of the first steps toward autism recovery and will only begin to occur if you consistently make compliance with your directions the best and fastest way that your child can meet with reinforcement. That means from the beginning do not let a good response of any kind pass without being followed by some form of reinforcement. There is always something reinforcing available to you--perhaps a tickle, a swing in the air, or a long loving deep pressure hug. Every time you reinforce a behavior you are making a statement that this is a behavior you want to see again in similar circumstances. Once your child understands this, he will also recognize that when you do not reinforce a behavior, it is that you would not like to see that behavior again.

Once earned, instructional control can be maintained by slowly thinning out the amount of reinforcement through an increase in the response–reinforcement ratio. The response–reinforcement ratio is the amount of acceptable responses a child needs to give before receiving a single presentation of reinforcement. To thin out the response–reinforcement ratio you would change from reinforcing every single response to reinforcing every second, third, or even fourth time your child complies with a direction. Eventually you can wait even longer. As your child's willingness to participate in learning improves, you should move from a reinforcement ratio of one (reinforcing every response) to a variable ratio (VR) of two or three. This means that on the average you will follow every two to three appropriate responses with tangible reinforcement. Next, you can move to a VR-5 (reinforcing an average of every five responses) and eventually a variable ratio of ten or more. The reason we use a variable ratio schedule of reinforcement is that scientific study indicates that using variable ratio (unpredictable) reinforcement schedules are more effective in evoking consistent and strong responding than set (predictable) schedules.

Instructional control can be easily maintained by slowly thinning out the response-reinforcement ratio.

Step 6: Demonstrate that you know your child's priorities as well as your own.

Track and record each of your child's favorite reinforcing items and activities. Then observe which he prefers in different situations. These preferences can be constantly changing, so you need to do the best that you can to know what he desires the most at any given time. Make a list of his current reinforcers and share this list with all the adults who regularly interact with your child. Divide your list into primary reinforcers (edible), secondary-tangible reinforcers (non-edible objects) and secondary-social reinforcers (interactions and activities). Work hard to find or develop enough reinforcers to fill up these lists. Your child needs to be able to work for a wide variety of reinforcement. Everyday you should try to find or develop a new reinforcer or two.

To find new reinforcing items or activities for your child, look at what currently functions as reinforcement and figure out why it is reinforcing.

The best way to find new reinforcing items or activities for your child is to look at what currently functions as reinforcement and figure out what aspect of those reinforcers your child likes. Looking for new items or activities with similar attributes will often allow you to expand your child's reinforcer list. Your child's rituals and stims (self-stimulatory behavior) are fertile ground for developing reinforcement. For example, a child who likes spinning himself around in circles might like being swung in the air by his parents, spinning in playground swings or on a computer chair, bouncing on a large gym ball, or being pulled across a hardwood floor on a blanket. Children who like opening and shutting doors or lining up objects might love playing with toys that allow for such activity. Children who like streetlights might work for toys with flashing or spinning lights, flashlights and mirrors, or games like Super Simon and Lite-Brite. The truth is there is no right way to find reinforcers for your child. The only way to find a new reinforcer is to keep trying new things until you do.

Differential reinforcement is the process of applying different amounts of reinforcement to different types or levels of behavior.

Always rotate your use of specific reinforcers to keep from diluting the reinforcing value of any one item. It is also a good idea to save your child's most valued items and activities to be used as reinforcers for difficult or important skills such as language acquisition or toilet training. Be sure to consider social reinforcement as well as those that are tangible. Knowing how to manipulate what your child desires is one of the important parts of using differential reinforcement to improve your child's decision-making skills. Differential reinforcement is the process of applying different amounts of reinforcement to different types or levels of behavior.

By knowing what your child prioritizes as his favorite items, you will be able to decide which items to give him as a consequence for weaker responses, which to use for good responses, and what type of reinforcement is deserved for terrific responses. By differentially reinforcing the type of responses your child makes, you will be able to better shape the type of responding you will receive from him in the future. In addition to knowing what your child wants, you must also remain aware of your priorities. What is the most important thing for you to be teaching your child? Normally, when you work with your child, you will have several different goals in mind at any one time. When this is the case, it is possible that a single behavior choice your child makes may be appropriate for one goal you are trying to meet but inappropriate for another. In these instances you need to know what target goals are your priorities. If your goal is to pair with your child, you might respond to a behavior differently than if you are trying to focus on skill acquisition. There is seldom only one correct way to respond to a behavior choice your child makes. It is important to know what your priorities are at any given time and make reinforcement choices based on these priorities.

The ability to earn instructional control with your child is extremely important. It is what helps you to transfer your child's world into a learning environment. This chapter has walked you through six of the seven important steps involved in earning and maintaining instructional control without the need for manipulating your child with escape extinction. These six steps allow you to begin building your child's internal desire to make positive behavior choices. The next chapter discusses Step 7, the other side of instructional control-- decreasing problematic behavior.

Summary of Chapter 5

The scientific study of behavior has shown that the reasons your child needs to build better attention, focus, and interaction skills must come in the form of reinforcement and/or motivation and can only be earned through good instructional control (page 50).

The overall goal of any child's behavior plan should be to show the child that the fastest and easiest way to get what he wants is to follow directions while using appropriate language and behavior skills (page 51).

Regardless of what other therapists and therapies have promised, recovery from the diagnosis of autism is not a realistic possibility without successfully earning and maintaining instructional control (page 51).

Pairing is a behavioral principle which states that when two items or activities are experienced together the perceived value of one will influence the perceived value of the other (page 52).

The Goal of Pairing is to establish yourself as a reinforcer for your child's behavior choices allowing you to become a generalized reinforcer for good behavior (page 52).

Escape extinction is the process of not letting a child's use of escape behavior lead to actual escape of the task or teaching setting. In most cases captive learning through escape extinction should be used as a last resort and then only with a plan in place to reduce its need in the future (page 53).

It is only when your child is making the *independent choice* to maintain and prolong your interactions that you can begin teaching beyond the limits of what he was formerly willing to learn (page 55).

All seven steps of instructional control must be in place if you are to successfully develop the best possible learning relationship with your child. The failure to adhere to even one step upsets the entire balance and your child will consistently be able to find a way to avoid the benefits of your teaching (page 56).

Try not to consider reinforcement a thing. It is better thought of as a free flow of positive items and experiences moving in both directions between you and your child (page 61).

Once earned, instructional control can be maintained by slowly thinning out the amount of reinforcement through an increase in the response–reinforcement ratio. The response–reinforcement ratio is the amount of acceptable responses a child needs to give before receiving a single presentation of reinforcement (page 67).

Differential reinforcement is the process of applying different amounts of reinforcement to different types or levels of behavior (page 68).

Seven Steps to Instructional Control

Step 1: Show your child that you are the one in control of the items he wants to hold or play with and that you will decide when and for how long he can have them (page 56).

Step 2: Show your child that you are fun. Make each interaction you have with him an enjoyable experience so that he will want to follow your directions to earn more time, sharing these experiences with you. (page 57).

Step 3: Show your child that you can be trusted. Always say what you mean and mean what you say. If you instruct your child to do something, do not allow him access to reinforcement until he has complied with your request. This step allows for prompting him to completion if necessary (page 59).

Step 4: Show your child that following your directions is beneficial and the best way for him to obtain what he wants. Give your child easy directions as often as possible and then reinforce his decisions to participate by following them with good experiences (page 64).

Step 5: Provide consistent reinforcement. In the early stages of earning instructional control with your child, reinforce after each positive response. Eventually change to an ever-increasing variable ratio of reinforcement. (page 66).

Step 6: Demonstrate that you know your child's priorities as well as your own (page 67).

Step 7: Is detailed in Chapter 6.

Chapter 6

Decreasing Problematic Behavior

Choices with Instructional Control

Chapter 5 outlined the first six steps to instructional control. These steps combine to form a series of guidelines that detail how to interact with your child so that he will quickly begin to make better learning choices. However, for many parents this is only half the battle of gaining cooperation and building a positive learning relationship with their children. The seventh and final step in earning instructional control explains how to best respond when your child chooses not to cooperate.

Empty threats quickly become meaningless. Your words will only have meaning if they are paired with actions that correspond to their intended meaning. Saying the word "no" to a child has no effect when the child can choose to participate in the activity anyway and still find positive outcomes. Any child's consistent ability to attend to and to obey instructions will ultimately depend on if those instructions are supported by a meaningful consequence. There needs to be a noticeable difference in your child's post-decision environment that will demonstrate that the choices you want him to make are in his best interest and that "bad" choices carry no benefit. Once this is the norm, your child will begin willingly making the choice to increase the

Your words will only have meaning if they are paired with actions that correspond to their intended meaning.

frequency of his positive decision making while decreasing the frequency of inappropriate choices.

Attention, escape, and self-stimulation are all behavioral outcomes that a child may find reinforcing. If a child's most effective way to find and maintain these reinforcing outcomes is to break rules or ignore instructions, he will. Adults tend to become more demanding when a child ignores their demands. As a result, the more demanding the adult becomes the more determined the child is to refuse the demands. This ever-increasing cycle spirals out of control in far too many teaching relationships. The process of breaking this cycle has two parts. The first is to make your instructions worth following. Accomplishing this requires a comprehensive use of the instructional control steps 1 through 6 detailed in Chapter 5. The second part removes any benefit coming from ignoring or refusing your rules or instructions. This is addressed with the seventh step of instructional control.

Step 7   Show your child that ignoring your instructions or choosing inappropriate behavior will *not* result in the acquisition of reinforcement.

Pairing yourself with your child's favorite items and activities during 75% of your interaction with him will allow you to become his major source of reinforcement. In concert with comprehensive restriction of his reinforcing items, pairing in this fashion will allow you to hold your child to high behavioral expectations during the 25% of the time you are giving instructions. Avoid allowing your child to meet with reinforcement when he specifically chooses to refuse a direct instruction or knowingly engages in inappropriate behavior. **Inappropriate behavior** is anything your child does that you would not like to see repeated under similar circumstances. Behavior choices such as yelling, grabbing for reinforcers, pulling mom or dad, stomping one's feet, demonstrations of frustration including self-injurious behaviors, pushing someone away, and ignoring parent requests are examples of inappropriate behavior. You must consistently recognize when your child is behaving inappropriately and intentionally make that behavior unsuccessful. You do this simply by *not* reinforcing it.

Every behavior your child is currently using was in some way reinforced in the past. If not, there would have been no reason for him to use this behavior again. Anthony was a boy with whom our team worked very hard to earn instructional control. Whenever Anthony was unhappy he would begin yelling "Ow, ow, ow!" Since Anthony did not have the ability to express himself with many words, his parents wondered if he was saying "ow" because he had been emotionally hurt. Other theories were that he was scared, confused, dealing with sensory issues, feeling internal pain, or that he did not know what the sound "ow" typically meant. All of those theories were potential causes of this behavior, but a study of the antecedents and consequences of this behavior demonstrated that Anthony was using this behavior as a way to gain the attention of others or avoid/escape situations in which he would rather not stay. Anthony had likely heard others say "ow" when they were hurt. Additionally, he had found that when he expressed getting hurt with the "ow" sound, people would immediately stop what they were doing and come to his aid. Not only did he receive attention and comfort for his pain, Anthony also realized that saying "ow" had value as an escape from demands. Over time, Anthony began to say "ow" whenever he was unhappy with his situation and wanted it to change. The more this behavior was reinforced (successful in gaining what he wanted) the more he used it. Eventually, he would yell "ow" if he wanted a different color pencil than the one that he was given. The best way to affect Anthony's inappropriate use of the sound "ow" was to deny it further reinforcement. The way that our team solved this problem was by applying a consequence called **extinction**. Extinction is the process of not reinforcing a previously reinforced behavior. Whenever a behavior has developed a history of being reinforced, you can put that behavior on extinction by no longer allowing reinforcement to follow it. Any behavior that is put on extinction will reduce over time.

Extinction is the process of not reinforcing a previously reinforced behavior.

Anthony had been receiving reinforcement for the sound "ow" because it was often followed by attention, escape, and increased control over his environment. To extinguish this behavior we had to withhold the reinforcement that had previously followed it. By refusing to allow Anthony to meet with reinforcement when he used "ow" (unless Anthony was truly hurt) we took the value out of the sound. Without reinforcement to support its use, the sound began to disappear. In a very short time Anthony gave up his inappropriate use of the "ow" sound that was getting in the way of his learning. In effect, we maintained his use of the sound "ow" at times it was appropriate but extinguished its use at inappropriate times. This type of extinction procedure can be used for an unlimited number of less effective or problem behaviors.

Any behavior that is put on extinction will reduce over time.

Depending on the child and situation, extinction can look very different. There are two major types of extinction. The first type of extinction that needs to be addressed is when your child wants something from you. For example, you are on the phone and your child wants your attention. If your child's crying has gotten your attention in the past, your child will likely cry whenever he wants you to hang up the phone. The way to reduce this behavior is to put it on extinction. Refuse to hang up the phone when your child is crying. Then when your child stops crying for even a short time have someone prompt him with a more appropriate way to get this desire met. It could be by calling your name or tapping you on the shoulder. It might just be to find something else to do while you are on the phone. As soon as your child demonstrates one of these competing behavior choices, you can quickly hang up and give him your attention as a reinforcer for his new more appropriate behavior. Pretending to use the phone many times per day will allow the desired result to occur more quickly than would happen if you only use the procedure on occasions you receive phone calls.

Often your child uses inappropriate behavior when he already has your attention. For instance, your child wants something from you that he cannot have either by parental choice or because he refuses to appropriately respond to an S^D (instruction). This includes an unwillingness to ask for the item appropriately or wait patiently for you to deliver the item in the manner you see fit. If, while your child already has your attention, he chooses to engage in any behavior below your current level of expectation, you must consider this an extinction situation. The way to apply extinction in this case is to immediately make an observable physical statement. You must clearly demonstrate that his choice is unacceptable to you. In many cases, you could stop yourself mid-sentence and turn away from your child. When a child loses the attention of his parents at a time when he wants something from them, it is a clear statement that he is now on the wrong path.

Here is how extinction looked with a 16-year old boy our team was asked to help named Max, who had the ability to use individual words to ask for things but seldom chose to do so. Instead, he pointed at or pulled his mom to the desired object. In this case, it is both the item and Mom's assistance that Max wants. Our goal was to teach Max to vocally ask for things that he wanted in his environment. In developing instructional control, we showed Max that he could always have what he wanted if he followed our instructions and used appropriate vocalizations to ask for things. In addition, we also had to take the value out of pulling mom to the items he wanted. Using the seventh step to instructional control in this context meant not allowing Max to have what he wanted when he tried to pull his mom. Whenever he tried, mom was instructed to fold her arms in a way that he could not grab hold. She was then instructed to say the word of the object that he wanted and wait for him to echo instead. If he tried to pull her instead of repeating the echo request, mom turned away from him. Once he stopped trying to pull her, mom would turn back to him and restate the word he was to echo. This procedure was repeated as often as necessary. When Max did repeat the name appropriately or made an acceptable approximation, she would take his hand and walk with him to get the item. If she was unaware of what he wanted she would have him echo, "Come with." Once he did, mom would go with Max until he demonstrated what he wanted. Then, when she could ascertain what he was motivated to have, she would give him the name of that item to echo. As soon as Max understood that using words would be reinforced and pulling would not be reinforced, he began happily using words to ask for things and his pulling behavior vanished. This procedure has worked just as well for non-vocal children. However, instead of prompting these children to echo the word "come here" we prompt them to make a sign language symbol for "come here" and then the sign for the item they want.

Extinction is relatively easy when your child uses inappropriate behavior to ask for something. You have control of what your child wants and he can only have it if you give it to him. Reminding yourself who is truly empowered in this situation should help you to remain calm and capable of responding appropriately regardless of his behavior choices. One of the simplest techniques to use when a child wants something from you and is ignoring an instruction or attempting an inappropriate behavior to obtain it is to turn your body away from him. If he wants something from you, he needs your attention to gain your willing participation. Turning away from him is an unmistakable statement that his behavior choice has lost your attention. As soon as he has stopped the behavior or any new inappropriate behavior, you can turn back to him and restate the instruction. You should be willing to repeat this procedure for as long as he continues to make inappropriate choices. Depending on the level of instructional control you are trying to obtain you can even begin to make decisions on the acceptability of his behavior while complying with your

Extinction is relatively easy when your child uses inappropriate behavior to ask for something. If you have control of the item, you can withhold it until he makes a better choice.

Turning away from your child in response to an inappropriate behavior is an unmistakable statement that his behavior choice has lost your attention.

instructions. Was his response loud enough? Clear enough? Was he whining? Did he make eye contact with you while answering? In the beginning stages of instructional control, these questions would not be a consideration as you are only looking for basic levels of participation. However, the better your instructional control becomes the more you can begin to focus on other important concerns such as volume, clarity, and eye contact, among others. This type of decision-making refers back to the sixth step of instructional control and will depend on your current teaching priorities. For example, is your teaching priority to gain your child's cooperation or is the quality of his response more important at this time?

Even when your child follows a direction, you still need to be allowed to deliver the reinforcement in a manner you feel is appropriate.

Even though your child follows a direction, you still need to be allowed to deliver your reinforcement in a manner you feel appropriate. If after following a direction your child chooses to grab at the reinforcer before you can deliver it, stop and have him demonstrate a competing behavior. A **competing behavior** is any behavior that cannot be demonstrated at the same time as the behavior in question. Something such as telling your child to wait or put his hands at his sides would be appropriate. Then you can provide the reinforcer the way you want it to be delivered.

You should also use extinction when you have decided your child cannot have an item but he refuses to accept the answer "no."

Sometimes your child will want an item from you that you have decided he cannot have. If he does not accept the answer "no" and continues to ask for it, complain, or engage in any other inappropriate behavior, you must also consider this an extinction situation as well. Extinguishing complaining behavior or inappropriate attempts to convince you to change your mind is similar to what was described above. The main difference is that after you have turned away from your child, you need to wait for him to cease his efforts to change your mind. As soon as he is quiet, you can approach him about playing with another object or doing something else. If he starts asking for the "off limits" item again or engages in any other inappropriate behavior, you need to immediately turn or walk away again. Repeat this procedure until your child has accepted the answer and moved on. As soon as he does, reinforce this positive choice with something great. Once your child begins accepting your answer "no" without a fuss, you might want to occasionally give him the off-limits item as a reinforcer for the behavior of accepting your decision. Just be sure it is very clear that he is getting the item as a reinforcer for the behavior of willingly accepting your answer "no." This will give him even more motivation to fight through the unusually strong desires that come with autism and accept your refusals in the future. The first few times you use this procedure you should only expect your child to be quiet for a few seconds before trying to engage him in another activity. However, as his understanding of the procedure grows so should the length of time you expect him to be quiet before returning your attention to him.

The two examples above demonstrate how to use extinction when your child is looking for something from you. The second type of extinction to consider occurs when you need your child to do something for you and he refuses, or tries to escape the demand. For example, you want your child properly attired before he leaves for school and he refuses to put on his shoes. Step 7 in this situation is trickier because, you are not in physical control of your child's current desire. Thus, you cannot use this desire as motivation or reinforcement. In this case, you are left with what is called escape extinction. When using escape extinction, you cannot turn or walk away from your child after presenting an S^D (instruction) and obtaining an inappropriate response. In fact, you must do the exact opposite. When you have a direction for your child and he is not complying with it, you need to keep giving that direction until he complies. Chapter 5 speaks against the use of escape extinction procedures. Escape extinction involves maintaining your S^D while blocking your child's attempts at escaping the demand. It is extremely difficult to use escape extinction without physically forcing a child to submit. Doing so will often damage the positive connection you are so carefully trying to build with your child. Additionally, escape extinction doesn't allow your child to escape so it does not allow him to make a conscious choice to stay. However, it is important to note that if you are willing to allow your S^Ds to go unfulfilled in this type of situation, you will be reinforcing inappropriate behavior and your child will not learn to follow your directions in the future. Regardless, It is always better to avoid this type of extinction.

Escape Extinction involves maintaining your S^D while blocking your child's attempts at escaping the demand.

Using all seven steps of instructional control in concert will normally make the use of escape extinction unnecessary. However, if at any time you do choose to use escape extinction, it is best that you follow through with it until your child has complied with your instruction. The best way to make sure your child fulfils your requests appropriately and in a timely manner is to prompt him through the required response. If you need to use escape extinction, you should analyze why your child did not follow your direction to begin with. Was your S^D clear? Have you not paired this specific activity with enough reinforcement

Using all seven steps of instructional control in concert will normally make the use of escape extinction unnecessary.

in the past? Were you trying to fight past too strong of a motivation with too little reinforcement? Was your child capable of answering that S^D? Maybe you are not using differential reinforcement appropriately. To use **differential reinforcement** in this case you could begin to reinforce your child differently depending on how the task is completed. Give him a small amount of reinforcement when you have to prompt him through the skill, give him more reinforcement when he does a skill independently, and give him the most when he does it quickly and completely without prompts. The larger amount of reinforcement earned will act as the reason your child will want to perform the skill in the best possible way in the future. It is the repeated pairing of this better response with better reinforcement that will motivate your child to continue using this new behavior beyond the current teaching trial.

Give small amounts of reinforcement when you have to prompt a skill, more when your child does the skill independently, and the most when he does it quickly and completely without prompts.

In most cases, you can avoid using the more difficult and less desirable escape extinction by understanding the power structure of interactions and taking the time to plan. Once an imperative (directive) has entered an interaction, there is an immediate power imbalance. Interactions involving declarative language are always balanced. Without a request, neither party has an expectation to live up to in that moment of the interaction. This keeps an interaction purely social. This is why in the ABA/VB program developed by Knospe-ABA, we strongly recommend that interaction between you and your child consist of 75% pairing with the use of declarative and non-verbal language to build your child's social determination skills. In other words, for every minute you are with your child only 15-seconds of that time should involve giving and answering S^Ds. The other 45-seconds should be for pairing and reinforcement only.

Making a request that requires a response from the other person puts that person in a position of power in the interaction.

Anytime someone makes a request that requires a response from the other person, he willingly puts that person in a position of power in the interaction. The person receiving the request is in power because he knows what the other person wants and can now decide if he will respond to the request or not. The reason extinction works so well is that it stems from your child's desire to have something from you. He is used to being reinforced for a specific behavior and now you are withholding this reinforcement until he chooses a different behavior. When your child wants something from you in an interaction you are in the power position. You can decide if, when, how long, or to what degree he can have what he wants. Conversely, trying to get your child to do something when you do not control his current motivation puts him in the power position. This means that he can now decide if, when, how long, or to what degree you can have what you want.

Without a good understanding of ABA/VB, most parents, teachers, and therapists frequently give instructions to a child when they have no way to ensure compliance because they do not control the child's motivation. This keeps the child in a constant state of control over their interactions. Regardless of what you need from your child, in developing instructional control your best decision is usually to wait until he wants something from you before you ask. If he refuses, you are now dealing with an extinction situation that *you* can control. Here is a good example of the way you can turn a low power position into a more advantageous teaching situation. If you want your child to put on his shoes you can ask him to comply. Then you are left to wait and see if you have done enough pairing that he responds out of the hope that you will continue a reinforcing behavior exchange. If he does not respond, you are now forced to use escape extinction and apply direct pressure to your child in the form of repeated instructions and forced physical prompting until he complies. Your only other choice is to give in on your demand. Either eventuality is far less than ideal. A better choice is to wait until your child asks you for something such as a favorite toy to play with or a snack. Remember, thanks to comprehensive control of your child's reinforcement, this will be a regular occurrence. Then when he has demonstrated a motivation for something you can control, you are in the power position and can use that motivation as the reason why he will respond to your S^D (instruction). In situations where your child is already enjoying a reinforcing item or situation you can temporarily block access to it and give the request to put on his shoes. If he does respond by putting on his shoes, you can reinforce him with the toy, snack, and any other social reinforcement you want to add for good measure. Remember pairing social praise such as "great job" or "thank you" with tangible reinforcement will allow you to develop more social reinforcers that you can use in the future. However, even if your child does not respond to your request, you are now in an advantageous position in which you can use extinction by withholding something he has demonstrated that he wants until he makes a better choice.

Barry is a little boy diagnosed with PDD-NOS (Pervasive Developmental Delay -- Not Otherwise Specified.) This label is applied to children who have many, but not enough of the behaviors necessary to receive an autism diagnosis. At age four Barry seemed to enjoy making his mom's life miserable in the mornings. She said that it was a nightmare trying to get him ready for school each day. She described the normal routine. Barry was an early riser and he would wake her up for his morning milk as soon as he was out of bed. Then, with milk bottle in hand, Barry watched cartoons with his sister as mom prepared herself for work. The problem started when it became time for Barry to get ready for school. At this point, Barry would run, scream, kick and generally indulge in any behavior that enabled him to escape mom's demands. Some mornings, it took mom over two hours to get Barry dressed and she would have to start before five every morning not to be late. Barry used an infinite number of different behaviors for the purpose of escaping mom's instructions but he also had developed a great love for the play aspect of their morning interaction. He was in complete control of the actions and emotions of his entire family. He was able to watch his cartoons, eat his breakfast, drink his milk, and still got to play chase with mom for as long as he wanted.

The first thing our team did was to explore what types of reinforcement were available for Barry in the morning. There were several obvious choices. First, he loved watching cartoons with his sister. Second, he insisted on his bottle of milk before doing anything else in the day. Third, he wanted to eat his bowl of cereal. Additionally he liked to play a chase game with his mom. All of these reinforcing items were motivations that Barry had in his environment that were not being explored for their teaching value.

We started by unplugging the television so that mom would have complete control over its use. If Barry wanted to watch television or relax with a bottle of milk, he would first be instructed to go into the bathroom and begin getting ready for the day. If he refused, mom would take his milk into the bathroom and begin getting herself ready for work. Instead of using escape extinction by forcing Barry to follow her direction, mom instead allowed him to make an inappropriate choice but calmly demonstrated that this choice would not lead to the reinforcement he desired. Without access to milk or the television, Barry began trying to engage his mom's attention. When he asked again for milk, he was told he could have what he wanted but he first had to wash his hands and face. In the beginning, he would run out of the bathroom. But that refusal/escape behavior was no longer followed by reinforcement. Yes, he temporarily escaped the demand; however it was not leading Barry to what he truly desired, milk and time watching television. Barry was instead given the opportunity to make the most of a difficult choice (a skill he would need to possess in life). If he wanted milk, television, and a chase game with mom, he would willingly have to follow her directions. Whenever Barry tried to gain mom's attention, she repeated the instruction, "Wash your hands and face." Eventually, the desire to have his milk and television the way he liked it developed enough motivation in Barry that he was willing to follow her direction. Once he did, mom gave reinforcement to this new behavior choice by tickling and chasing him for fun, giving him his milk and then plugging the television in for him. After 10 to15 minutes of television reinforcement, it was time for Barry to dress. Mom unplugged the television, took his empty milk bottle, and instructed him to put on his clothes. If Barry refused, she left the clothes for him but the television remained unplugged and mom returned to her morning routine. Any attempt by Barry to convince mom to turn the television on or engage in morning play activities were met with the instruction, "Put your clothes on." With all other forms of reinforcement controlled by mom, and little else to do, Barry, after a few tantrums, eventually made the choice to dress. Mom cheered this decision, ran to him and helped him put on his clothes. She gave him the attention he wanted and immediately turned the television back on for him.

Barry was allowed to enjoy his cartoons until breakfast was ready. Mom then unplugged the television and announced that it was time to eat, but when Barry arrived at the table, he saw that his coat and shoes were on his chair. Mom used the fact that she knew Barry wanted to eat as an opportunity to give him an instruction, "put your coat and shoes on." Again, when Barry refused, she ignored him and nonchalantly ate her breakfast. With no television and mom not responding to his attempts at gaining her attention or control of her emotions, Barry had little else to do but think about his breakfast on the table. Eventually he made the choice to put his coat and shoes on, ate his breakfast, and his mom praised him for his good decision making as they went out the door to school. Had he not chosen to comply, mom would have put his breakfast away uneaten. After all, it was Barry's choice whether or not to eat. Once Barry realized that mom meant what she said and that he would find little reinforcement with any behavior other than following her directions, he began to comply more rapidly each day. Eventually mom no longer needed to unplug the television. Just the knowledge that she would, with no benefit coming to him, was enough for Barry to begin making better early morning choices without the constant need for extinction. The better mom used extinction, the less often she needed to use it and the more normal her morning interactions with Barry became.

The better you use extinction, the less often you will need to use it and the more normal your interactions with your child will become.

As much as extinction can be a valued form of behavior reduction, it is important to emphasize the problems that accompany the use of <u>escape</u> extinction. As stated in Chapter 5, escape extinction is the process of not allowing a child to escape a teaching setting or demand. In the first example, mom did not stop Barry from escaping her demand. She allowed him the choice to leave but through environmental control made that choice undesirable. In other words, avoid giving your child reinforcement in the form of attention or control (power over you) when he uses behavior meant to avoid learning. Do not physically stop your child from leaving the teaching setting or refusing your demands. Instead, when your child decides to leave a teaching setting, make sure that his choice has no visible controlling effect on you. This can be best done through declarative statements such as, "I guess we are done playing," "Bye," or "Oh well, I guess you do not want to watch television anymore." Non-verbal reactions are also beneficial. Gather your teaching and reinforcing materials and walk to another part of the room. Divert your eyes and/or turn your body away from your child. Continue playing with the items either by yourself or with other children. Make sure that your child has no access to reinforcing objects and actions until he returns to finish the activity he left. This encourages your child to make a conscious choice to follow your directions and return to participate in joint learning activities. Letting your child go and waiting until he chooses to come back is much more effective than trying to pull him toward your activity or holding him there against his will. Every action has an equal and opposite reaction. Pulling your child toward work will only increase your child's motivation to escape work. For your teaching to be as productive as possible, your child must decide that it is in his best interest to learn from you. Do not force this decision. Instead, set up the environment through the seven steps of instructional control so that learning from you is your child's most beneficial option. Then give him the opportunity to realize it. Whenever possible avoid escape extinction: Children who *choose* to rejoin the teaching process are less likely to leave it again and more likely to display maximum effort.

Children who choose to rejoin the teaching process are less likely to leave it again and more likely to display maximum effort.

Although you will only need to think about Step 7 and the use of extinction procedures in the relatively small percentage of time you are not engaged in steps 1 through 6, any talk of power positioning when dealing with children is distasteful. Nobody wants to spend time thinking about how to maintain a position of power when interacting with a child. However, children with autism are extremely bright and generally intuitively aware of the principles of behavior. This book has already discussed many of the ways your child might be using ABA to change your behavior choices on a daily basis. If you do not begin to understand how to respond in kind, surrendering constant control to your child will allow his problematic behavior to grow until you can no longer care for him or help him to become a happy independent adult.

Although the process of using extinction is often difficult, it is one of the most useful strategies available to help a child decrease his use of inappropriate behavior and to accept instructional control. Steps 1 through 6 are designed to help increase the frequency and quality of your child's positive behavior choices. When used correctly, these steps make life immediately easier for you and your child. He is following directions and participating in positive interactions with you and, subsequently, you are playfully giving him all of his favorite things. It is this part of instructional control that you want to spend the most time with as it is usually filled with joy and laughter. Conversely, the benefits of extinction procedures are not immediate. The results occur over time and exist in the absence of reinforcement. However, this seventh step of instructional control must come into play whenever your child makes a choice that you do not want to see again.

An extinction burst is the period during which a behavior on extinction will intensify or increase before finally decreasing.

A behavior choice that consistently meets with reinforcement will increase in frequency. By definition, something in your child's environment has consistently reinforced all of his problematic behavior choices. Extinction reverses this process of inappropriate choices eliciting access to reinforcement resulting in increased frequency. When used correctly, extinction blocks reinforcement rendering the behavior obsolete. Extinction allows you to reduce problem behavior without the need for aversive punishment procedures. You need to realize however that extinction always comes with a cost; the extinction burst. An **extinction burst** is the period during which a behavior on extinction will intensify or increase before finally decreasing.

The extinction burst is composed of behavior more severe than the one you are trying to extinguish. Initial periods of extinction burst are often long and difficult to endure. However, your child needs you to help him get past his extinction burst. Working through each extinction burst with your child is the only way you will ever fully earn instructional control and develop a best-case working relationship with him. As soon as you make a request of your child to which he does not choose to comply, you must put that behavior on extinction and ride out the extinction burst no matter how severe the behavior becomes. If your child is endangering himself during the extinction burst, you should protect him. If he is endangering your safety, you can leave the room. However, once you make the decision to use extinction, you cannot give in to your child's extinction burst behavior choices. If you do, you will be teaching your child that the behavior that caused you to give in is the one he can use the next time he does not want to do what you have asked. Your child might verbally or physically threaten to damage one of your possessions during an extinction burst. Do your best to keep important items out of reach *before* going into an extinction situation with your child. However, if you have not done this and you need to protect an item, you should calmly and without showing any distress, get between your child and the object. Avoid giving him any reinforcement including your attention during this time. Showing distress over an object or action that your child threatens during extinction will likely cause your child to use it as a distraction tool during his next extinction burst. The more distraction tools you give your child, the more difficult the extinction process becomes.

Showing distress over an object or action your child threatens during extinction will likely cause your child to use it as a distraction tool during his next extinction burst.

When we began working with Anthony, our team found that he was dead set against participating in any parent-guided activity. We began by taking control of all of Anthony's favorite things. Then we began pairing ourselves with those items in fun and reinforcing ways. When a member of the team had Anthony's strong motivation to continue a pairing activity, he stopped and gave Anthony a simple instruction "Do this," which was then prompted to completion. Then Anthony's prompted behavior was reinforced with more pairing fun. After a few of these simple directions with prompted responses, Anthony began to realize that he was actually following instructions and suddenly chose to refuse any attempt to prompt his next answer. As a result, we turned away from him, kept control of all of the reinforcing items, and waited for him to try to engage one of us in activity again. With nothing else to do, it did not take long for Anthony to begin looking for ways to steal back control of the situation. He began yelling "Ow, ow, ow!" He began running through the house throwing himself into the furniture. He cried, screamed, tried to take the toys, knocked over chairs, threatened the big screen TV and generally chose to tantrum his way through the next two to three hours. Since we were now using an extinction procedure, it was imperative that this learning situation end with a positive choice on Anthony's part. We avoided giving him attention and worked

The more distraction tools you give your child, the more difficult the extinction process becomes.

hard not to let his distraction techniques work to steal our focus on the original instruction. Every time he quieted down or came to any of us for something he wanted, we would calmly repeat the original instruction, "Do this." If we thought Anthony would let us, we would try to prompt the correct response. If Anthony pulled away, we would turn away from Anthony again and wait. Anthony had to see that his inappropriate choices were counterproductive and did not get him what he wanted. He had to see that the more he shared control with the people in his environment the better life was going to be. Additionally, he had to find out that trying to maintain complete control was no longer to his benefit. At some point as Anthony closed in on his third hour of extinction burst behavior he stopped, took a deep breath, and walked over to his mom. She said, "Do this" and while looking her straight in the eyes, he copied her instruction without even needing a prompt. Mom was so shocked that she stood there not sure what to do. The rest of us cheered for him and told her to start playing with him again. She tickled him, swung him in the air, offered him his favorite toys, and went back to a long period of pairing with no new demands. To help Anthony make the difficult decision to fight past his controlling behaviors, the team had to make his positive choice a worthwhile experience that would motivate him to repeat this choice in the future. In short, we had to reinforce the choice. After about one-half hour of play and pairing, mom once again began giving easy instructions. As before, Anthony put up with the first few but eventually had enough and made a choice that required us to use extinction again. The team repeated the extinction procedure but this time it only took Anthony about one-half hour to make a better choice. After a three-day consultation, our team left Anthony's parents with the seven steps to instructional control and a few basic teaching programs. After about two weeks of using these steps, Anthony was no longer fighting against instructions. He had demonstrated a couple of five-minute extinction bursts per day and only one half-hour extinction burst in the week. More importantly all the time he was not in extinction, he was participating in fun activities with his family and beginning to make progress on new learning goals. He was more socially attuned to his family's needs and he was beginning to learn how to use functional language. To top it all, his parents described Anthony as much happier and their lives as much improved.

Our team at Knospe-ABA is introduced to many children with autism who have developed incredibly difficult problem behavior. Just recently one of our new consultants called me on the phone for guidance. She was now heading into her third hour of extinction burst with a little boy who was determined to wait out her willingness to withhold reinforcement. I asked her to describe the situation and the procedures that were being used. After ascertaining that the procedure was most likely being conducted in the best possible way, I told her to focus on reinforcing the parents. This was their initial consultation and it was important that they get through this very first extinction burst and see the positive result at the end. I knew that if they lost their will to continue and reinforced the child after three hours, they would be setting themselves up for three hour extinction bursts whenever they refused to comply with their child's demands. I had our consultant remind the family that extinction was not an experiment that we were conducting. The methods of reducing behavior through the principle of extinction have been widely demonstrated scientifically. My experience guiding the programs of numerous children has given me the confidence to know that if I follow the procedures correctly I <u>will</u> find a positive outcome in the end. With the added boost of my unflinching confidence, our consultant and the family went back to work with Step 7 of instructional control. In this instance, the procedure took five hours and fifteen minutes to complete (a new Knospe-ABA record). But when it was done, the child had realized that mom, dad, and the education team were not going to give in. This left him with the resolve he needed to overcome his immediate desires and make a better choice. When he did, the entire team overwhelmed him with positive praise, tickles, games, sweets and fun. He returned to a positive flow of shared experiences and as of the writing of this book has never needed more than an hour to make a better choice again.

Most children with autism enjoy the use of repetitive self-stimulatory (stim) behavior. Many will choose this behavior over your reinforcing activities whenever the workload becomes too difficult. However, it is actually only a very small percentage of children with autism who truly find their ritualistic self-stimulation behavior the <u>most</u> reinforcing behavior in which they can participate. When a child would rather stim than participate in any fun pairing activity with others, there needs to be additional instructional considerations. If your child truly would rather engage in repetitive self-stimulation over any fun activity that you can provide, extinction is more difficult. This is because you cannot control the delivery of the reinforcement through environmental manipulation alone. For this small subgroup of children with autism, you may

It is actually only a very small percentage of children who find their self-stim behavior the most reinforcing behavior in which they can participate.

be forced to disrupt their ritualistic stim behavior until they make an appropriate response to your S^D (instruction). For example, children who would rather look out the window for several hours than participate in any other fun activities with you might need to have their view to the window blocked until they choose to respond. This is a form of negative reinforcement.

Negative Reinforcement is the removal of an aversive stimulus to increase the use of a specific behavior. In other words, stop the ritualistic behavior until the child responds and then reinforce that response by removing your unwanted influence from the environment allowing the child to resume the ritualistic behavior if he so chooses. Negative Reinforcement usually carries with it a built in motivation for the child to escape your interaction. This book suggests that procedures that motivate a child away from interaction with others also educate away from recovery. After all, the behavior of atypically choosing solitude over interaction is considered a characteristic of autism. Using strategies that encourage a child away from interaction reinforce this autistic behavior making it more likely to reoccur. Similar to escape extinction, it is recommended that you avoid using negative reinforcement in a good ABA/VB program whenever possible.

Procedures that motivate a child away from interaction with others also educate away from recovery.

Positive Reinforcement is the addition of something to the child's environment that increases the use of a behavior. Positive reinforcement motivates a child to want to be with you and, therefore, educates toward recovery. If you are being advised to use negative reinforcement procedures (blocking and then releasing your child's self-stimulatory behavior), be sure to add as much positive reinforcement and fun pairing experiences into your interactions as possible.

Positive reinforcement motivates a child to want to be with you and therefore, educates toward recovery.

When using extinction it is extremely important that you do not inadvertently reinforce your child's inappropriate behavior. During an extinction procedure, it is common for a parent to want to say "no" or try to explain to a child why he should not do something. However, words are not actions and they often do not mean the same thing to the child that they do to the adult. You may be saying the word "no" to your child, but talking to him could be giving him the attention he seeks. If you use the word "no" or any words during these times of extinction burst, you are running the risk of severely increasing the behavior you are trying to extinguish.

Be aware that extinction bursts may bring about behavior that is new to your child. You may see him throw his body to the ground or threaten to break something. A non-vocal child might try to hit or bite himself. A vocal child might tell you that he hates you or that you are being mean or acting crazy. This new behavior is just a higher-level attempt at helping him obtain his objective. As long as you do not give any appearance that this new behavior could be successful, your child will have no reason to use it again. Regardless of the difficulty level of your first few extinction bursts, the principle of extinction tells us that if you can outlast the extinction burst, the resulting behavior will decrease. More importantly, if used consistently, this behavior will disappear from your child's future behavior repertoire as well.

Extinction can be used to reduce extreme behavior choices in a matter of days or weeks.

Extinction bursts will quickly begin to decrease in duration and veracity as your child realizes that the benefit of using that inappropriate behavior no longer exists. This is the reason ABA/VB calls for the use of extinction. Fighting through some tough spots with your child in the short term with extinction is generally better than trying to use punishment procedures. Punishment procedures include purposely applying consequences to a behavior that you know will make the behavior less likely in the future. These consequences are frequently aversive to the child and result in an animosity toward the person using them. Extinction is generally better because it is not the application of an aversive. It is merely the lack of applying unearned reinforcement. This difference is what will allow you ethically to alter your current working relationship with your child without destroying his trust or desire to be with you. Using extinction to reduce problem behavior can be a powerful tool but used inconsistently, it has the potential to be as damaging as it is beneficial. When used correctly, it can reduce extreme behavior choices in a matter of days or weeks. However, if you are not fully prepared to ride out all extinction bursts along the way, you will end up increasing the duration and severity of these behavior choices that you are trying to extinguish.

If you are not prepared to ride out all extinction burst behavior, you will increase the severity of the behavior you are trying to extinguish

The final step of earning instructional control calls for extinction because even with the most advanced and ethical procedures available, reducing problem behavior is no fun for anyone. You will see a series of new and difficult extinction burst behavior you would rather not have to witness and your child could potentially have to go through extended periods without the reinforcement he would like. However, once your program begins taking shape, you should become better about keeping the reinforcing value of your teaching high enough that your child will not make choices that lead to extinction situations. Additionally, as long as you are willing to commit to extinction when necessary, your child will become increasingly better about earning his way out of any extinction situation he finds himself in.

Many parents report that their children's behavior is not problematic. But, after arriving in the home for a consultation, it becomes immediately apparent that the parents have been willing to hand complete control of the household over to the child in an attempt to avoid the extinction burst. Although fear of the extinction burst is understandable, parents who make allowances for disruptive behavior are not educating toward recovery. Rather, they are merely managing a problem that will only become worse. Giving control to your child in an attempt to manage his behavior may make life easier in the short term but ultimately you are reinforcing controlling behavior choices. These controlling behaviors will continue to grow until your child begins demanding so much control that you can no longer coexist. At some point you may be forced to put controlling behavior on extinction in an attempt to keep your child at home. The only difference is now you might be attempting extinction with a 15-year old that outweighs you by ten pounds instead of a more manageable three-year old. In addition, the behavior you will be attempting to extinguish will have had the benefit of receiving many years of reinforcement instead of just a few making the behavior more resistant to extinction.

Giving control to your child in an attempt to manage his behavior only reinforces his controlling behavior choices.

Parents and professionals sometimes avoid using extinction because initial extinction bursts can be severe and disruptive. Extinction can be scary when you do not know how most effectively to perform the procedure. Additionally, it is difficult to use a procedure that might lead your child to use all of his most undesirable behavior, especially when you have not had the benefit of seeing the worthwhile result of this procedure with other children. If you allow yourself to avoid using extinction because you fear extinction burst behavior, you will likely be able to avoid your child's use of those behavior choices. However, you will not remove the extinction burst behavior from your child's repertoire. In fact, you will only be delaying the use of the behavior until you can no longer accept the growing severity of your child's inappropriate behavior choices. Bad behavior does not just go away. Your child will only learn that extinction burst behavior will not be effective if he has tried the behavior enough times without success.

Your child will only learn that extinction burst behavior will not be effective if he has tried the behavior enough times without success.

When consulting with a family for the first time, it is usually obvious exactly what behavior the parents are least likely to keep on extinction. Whether it is a child who cries, hits himself, screams, or threatens the furniture, it is always the behavior that the parents cannot allow themselves to keep on extinction that the child will engage in most. For example, parents who cannot bear to see their child cry are usually the ones whose children most frequently cry. Parents who are easily embarrassed when their child yells will ultimately have a child who yells whenever he does not get what he wants. The same is true for parents who are terrified of their child hitting himself. The fact is, when you try to teach your child to use more effective behavior, you will naturally use extinction on his less effective behavior. However, by not understanding the principle of extinction and planning for the extinction burst, you will likely give up and reinforce your child when he tries the behavior you least want to see. Anytime you choose to manage a behavior instead of extinguish it, you will have no choice but to reinforce it. Reinforcing this least desirable behavior only increases its use. Remember, your child with autism is very smart about getting what he wants. Once your child knows what behavior will be most successful, he will use it most often.

Extinction is a powerful tool in decreasing inappropriate behavior but it only helps you earn instructional control if you also have the preceding six steps in place. Extinction without restriction of reinforcement is almost impossible. Extinction without a strong paired relationship is exhausting. Extinction used by parents who do not mean what they say and say what they mean is inconsistent. Extinction used by people who do not know what a child finds reinforcing cannot offer him better alternatives to his extinction burst behavior. Extinction without the use of all of the steps of instructional control will often prove unsuccessful.

Many children with autism love watching videos. If this is true for your child, teaching with video as a reinforcer is one of the best ways for you to begin earning instructional control. Start by turning on one of your child's very favorite videos. Make sure that you have the remote control and can decide when and why the video is played or paused (instructional control step 1). Next, play the video for your child and bounce him on your lap, or rub his head or back while he watches making the experience more fun with you than without you (step 2). Turn the video on pause and give your child a simple S^D such as "give me five" (step 4). When he follows the S^D, immediately turn the video back on (step 5). If your child chooses not to respond to the S^D, immediately turn the video off or stand in front of the TV to show that you mean what you say (step 3). If your child begins to get up from his seat, cry, hit, or try any other inappropriate behavior you should not turn that video back on (step 7). However, as soon as your child is quiet and chooses to follow your direction, with or without prompts (step 4), you can turn it back on again (step 5). Then begin bouncing and massaging him again (step 2). If your child is not using vocal language, teaching him to use a sign language request for video is a great skill to use for instructional control. If he talks, you might try simple motor imitation skills such as telling your child, "do this" while you are touching your head, tapping the ground, or clapping your hands. Applying these seven steps of instructional control in this controllable teaching setting that is usually highly motivating will give you the practical experience you need to incorporate them throughout your child's entire day.

When used correctly extinction can reduce even severe behavior quickly. Step 7 of instructional control is used to decrease a behavior that you do not want to see again in a given situation. However, extinction alone is not useful for teaching new skills and should not be used if your child cannot perform a skill you have asked of him. When you reread the first six steps of instructional control you will always see mention of a prompt. Appropriate prompting methods are important in ABA/VB and are discussed in later chapters. When necessary it is recommended that you use prompts to help your child follow your directions. This could include the use of physical prompts that help your child to complete the task without error. Using prompts in your teaching offers your child an easier path to demonstrating a new more desirable behavior. However, if your child refuses to allow you to prompt him, he is demonstrating an unwillingness to give up control and is choosing not to participate. When this is the case, you must use extinction or you will not be able to gain your child's willing participation in learning.

Extinction can reduce even severe behavior quickly but by itself is not useful for teaching new skills.

Although extinction reduces problem behavior, some children use extinction burst behavior that is beyond a parent's ability to control. Before age seven or eight, most children can easily be taught to differentiate appropriate and inappropriate behavior with the use of extinction alone. However, older children are sometimes strong and determined enough to seriously damage items or injure themselves and others during the extinction process. It is more difficult to avoid reinforcing a child's extinction burst behavior when he has the ability to break glass windows, knock over a chest of drawers, or severely hurt his siblings. For children whose extinction burst behavior is too varied and severe, you may need to add some form of punishment procedure to the extinction process. There is nothing unethical about the use of punishment procedures. In cases where children are putting themselves or others in dangerous situations, punishment might be the most ethical and appropriate procedure you can apply. The seventh step of instructional control does not preclude the use of punishment procedures. Step 7 states "Show your child that ignoring your instructions or choosing inappropriate behavior will *not* result in the acquisition of reinforcement." Although extinction is the main reduction technique, punishment procedures also fit the Step 7 criteria.

Positive punishment encourages a child away from further interaction teaching him away from recovery.

As with reinforcement, you have a choice between positive and negative punishment. **Positive punishment** is anything <u>added</u> to a child's environment after a behavior that decreases the use of that behavior in the future. For example, spanking, yelling, and adding to a child's workload are forms of positive punishment. Since positive punishment such as spankings are added to the child's environment by the parent or teacher, the child's natural reaction is to escape or avoid further interaction with the punisher. This book suggests that any procedure that encourages a child <u>away</u> from interaction also teaches a child <u>away</u> from recovery and, therefore, should be avoided.

Negative Punishment requires a child to move toward further interaction therefore teaching toward recovery.

Conversely, **Negative punishment** is anything <u>removed</u> from a child's environment after a behavior occurs that decreases the frequency of that behavior in the future. When negative punishment is used, the parent or teacher removes something from the child's environment. For example, choosing to stop reinforcing activities or take back reinforcing objects is a form of negative punishment. Negative punishment procedures require a child to move <u>toward</u> interaction with the parent or teacher to regain access to the desired reinforcement. Therefore, negative punishment procedures teach <u>toward</u> recovery because they increase the child's desire to interact. If you follow all of the many procedures of this book, you will find yourself using pairing, positive reinforcement, extinction, and negative punishment procedures in almost all of your interactions with your child. It is strongly recommended that if you choose to use negative reinforcement or positive punishment in your teaching that you plan quickly to fade the use of these procedures while vastly increasing the amount of time you engage in pairing yourself with reinforcement. This book prioritizes the use of positive reinforcement, negative punishment, and extinction procedures over the use of negative reinforcement, positive punishment and escape extinction procedures. By doing so you will find your child is consistently filled with motivation to prolong his interactions with you. This insures that your program is consistently teaching your child toward recovery. Instructional control is the method behind how you can fill in the many cracks in your child's sand wall that currently allow him to obtain reinforcement without getting over his learning barrier. Having all seven steps in place concurrently is the only way that you can completely fill in those cracks. Once filled, you can begin to pour in all the motivation that your child will need to achieve new levels of skill acquisition.

For some parents of children with autism, learning how to understand their child's behavior and using that understanding to gain instructional control can be all it takes to put their child on the right path to recovery. This was the case for a little boy named Dennis who will be discussed more in the next chapter. Earning instructional control with Dennis was about 90% of what he needed to recover from autism. After his parents, teachers, and therapists learned how to earn instructional control with him, Dennis was able to learn enough skills to be considered medically recovered from autism in just under a year. For others, good instructional control might only be 50%, 10%, or less than 2% of what they need (as if this could ever be measured at all). The important thing to remember is that without first earning and maintaining instructional control with your child there is no way that your program can be considered optimal. Without an optimal program you will not know if your child is learning everything that he can as fast as he is capable. The inability to gain instructional control is usually at the root of all the severe behavior with which you now deal. Unfortunately, children with autism are rarely behaviorally still. If you are not using these seven steps to capture the environment for the purpose of teaching your child more effective and desirable skills, autism will continue using the environment as a tool to help your child get away with increasingly less effective and desirable behavior.

Escape extinction creates a captive learner looking to escape. So does negative reinforcement and positive punishment. The ability to avoid these procedures in your teaching is important as it quickly creates a willing and motivated learner looking to interact. The Verbal Behavior approach to ABA is based on making teaching more reinforcing than escape. The procedures of VB

For some parents of children with autism, gaining instructional control can be all it takes to put their child on the right path to recovery.

taken to their fullest extent help make escape extinction, negative reinforcement and positive punishment a part of ABA's past. When this is the case, you will finally be teaching your child to his true potential. Implementing and maintaining the seven steps to instructional control throughout your child's day is the best way to reach this goal.

There is no substitute to an experienced eye when it comes to the complex understanding of behavior. If you are attempting to use the seven steps to instructional control or any of the procedures recommended in this book, first attempt to find a board certified behavior analyst to oversee and guide your program.

Summary of Chapter 6:

Instructional Control:

Step 7   Show your child that ignoring your instructions or choosing inappropriate behavior will *not* result in the acquisition of reinforcement (page 74).

Extinction is the process of not reinforcing a previously reinforced behavior. Whenever a behavior has developed a history of being reinforced, you can put that behavior on extinction by no longer allowing reinforcement to follow it. Behaviors that are put on extinction reduce over time (page 75).

Extinction is relatively easy when your child uses inappropriate behavior to ask for something. You have control of what your child wants and he can only have it if you give it to him. Reminding yourself who is truly empowered in this situation should help you to remain calm and capable of responding appropriately regardless of his behavior choices (page 77).

Sometimes your child will want an item from you that you have decided he cannot have. If he does not accept the answer "no" and continues to ask for it, complain, or engage in any other inappropriate behavior, you must also consider this an extinction situation as well (page 78).

Whenever possible avoid escape extinction: Children who *choose* to rejoin the teaching process are less likely to leave it again and more likely to display maximum effort (page 84).

An extinction burst is the period during which a behavior on extinction will intensify or increase before finally decreasing (page 85).

Showing distress over an object or action that your child threatens during extinction will likely cause your child to use it as a distraction tool during his next extinction burst. The more distraction tools you give your child, the more difficult the extinction process becomes (page 86).

When using extinction it is extremely important that you do not inadvertently reinforce your child's inappropriate behavior (page 89).

Using extinction to reduce problem behavior can be a powerful tool but used inconsistently, it has the potential to be as damaging as it is beneficial. When used correctly, it can reduce extreme behavior choices in a matter of days or weeks. However, if you are not fully prepared to ride out all extinction bursts along the way, you will end up increasing the duration and severity of these behavior choices that you are trying to extinguish (page 90).

Bad behavior does not just go away. Your child will only learn that extinction burst behavior will not be effective if he has tried the behavior enough times without success (page 91).

When used correctly extinction can reduce even severe behavior quickly but by itself it is not useful for teaching new skills (page 93).

This book prioritizes the use of positive reinforcement, negative punishment, and extinction procedures over the use of negative reinforcement, positive punishment and escape extinction procedures. By doing so you will find your child is consistently filled with motivation to prolong his interactions with you. This insures that your program is consistently teaching your child toward recovery (page 94).

For some parents of children with autism, learning how to understand their child's behavior and using that understanding to gain instructional control can be all it takes to put their child on the right path to recovery (page 95).

There is no substitute to an experienced eye when it comes to the complex understanding of behavior. If you are attempting to use the seven steps to instructional control or any of the procedures recommended in this book, first attempt to find a board certified behavior analyst to oversee and guide your program (page 96).

Chapter 7

Teaching the Control Child

You may recall that before learning about ABA and then Verbal Behavior, I worked with a young boy named Aaron who was, without question, my biggest failure as a teacher and inclusion specialist. However, it was not from lack of effort. Our school based special education team did everything we knew how to do at the time to help Aaron. We tried using visual schedules based on the TEACCH program, a sensory diet based on the sensory integration advice of our Occupational Therapist, a positive behavior support plan developed by our school psychologist. We accommodated him and modified for him. We punished him and forgave him. On the advice of experts, we let him chew gum in class, use pens instead of pencils, and even gave him a comfortable place of his own under a table to help make him feel safe and secure. We reasoned with him and excused him. We put him in the principal's office. We even allowed him to run around outside during class time. Absolutely, nothing had any effect on him. We could not make an important difference in the way that autism was negatively impacting his relationships or his ability to learn. It is now obvious that the reason we were never able to help Aaron was two-fold: We were working unaware of the seven steps to instructional control outlined in Chapters 5 and 6, and we misdiagnosed what was reinforcing his behavior as discussed in Chapter 4.

The behavior analyst who was then working with Aaron did an exhaustive functional analysis to determine the cause of Aaron's inappropriate behavior. We then developed our treatment plan based on the analysis that Aaron's behavior choices had multiple purposes. Sometimes, he behaved inappropriately to gain attention. Other times he behaved inappropriately to escape demands. But he also had periods where he behaved inappropriately for self-stimulation purposes. So in response to the recommendations resulting from this functional behavior analysis, every time we thought Aaron was looking for attention, we made our attention contingent on following a direction. Every time he was looking for escape, we tried to make his ability to be left alone contingent on following directions. Whenever we thought his behavior was dealing with self-stimulation, we tried to use a sensory integration approach recommended by our school Occupational Therapist. Nevertheless, we were never able to get Aaron to accept instructional control in the school setting.

I have more recently come to realize that the reinforcer for nearly all of Aaron's behavior was control. Aaron was a classic control child. He knew how to use ABA to get what he wanted better than any child I had met before and possibly since. When our team thought he behaved inappropriately to gain our attention, we would turn away from him to make his behavior unsuccessful. In response to this he would just go off by himself and engage in self-stimulation. When our team thought he wanted to escape, we would not allow him to and tried to maintain our instructions. In return he would only laugh and play games with us. When we thought his behavior was a form of self-stimulation, we assigned him a sensory task to help him and we found that he used this task as a way to escape work and get attention from us or from his classmates. Aaron was as slippery as a fish and we never really understood him well enough to consistently manipulate his environment in beneficial ways. Without the ability to manipulate his environment effectively our only option was to try to manipulate him physically. However, any attempts to force Aaron to comply with a direction resulted in endless screaming, and aggressive behavior.

The reason it was so difficult to offer Aaron's behavior meaningful consequences is that he was never truly looking for attention, escape, or self-stimulation. What Aaron was looking for as a result of his behavior choices was some form of control over his environment and the people in it. He had an unusually strong desire to be in control of his every interaction. Not understanding this at the time, we were helpless in our efforts to improve his behavior repertoire. Regardless of what we tried to do in response to his behavior, he could always make a choice that would keep control in his favor. This was extremely successful in keeping us from ever earning the instructional control we needed to be able to teach him. I have come to believe that children who regularly demonstrate more than one purpose for behavior are "Control Children." Nearly every behavior and interaction they engage in is in someway based on how they can obtain or maintain control of their environment.

I touched on the subject of control as a possible reinforcer of behavior in Chapter 4. However, I must strongly restate that in the science of behavior there is no identified function of control. In fact, most behavior analysts suggest that thinking about your child's behavior in terms of its controlling element is counterproductive and can obstruct the analytical benefit of ABA. Instead, most BCBAs encourage parents to pinpoint which of the three major functions of behavior (attention, escape, self-stimulation) the child is attempting to gain from each of his behavior choices. For example, if you can determine why your child hits others while at play, you will be able to develop an effective plan to reduce this inappropriate behavior. This can be achieved by making the behavior unsuccessful at achieving its intended function while teaching more appropriate replacement behaviors. Although only a trained behaviorist is equipped to complete a functional analysis of behavior, Chapter 4 will help you identify and address your child's negative behavior choices by approximating a functional analysis in a home, school, or community setting. However, when working with Aaron, the boy discussed at the start of this chapter, traditional functional analysis was ineffective in leading to the earning of instructional control.

Some socially mediated behavior is not intended solely for the purpose of escape or attention. Often escape or attention behavior occurs purely as a means to an end--that end being the goal of maintaining a controlling position in the interaction or relationship. In my experience, I have found that in some situations, considering "control" as the maintaining reinforcer of a child's socially mediated behavior is a more effective way to develop a comprehensive solution to his inappropriate behavior choices. In these cases, focusing solely on the escape or attention function of individual behaviors serves only as a distraction that leaves you unable to remove the controlling value of an entire behavior stream.

When speaking of control as a reinforcer of behavior, I refer to a desire for power or dominance in an interaction or relationship. I believe that the desire

Children who regularly demonstrate more than one purpose for behavior are "Control Children."

When speaking of control as a reinforcer of behavior, I refer to a desire for power or dominance in an interaction or relationship.

to obtain or maintain control or dominance is responsible for many of the difficult to explain behaviors demonstrated in life. For example, a person may refuse to accept the help of a rival not because the person does not need help but because the person wants to deny the rival the satisfaction of having helped. The behavior of refusing assistance may serve to gain attention or escape a demand but more importantly it occurs as a reflexive response meant to avoid losing standing in the relationship. To consider the behavior of "refusing help" an escape behavior and attempt to give consequence to it without considering the reinforcing value of maintaining the current relationship status will likely result in less than optimal results. A reporter's refusal to divulge a source leading to jail could be analyzed as a desire for more attention coming from publicity or as a means to escape the demand of the court. However, analyzing that this behavior is most likely due to a desire to maintain a credible relationship with future sources is potentially a more effective way to begin developing a plan to deal with this behavior. Why would a person resort to physical violence when losing an argument? If he already had the other person's attention why would he choose a behavior that would likely cause personal pain, regret, or possible legal repercussion? This behavior is likely multiply controlled offering some combination of self-stimulation, attention, and the potential avoidance of future demands. However, I argue that this behavior is easier to program for when you consider its ability to regain dominance, power, or control in the interaction or relationship. Punching someone when losing an argument reasonably occurs out of a desperate desire to turn a losing situation into a winning situation. In these situations, programming to this larger picture desire offers valuable insight.

The same types of questions abound when working with children who have strong control desires.

- Why would a child, who does not want to participate, close his eyes or turn his head away when being physically prompted? These behaviors do not escape the demand nor are they meant to, but instead they act as a demonstration that compliance is not being given freely and the parent has not won.

- Why would a child who wants to swing, refuse to say "swing" when you ask him to but immediately begins using the word "swing" when you make his required response something other than saying the word? Following the direction is easy for him to do and the reward is worth the effort, but doing so on command will mean that the child must give in.

- Why would a child who is responding well to a set of skills choose to purposely begin making mistakes as soon as the video camera is turned on or the parents try to show others what their child can do? Not allowing others to have satisfaction at your expense is a controlling behavior.

- Why would a child being asked to touch his nose, purposely touch right next to it in the hopes of removing the demand, but not directly on his nose? The difficulty level of the response is the same, but touching the actual nose has the added difficulty level of choosing to succumb.

- Why would a child who desperately wants a gummi bear refuse to take one once he has been given a forced physical prompt to do something he had been refusing to do as a prerequisite to earning a gummi bear? There is no longer a demand and no further attention is gained. The value of the gummi bear has temporarily been lowered due to the child's desire to find a way to exert his will in the situation.

The types of behaviors that are listed here are described in every day language as a desire to "win," "not give in," "not let someone get the best of you," "save face," or "get revenge." People who have these desires in large quantities are typically said to "have too much pride," "be thick headed", "act out of spite," "be overly competitive," or "refuse based on principle." As discussed in chapter 4, all of these behaviors can be behaviorally explained as being socially mediated positive or negative, or automatically reinforcing positive or negative. In fact, it can be argued that each of these behaviors can be identified through a traditional functional analysis as being attention seeking, escape/avoidance seeking, or self-stimulating. However, although it goes beyond the current constructs of a functional analysis of behavior, I believe these socially mediated behaviors that are meant to avoid future demands or to retain the current status quo of a relationship, are reinforced by their ability to maintain dominance, power, or control. Attempting to understand these behavior choices within the context of their relationship to winning control offers you additional support in your attempts to earn instructional control with your child.

Attempting to understand these behavior choices within the context of their relationship to winning control offers you additional support in your attempts to earn instructional control.

The dominant figure in any environment is the one who makes the rules by which everyone lives. Frequently, the child with autism is the dominant figure at home or in a classroom. This was certainly the case with Aaron. Aaron had decided that he would not participate in learning activities unless (what eventually became) a team of about seven adults was seeing to his every whim.

Dominance in any relationship is seldom given freely. Generally, it is won through a series of power struggles. Highly motivated children, who are not constrained by the same social, legal; and ethical considerations as adults, are usually capable of winning these power struggles with the adults in their environment. The spoils of these victories come in the form of complete control over one's life and most everything in it. In this way, control acts as a generalized reinforcer for all the behaviors that allowed a child to gain and maintain this dominant position. With enough of this reinforcement, these behaviors become more than individual choices to gain attention, escape, or self-stimulation, instead they become a complex symphony of constantly changing intentions whose only real goal is to maintain control.

When a child is in control he is able to do exactly what he wants whenever he wants.

When an adult is in control, the child is required to meet expectations that are almost always counter to what the child wants. Additionally, children find that the more control they give to others the more control others tend to take--which, as far as the child is concerned, becomes an ever-worsening situation. When a child is asked to relinquish some form of control and participate in the activities of others, he sees this as a harbinger of rough times ahead. Behaviorists know that any reliable signal to a worsening set of conditions creates a reflexive motivation in the child to remove or abolish this worsening set of conditions. So, even when a child might not mind the actual task he is asked to perform, he may see the behavior of following your instruction as a sign of worse things to come. When this occurs the child automatically begins refusing any direction given to him regardless of how mundane or simple. It is these children who have developed this sort of reflexive impulse to refuse even fun instructions based on the fear of these instructions leading to a loss of more control that are likely the ones being diagnosed with Oppositional Defiance Disorder (ODD).

In terms of their persistent behavioral objective of maintaining dominance or control in their relationships, I have affectionately identified children with a reflexive motivation to refuse all attempts at sharing control as "Control Children."

When a child is in control he is able to do exactly what he wants whenever he wants. This freedom from outside pressure will then motivate an even stronger desire to hold the dominant position and maintain control. For a strong control child this refusal to relinquish control will occur regardless of any immediate reinforcement that giving up control in the current situation might afford. A contributing factor is the child with autism's inability to understand the complex, ever changing rules of social interaction. To combat the feeling of being inadequate in social interactions, the control child begins to establish sophisticated and often subtle ways to steal control in his every interaction. Many children with autism can become so good at this that it is almost completely undetectable to the untrained eye. When control children are allowed to gain control through inappropriate behavior, those behavior choices are reinforced and the child uses them to become more controlling. The control child becomes expert at switching his purpose and desires immediately in response to our attempts to give consequence to them. The more an attempt is made to take control away from the child, the more out of control the child feels and the more he becomes adept at stealing control back. Regardless of what leads a child to desire this need for dominance or control, many children with autism have an unusually strong desire to maintain a dominant position in their environment. They do not easily relinquish control nor are they easily dissuaded from reaffirming their position of power.

When a child does have control and people are behaving in a way that he can predict, it allows him to feel comfortable and safe in the world. For some, the more out of control the people in his environment become the more in control the child feels. Once people are running around trying to do exactly what a control child wants, they make sense to him. A control child uses ABA to make the social world increasingly more like his inner world of autism. He becomes gifted at offering consequences that force order and consistency upon his parents, teachers, siblings and potential friends. So when parents begin to follow their child's directions and give up instructional control, the child will feel comfortable enough to remain engaged with his parents on a more regular basis. This added attention is reinforcing to the parents so they become more willing to relinquish control in the future. Ultimately, the child becomes more adept at finding stronger ways to satisfy this need for control until the parents find themselves performing some form of nightly half-hour bedtime ritual, two-hour morning dressing ritual, or worse.

Many families live by rules established to keep their control children calm. This attempt at managing behaviors often offers immediate relief (which is why parents do it) but ultimately creates an even larger ever-increasing control problem. In one initial consultation, our team was trying to help parents teach their six-year old son Jack to ask for his favorite food items with sign

Many families live by rules established to keep their control children calm.

language. However, the more we tried to set up the eating environment in a way that we could control, the more concerned the parents became. We eventually stopped our consultation and asked what was wrong. We were immediately presented with a comprehensive list of Jack's eating demands. First, it was explained that Jack would never eat unless he was sitting in <u>his</u> chair on the correct side of the table. He also needed a specific cup and spoon, a favorite toy on the table next to him, and a singing jukebox. As Jack's singing jukebox, mom had developed a repertoire of almost 50 different songs that she would sing for Jack while he ate. Since Jack could not ask for the song he wanted, mom would hold out a spoonful of his food and begin to sing. Jack would then shake his head no and mom changed to a different song. Whether it took mom two tries or ten, this would continue until she found the exact song that Jack wanted to hear. Once she did, he would open his mouth and allow her to feed him until he wanted a new song. Then the procedure would repeat for the length of the meal. We had to explain to the family that accepting this type of controlling behavior would only reinforce it causing it to increase in frequency and severity. A member of our team even joked to Jack's father, "If you are not careful, Jack might not let you sit at the same table with him soon." The parents became very silent. As it turns out, Jack's father had not been allowed to eat meals with his wife and son for over a year.

Children like Jack are not born with any of these demands. The more they are allowed to control the home environment, the more controlling they become. Eventually parents become convinced that their child is incapable of interacting in any other way. They begin to think that their child needs these rituals and routines to feel comfortable and if the parents do not follow these rituals to the letter they are in some way hurting their child. But what happens when a control child goes to school? What happens when he tries to make friends? What happens when he tries to keep a job and this need for control is still causing him to push the buttons of everyone around him until he is able to obtain control of his every desire? Is giving in to a control child's every "need" really helping him to be comfortable in our world or are we instead just modifying our world to fit the wants of the child? Are we allowing him merely to expand the parameters of his inner autistic world to include us? More importantly, will others be willing to allow this as well? If a child controls an interaction he feels "in control" and will stay engaged. However, when adults refuse to relinquish control to a child, the child will use extinction burst

Is giving in to a control child's every "need" really helping him to be comfortable in our world or are we instead just modifying our world to fit the wants of the child?

behavior to gain what he wants. Then, when all else fails, the child can always resort to the ultimate power play and retreat into his private inner world. He can stay there seemingly content and happy leaving us behind to wonder why.

If you are dealing with a control child, you need to understand that there is a better way. Your child's desire for control should not run the household or ruin your family life. You do not need to choose to follow your child's every demand or bear the brunt of the consequences. You do not need to let your child take increasingly more control of your interactions until he becomes big enough and strong enough that you can no longer live safely in your own house with him. What you can do is learn how to use ABA with Verbal Behavior. This simple understanding of antecedents and consequences, reinforcement and motivation and the many associated techniques will enable you to interact with your child in a way that he can understand. When your child understands you, he will begin to believe that he can communicate with you. Then he will not feel as out of control in the larger environment. Once you can apply the practices of ABA and Verbal Behavior and begin to implement the seven steps to earn instructional control, your control child will know how and where he fits into the social world. He can stay engaged with you for the right reasons rather than out of the desperate need to control your every interaction. He will begin to interact with the desire to experience the joys that only positive social interactions can bring. Once this is the case, your child with control issues can learn more ways to appropriately communicate his needs and desires. The better he can communicate with us the more appropriate control he will receive and in turn, he will rely less on inappropriate behavior choices to get what he wants.

So, how do you know if you are working with a Control Child? Ask yourself these questions:

1. Does your child seldom want to do anything you ask but will gladly do those same things five minutes later when it is *his* idea?
2. Is it difficult for you to find reinforcers that seem to be strong enough to keep your child's interest for more than a minute or two?
3. Does your child seem to like everything, but chooses to play alone with the curtains rather than follow a direction to earn time playing with a favorite toy?
4. Does your child always have to carry things or have things in his hand or mouth?

5. Does your child's behavior seem to have no reason?

6. Does your child's behavior seem to have an unlimited number of reasons?

7. Does your child need to keep things in a specific order or put things into a line and get upset when you interfere?

8. Does your child, not only like to watch TV or listen to the radio but must be in control of the volume, channel, and/or remote control?

9. Does your child only accept specific foods and will resist any attempt to get him to try anything new?

10. Does your child expect you to behave in a certain way around him or follow specific rituals or routines?

11. Would your child choose to go hours without food rather than say the word "please?"

12. Does your child make you carry him, sing to him, or do anything more than you would like to?

13. Does your child say words many times until you give in and repeat them back to him?

14. Does your child constantly point to or tap on items in books or on photographs for you to label for him?

15. Does your child have items that only he is allowed to touch or play with?

16. Does your child immediately tune out, tantrum, or walk away when you do not give him what he wants?

17. Does your child purposely do and say things that he knows will make you angry or feel embarrassed?

18. Does your child constantly change the subject of conversations and/or ask repetitive questions?

19. Does your child subtly refuse to give you exactly what you ask for but always finds ways to give you close enough to what you want so that you accept it?

20. Does your child walk away from or refuse reinforcement after you have forced him to complete a task?

After reading this list of control type issues, it becomes obvious why I believe that the largest percentage of children with autism fall into the category of control child. If you answer any or many of these questions with a "yes," you should consider the possibility that although your child might be looking for attention, escape, or self-stimulation with his behavior, it is possible that dominance in your relationship is your child's true reinforcer of choice. When this is the case then everything your child does likely becomes a tool to help him obtain and maintain a dominant position in his environment.

As was explained in Chapter 2 "Understanding the Label of Autism," the autism label describes a set of behaviors that a child has developed. The fact that the cause of autism has become so difficult to pinpoint and that an increasing number of children are diagnosed every year leads me to believe that autism likely has several possible causes. One of these causes for a subgroup of children developing autism, that 20 years ago might not have been labeled as such, is this utter refusal to accept instructional control. When a child is capable from an early age to fight off any coercive attempts to teach him beyond his interests; communication, behavior, social, and general learning skills are bound to become severely delayed often leading to a diagnosis of autism. Seeking the help of professionals trained to understand the motivations of a control child and systematically teaching the benefit of giving up increasingly larger amounts of control through motivation and reinforcement procedures can help a child very quickly move beyond the diagnosis of autism and on to a more successful and rewarding life.

This was the case with Dennis, the first child that Knospe-ABA was able to help recover from autism. His story begins in early 2004 when Dennis' family realized that there was something drastically wrong with the way that he was developing. Dennis knew many words but his functional language development was extremely delayed and uneven. When he did initiate verbal interactions, he was constantly obsessed with the topic of flowers, plants, and gardening. His favorite item in the world was a flower that he would carry in his hand at all times. His behaviors were becoming increasingly more demanding and out of control. The family did not know what to do and began to realize that his problematic behavior was not just a phase he was going through. It was obvious that these behavior choices were consistently getting worse and Dennis' language, social, and general learning skills were becoming increasingly more delayed by the day. They took Dennis to the local medical clinic where he was given a battery of tests by a large number of doctors, therapists, and psychologists. Much to the family's relief and then horror, their then three-year-old son was diagnosed with autism. The reason they felt some relief was that they hoped that now that they had a name for what was wrong with Dennis, they would be able to do something to help him. The horror came when they were then told that autism was a pervasive developmental disorder for which there was no cure. One professional actually told them that Dennis' behaviors would only continue to grow more severe as he got older and the parents should begin preparing themselves for the fact that at some point, they would not be able to handle him anymore. Because of long waiting lists for institutional placements, it was recommended that they begin the process of selecting a long-term facility in which he could eventually be placed. Dennis' parents made the decision that they were unwilling to accept this well-intentioned advice from so-called experts. This "no hope" prognosis prompted Dennis' parents to receive two more opinions in the hope that this was not going to be the future for their son. Both opinions came back as diagnoses of autism and Dennis' parents were crushed. After a short period of soul searching, the family decided that giving up on their son was not an option. Like many other families in this situation, they began searching the Internet for any help they could find. That occurred when they found our informational website *www.autismusaba.de.*

Dennis was a puzzle. Sometimes he would do whatever he was asked and other times he would refuse even activities he normally enjoyed.

Dennis' parents arrived with ten members of their family and support team at our introductory workshop in July of 2004. I remember them at the workshop, not only from the sheer size of their group, but by the quiet determination that they carried with them to help their son. A week after the workshop my wife and I visited the family home and met with Dennis for the first time. Dennis was similar to many of the children we meet when we go into a home for a first consultation. He had many words but used them without full benefit of their function. He was incapable of answering simple basic questions with a yes or no response. His interests were limited and he loved to look at spinning objects such as windmills, helicopters, and fans. Two of his favorite items were his mom's brush and hair dryer, although he never played with these items in any functional way. Rather, he developed an atypical attachment to them. Dennis was unable to answer simple questions such as, "What is your name?" or "How old are you?" In many ways he was partially echoic. He was able to generate words independently but often repeated the words of others instead of responding to them. He was sweet and interested in the world around him; however, he was definitely in charge of the household. As soon as he did not get exactly what he wanted he began to whine, cry, and throw a tantrum until the situation was rectified to his satisfaction. Dennis' autism was certainly causing deficits in all four major categories of behavior, communication, social/relationship development, and general learning skills.

The first step was to teach Dennis' parents the seven steps of instructional control while analyzing the main purposes of his behavior. While doing so, I noticed that Dennis seemed to like the attention of others but seldom enough to be willing to follow directions to obtain it. He was motivated to escape activities that he did not prefer, but seldom enough to follow simple directions that would give him a way to avoid these activities. He demonstrated some self-stimulating (stim) behavior but seldom seemed content to focus only on the stims for any length of time. Dennis was a puzzle. Sometimes he would do whatever he was asked to and other times he would completely refuse to participate in anything, even activities he normally enjoyed. Then at one point in the consultation process, it became apparent that what Dennis needed in order to participate in positive interactions with others was the ability to somehow control the object or interaction. As a team, we realized that if we could manipulate the conditions of the environment so that even though he was following directions, Dennis could choose and physically manipulate the reinforcement that he was given; he could have the feeling of control that he desired. By understanding what the team needed to give Dennis in return for his instructional control, we were able to put Dennis on the correct path to recovery.

When you deal with a child whose behavior choices are mostly based on a desire either for attention or escape, you can easily follow the examples outlined in Chapter 4, "Understanding the Purpose of Behavior," to make the inappropriate behavior unsuccessful and teach positive replacement behavior. However, control children with or without autism have never really been understood in even the best of ABA programs. When behavior does not tend to fall easily into one of the three categories of self-stimulation, attention, or escape, people tend to overlook "control" and assume other immeasurable phenomena such as sensory deficits, apraxia, and hyperactivity are responsible for this behavior. However, when looked at behaviorally, these labels frequently become a way to explain or excuse a child's attempts at maintaining dominance or control in his relationships.

Life demands that we all develop our sensory abilities and overcome our sensitivities to the environment. Some of us have more sensitivity than others and some of us are more adept at overcoming these issues. In most cases, people develop their own sensory abilities and find ways to cope with or overcome their own sensitivities to the environment. For those who cannot, a desensitization process containing the proper mix of motivation and reinforcement can help reduce or eliminate most if not all of these sensory issues. As a child I thought I would die if I was forced to eat spinach with my dinner. There were even times when I would uncontrollably gag or vomit when I attempted to eat a forkful. However, once my access to dessert was consistently made contingent on my ability to eat very small portions of spinach, my spinach consumption increased. Somehow, I found a way to overcome what seemed to be an uncontrollable reaction. Over time, these smaller portions of spinach were increased as well. With the addition of some lemon, I learned to enjoy and even request spinach with my meals. Had my parents been advised that my unusually strong refusals were due to sensory issues and I was unable to eat vegetables, I may have grown up without spinach and other vegetables in my diet. Once I had been successful at fighting off attempts to get me to eat vegetables, I am sure I would have used the same techniques to fight off soups and crèmes. If that was successful, I would probably have gained the confidence and techniques necessary to get my diet reduced to little more than pizza, chicken nuggets and French fries.

Accepting environmental sensitivities as unchangeable is counterproductive to your child's future.

Children with autism often have real and pervasive sensitivities to their environment. Accepting these issues as unchangeable is counterproductive to the child's future. Without your help, these issues are reinforced and often become more intrusive and problematic over time.

Joseph is a child with autism that Knospe-ABA supports. For two years, he refused to drink anything other than chocolate milk. His parents had become convinced by Joseph's behavior that his refusal to drink any other beverage was tied to a sensory issue. However, as part of his initial consultation, our team addressed this issue with a motivation and reinforcement plan that made playing with a highly motivating new toy we brought contingent on taking a tiny sip of water.

Joseph's first extinction burst lasted over a half-hour and included yelling "no," running out of the room, throwing his chair and then himself to the floor, and trying to convince us to let him play with the toy. Once convinced that his only access to the toy was by drinking, Joseph put the cup to his lips and took a tiny sip. According to the seven steps of instructional control, we immediately gave him the toy and played with him for several minutes. Then, when we made continuing to play with this toy contingent on taking another sip of water, Joseph made only a five-minute refusal before he took another sip. The team continued this procedure throughout the day and within three days

Joseph was no longer refusing to drink water. In fact, within a few weeks time, he was requesting water to drink and loved drinking out of water fountains and right out of the faucet.

Labeling and excusing your child's behavior choices becomes a self-fulfilling prophecy. Assuming a child cannot say a word or deal appropriately with a stimulus simply because he has not said a word or dealt appropriately with that stimulus may take the pressure off of you as a teacher but it does nothing beneficial for the child.

It is easy to expect a child labeled hyperactive to be unable to focus on a direction or remain on a task. Thus, the child is robbed of the consistent supply of motivation and reinforcement that he needs to overcome this issue. In the ABA/VB approach, children are put into situations where they will *want* to sit still so that they can consciously give effort to become better at sitting still for increasingly longer periods.

In a non-behavioral approach, a child's parents and teachers are advised that he is hyperactive and expected to accept his hyperactivity by never giving him the opportunity to learn to sit still. By choosing the second approach you will undoubtedly support the diagnosis of hyperactivity allowing it to endure. The behaviors described by the labels Attention Deficit Disorder (ADD), Hyperactive Disorder (HD), Oppositional Defiance Disorder (ODD), Obsessive Compulsive Disorder (OCD), Apraxia, or Sensory Integration Deficits are in many cases valid issues related to autism. They are descriptions of behaviors that many children display. But when you label a child and accept these behavior labels as unchangeable, you deny the child the opportunity to be educated toward recovery. In addition, accepting these labels and allowing them to change teaching procedures and expectations will give a control child all the power he needs to forever avoid learning beyond the scope of his interests.

Labeling and excusing the behavior choices of your child becomes a self-fulfilling prophecy.

Regardless of what labels your child has been given, if you feel that your child might be demonstrating an unusually strong desire for control here is a list of rules I have developed to help. The following list was originally designed to help Dennis overcome the learning deficits that evolved as a by-product of his severe controlling behavior. These rules have been modified and developed for many control children ever since. In some cases it is recommended to apply all of these rules while in others only one or two are necessary. If you suspect that your child's major motivation is control, here are seven rules you should consider implementing.

Rules for interacting with a control child

Rule 1: Remain calm and in control of your emotions. If you cannot, pretend to be calm or leave the interaction.

Parents of control children often spend their time worrying about their child's needs and feelings giving little consideration to their own. However, as the parent, teacher, or therapist working with a control child, it is *your* feelings that need to be more closely monitored. Your child's desire for control may cause you to feel nervous, angry, out of control, or even embarrassed. You must always pay attention to how your child is making you feel. If you find that you are becoming upset, you must not display your feelings. Remaining controlled when your child is out of control is important so that you can apply appropriate consequence to his behavior choices. Additionally, if your child can control your feelings, he will satisfy his need for control.

If this occurs often enough, he will learn that if nothing else works, he just needs to make you embarrassed, scared, or angry and he will win back his control over you. This was the case with Aaron. Aaron was the first grade boy with autism discussed in Chapter 1 who outsmarted the school district in California. Aaron had found that making his parents, teachers, and classmates, nervous, or angry was his strongest tactic to gain control of his environment. The constant reinforcement of the behaviors that led to this feeling of control created a child whose daily mission seemed to be finding unlimited ways to make others angry with him. Obviously, a situation like this is not good for your child, his teacher, boss, or any authority figure he will face in life. Like Aaron from California, Dennis also used his parent's emotions as a means to gain control. Knowing his father was easily embarrassed, Dennis would tell strangers, "Daddy was crying." This would cause his father to turn red and keep him from giving consequence to Dennis' behavior choices. The purpose of this type of behavior is avoidance of future demands but the only way not to give it power is not to let it appear to be successful in winning control of our responses.

Rule 2: Whenever possible, work choice into your directions including choices about the order of activities and reinforce every difficult choice the child makes quickly and appropriately.

People are generally not allowed to do whatever they want. If you want your child to live in a community that includes more than just your immediate family, you will have to teach him to accept this reality. Offering a choice to your child when he is not allowed to do exactly what he wants is an excellent way to give him a feeling of control. Whenever possible, let your child choose between two work activities. When he is finished, offer him a choice of reinforcing activities as a reward. Another way to give your control child opportunities to choose is to let him decide the order of the activities he is being asked to accomplish. The number of options you should make available to your child depends on the situation and his ability to make difficult decisions.

The ability to choose is not always reinforcing. To counteract the negative feelings involved with making a difficult choice, you need to spend time teaching your child that making choices in general is easy and fun. Take the pain out of making a difficult choice with other reinforcement such as praise, tickles, applause, and statements such as "that was a great choice." When educating a control child, spending time teaching the joy of choice making before giving the child any difficult choices to make is a useful first step. Most behavior consultants can help you design a program that will systematically teach this skill to your child in a fun and interesting way.

Rule 3: Know what behavior choices you want to reinforce and which choices you want extinguished. Offer more control as a reinforcer for choosing an appropriate behavior and do not allow the other behavior choices to be reinforced with any more control going to the child.

There are many different ways that we can successfully gain control in our interactions with others. Some would be considered appropriate while others would generally be considered socially unacceptable. The best way to teach your child to demonstrate appropriate behavior is to teach him how to get control in his environment in positive ways. Conversely, it is just as important to make his inappropriate attempts unsuccessful. Here is a partial list of appropriate ways your child can use to gain control. Be sure to notice every time your child uses one of these strategies and make sure that it meets with success.

<u>Appropriate ways to gain control</u>

1. Calling someone by name, saying, "Excuse me" or tapping a person on the shoulder to gain attention.

2. Using sign language or a PECS picture to ask for something.

3. Using appropriate requests for assistance such as, "Come with me," "May I have," or "Please help me."

4. Suggesting a fun game or activity during free time.

5. Making the choice to play with others the way they want to play or choosing to play alone.

6. Accepting the answer "No" and looking for another activity that is also fun.

7. Quickly and appropriately following a direction to get to a reinforcing activity faster.

8. Asking a question only one time and accepting the answer given.

9. Accepting help from others.

10. Accepting physical prompting when tasks are difficult.

This list is not complete or appropriate for all children. As you work with your child you will undoubtedly be able to identify your own list of ways that he can appropriately gain control in his environment. Share your list with all the adults working with your child.

There are also inappropriate ways to gain control in one's environment. These methods are common for many children and adults with or without autism. There is nothing especially unethical about your child's use of these approaches to gaining control. However, if you allow a child with control issues to use these methods to success, teaching to his deficits will be more difficult. For this reason, I suggest that you purposely make these following behavior choices unsuccessful.

Less appropriate ways to gain control

Develop and share your version of this list with every person working with your child as well.

1. Walking away from a direction and choosing something or someone else to be with during teaching.

2. Refusing to answer or intentionally giving incorrect or incomplete answers.

3. Answering slowly or quietly or with minimal effort.

4. Saying or shaking head "No."

5. Yelling or hitting.

6. Saying things to make someone unhappy, angry, or uncomfortable.

7. Refusing to let you physically prompt a correct response.

8. Purposely using the wrong sign or word for an item.

9. Repeatedly asking the same question.

10. Threatening to or actually breaking or spilling things.

Each adult you allow to regularly interact with your child should consider himself in a contract with your child. The contract states that whenever your child makes appropriate choices to satisfy a need for control, the person working with him will give up some level of control as a reinforcer. For example, when your child willingly gives you items that you have asked for, allow him to pick what items he can have in their place. Whenever your child makes a less appropriate choice to satisfy a need for control, the person working with him will allow no additional control and when necessary retract some. For example, when your child refuses to give you items for which you have asked, calmly restrict access to all reinforcing items. Additionally you can remove access to the items you asked him to give you, until your child willingly meets your next expectation. The goal of this contract is to teach your child that there is nothing wrong with wanting to feel a sense of control in his life. However, there are many ways to try to obtain this control. Some will bring him more control and some will not. When used correctly this contract allows but does not force your child to make specific behavior choices. As with all good ABA/VB teaching, it merely gives him good reasons to make the best choices for himself.

Rule 4: Whenever you see your child use an inappropriate behavior, consider him in an extinction situation until he makes a more appropriate choice (use prompts if necessary).

Extinction is a concept that was addressed in the previous chapter but it bears repeating. Once your child has chosen an inappropriate behavior to gain control, consider him in an extinction situation. This means that you cannot allow that behavior, or any other inappropriate behavior that follows, to allow him to achieve a feeling of having gained more control in any way. For example, if you give your child a direction and he yells "No" and runs to another area of the room, you also need to refuse him access to any form of reinforcement he might find including a feeling of having gained any control over you until the direction has been fulfilled. This can be done with or without prompts, but better choices should always be differentially reinforced with stronger reward. Normally, following this rule should not prove difficult, as you should already have good control over your child's reinforcers. If you have failed to control an important item, you need very calmly to follow him and refuse him access to this or any other reinforcement until the direction has been followed. If your child is very controlling, he might begin to move from one commonplace item to the next. This is usually done as a tactic to get you to forget about your direction and begin following him around engaging in power struggles over everyday objects. By changing your focus, he will have shifted control back into his favor. If you find that during extinction your child just begins to move from one normally unimportant item to the next, your best option is happily to allow him to have these items. It is true that the sooner you can get him to fulfill the original direction, the sooner you can return to productive learning. However, by giving him a way to gain control over your interactions during the extinction process, you will not be making his choice to refuse directions less likely in the future. Not giving this behavior power over you will keep you in control. The more you are capable of ignoring these pretend play activities the more quickly his extinction burst behaviors will cease.

Rule 5: Do not let "I don't care" Behavior stop your use of extinction.

The last chapter introduced Barry and his problematic morning behavior. As part of step seven to instructional control Barry's mom was taught to use extinction to help reduce this behavior. As expected, Barry demonstrated extinction burst behaviors as a result. However, Barry, being a strong control child, chose a very different type of extinction burst behavior to convince mom that extinction would not work. In fact, his first extinction burst behavior was to laugh at mom, climb under the table and pretend not to care. The more controlling a child is, the more likely it is that he will try to convince you that he does not care about your attempts to give consequence to his actions. "I don't care" behaviors include, but are not limited to the following; closing his eyes to show you he is not listening, staring out windows or playing with items he is normally not interested in, walking away from reinforcement he has just earned, smiling, laughing, or choosing self-stimulating behavior less reinforcing than the reinforcement that compliance with your instruction would earn him.

When Barry went under the table and pretended to have fun, he expected that behavior to be met with more attention and ultimately removal of the instruction. To make it unsuccessful, mom simply walked out of the room. Although Barry seemed to be content, mom knew he wanted his breakfast, mom knew he wanted his television, and mom knew he wanted things his way. Once again, Barry was left to make a difficult decision for himself. When Barry's "I don't care" play sounds were not being reinforced they became increasingly louder, in an attempt to bring mom back to him. The louder he got the more mom kept busy with other things. When it became clear to Barry that pretending not to care was not going to work, he started to come to mom again. At first it was with little looks or just walking past where she was. If mom looked over to him, he quickly diverted his eyes or turned away.

As with most of the children Knospe-ABA works with, the more it appeared that mom wanted him to come to her, the longer he stayed away. Conversely, as soon as mom convinced him that she was going to continue with her day whether he came or not, Barry began to change his behavior choices and eventually made the appropriate decision to put on his clothes. Although it may go against normal parenting instincts, this procedure is very effective with a child who uses "I don't care" type behavior.

When you change your behavior because of your child's lack of interest, you reinforce the power of his refusal. Thus, your child will resort to that behavior when he wants to avoid something. By understanding "I don't care" behavior as one of the many extinction burst behaviors a child might attempt, you can extinguish it from your child's repertoire as well.

Rule 6: Try to camouflage attempts to get your child to enjoy new things.

Developing new and more appropriate reinforcing items is an important aspect to the education of any child with autism. For strong control children this can be a more challenging task. Not only do you have to identify and introduce items that you believe have aspects that your child will like, but you also have to be very careful in how you go about the process. It is a common human instinct to want what you cannot have and to quickly lose interest in things that you can. This instinct seems to be magnified with control children. If your child recognizes that you are trying to get him interested in something, his natural suspicion and desire to resist coercion could cause him to refuse it. Consequently many items that might have excellent reinforcement value for your child can be lost to his control desires. Do not try to get your control child to play with new things. Bring these items into the environment and play with them yourself. Do not be obvious about your intentions. You might even try to hide the reinforcing value of the item from your child. The first time he tries to play with it, consider saying "no" but then later leave it somewhere that he can find it. Try to take it away a few times without reintroducing it. Let your child think of these new items as things with which he needs to find a way to gain access. Once he begins to use extinction burst behaviors to gain access to the item, you can begin to allow him to have it only as a reinforcer for good choices or learning behavior.

Rule 7: Always look after the safety of other students and siblings.

As adults working with a control child, parents, teachers, and therapists can be trained how to best interact with him and help him to meet his need for control in acceptable ways. However, other children in his environment should not be expected to know how to work with your child. They can, however, be coached to interact in ways that will keep them safe while helping their interactions with him to be as positive as possible. Aggressive behavior choices such as hitting should always be met with an immediate consequence. As previously discussed, this consequence should *not* include verbal attention or anger. It should include swiftly and carefully moving your child from the current activity to a lesser reinforcing one for a short period. This removal procedure is a form of negative punishment. Negative punishment causes a child to want to return <u>to</u> interaction and, therefore, teaches <u>toward</u> recovery. For removal to work, you need to be sure that the place to which he is moved is *not* reinforcing in any way. If need be, you could look for something like a cleanup area where your child will be prompted to clean up for a period of time. However this is a form of a positive punishment procedure. Positive punishment teaches away from recovery as it encourages escape behavior. Whenever possible it is recommended to choose some form of negative punishment procedure. For many children the sheer process of being removed from the setting with no other control or reinforcement value coming to them is enough to begin to reduce the aggressive behavior.

This was the case with Dennis. Once our team had developed a successful plan for Dennis at home, we were invited to his integrated kindergarten classroom. Dennis was considered by his teachers to be the most difficult child in his class. He hit children, threw toys, flopped to the ground, and followed few directions. Because we had determined that Dennis' behavior was being reinforced by gaining control of items or interactions, we instructed the teachers to pick Dennis up from under his arms without saying a word to him every time they witnessed him exhibit an aggressive behavior choice. They were then to take a few steps away from the interaction and put Dennis down facing away from the activity from which he was being removed. The teachers immediately returned to participate in a positive interaction with the child that Dennis had been aggressive with. There was no time limit put on how long Dennis had to stay away. He was simply removed from the activity he wanted to control. Other children may have needed a stronger program including a set period of time to be removed, but this simple removal procedure worked very well for Dennis. At first, the teachers felt uncomfortable picking him up and leaving him away from the others, but they saw immediate results. In less than two week's time, our team was told that the parents of the other children were asking what had happened to Dennis. The immediate loss of access to reinforcement after these aggressive behaviors was all Dennis needed to choose to stop using them. We are told that a child in his class asked if Dennis' twin brother was coming to school in his place. This positive result took away any reservations that Dennis' teachers might have had using new techniques.

A good ABA/VB approach should always recommend quick removal procedures such as the one used with Dennis before considering more aversive

For many children the process of being removed from a setting with no other control coming to them is enough to reduce aggressive behavior.

techniques such as having the child clean or do additional work. If your child is older and too large to remove in a quick and easy way, you will have to look for other negative punishment consequences such as removing yourself or the activity from your child instead.

In addition to the seven steps of instructional control, these rules designed for the control child will give you the very best chance at turning the tables on your child's controlling behavior. Please beware that the most persistent control children can be extremely frustrating and confusing to even an experienced professional. Back in the early days of ABA, providers might have recommended aversive punishment and escape extinction procedures such as putting a child in a cold shower, spraying him with water, forcing him to drink vinegar, strapping him down, holding him in a chair, or other questionable techniques. Most practitioners emphatically discourage these practices today. Without discussing the ethical concerns of procedures like these (which are beyond my comprehension), it is my belief and experience that children with and without autism learn best from positive experiences. The goal of teaching a child with autism is to show him that being involved in the social world is more enjoyable than being alone in his. If someone is overusing aversive techniques with your child, it is probably because this person has given up trying to find a better way.

An ultimate control child would rather not eat for a week than do one simple motor response for the right to run through a candy store.

There are children out there that I now affectionately refer to as ultimate control children. An ultimate control child would rather not eat for a week than do one simple motor response for the right to run through a candy store. If your child is this determined and difficult to work with, you must resist the temptation to use aversive techniques. In most cases these procedures including safe but aversive forced physical prompting procedures are not going to work and will be counterproductive to your ultimate goal of building and maintaining a positive relationship. Aversive techniques should only be used with parental permission after there is documented evidence that they are the very best way to affect a behavior that is severe in nature. It is my belief that aversive procedures should not be used merely to gain instructional control. Do not allow anyone to do anything to your child that you do not agree is absolutely necessary to help him progress. For some children punishment procedures will be necessary to safely reduce destructive behaviors. However, most aversive techniques have been replaced by positive methods that have shown as much or more success in getting the desired result. Whenever you are not sure what to do with your child, the best advice is always to try more pairing. You can never have too good a relationship with your child.

As your child's advocate, you should insist on knowing exactly what procedures will be used with your child. You should fully understand the purpose behind the use of any aversive techniques, as well as the possible alternatives, before giving your approval.

Dennis' removal procedure was not the only program given to his kindergarten teachers. In fact, our team offered many ideas and procedures to help Dennis participate appropriately with his peers. The use of these procedures in the kindergarten combined with the family's use of instructional control and the aforementioned rules for the control child had an immediate impact on Dennis' learning and behavior choices. Two weeks after meeting Dennis in July of 2004, he was able to answer simple questions with appropriate "yes" and "no" answers. He could answer his name when asked and could tell you his age. In a few months time he had developed to the point that he was becoming a bit of a mini-celebrity in his small German town.

Everyone who knew of Dennis wanted to know what was behind his sudden change. By January 2005, Dennis' mom was invited to speak to the local school district about Dennis' progress and ABA/VB. Then on Valentine's Day of the same year, came the call our team had been hoping for. Now four years old, Dennis (pictured on the cover) had just returned home from a visit to the local medical clinic. The same doctors, therapists, and psychologists who had diagnosed Dennis' autism and gave his parents a very grim outlook for his future were unable to explain what they saw. They had never seen it before and could not imagine how it had happened but after all of their testing and analysis, they could no longer find one major symptom of autism.

In about a year's time, through the help of good ABA/VB, Dennis had his label removed and became what our team has been told is the first medically documented case of autism recovery in Germany. I am firmly convinced that the reason this recovery was made possible developed from a willingness and ability to recognize and teach to Dennis' overwhelming desire to control. Along with the other recommendations of this book, understanding Dennis' attempts to find control in his environment and using those desires as a motivation to learn allowed his family to educate Dennis to recovery. More importantly it taught

As your child's advocate you should insist on knowing exactly what type of technique is going to be used with your child.

them how to give Dennis the tools necessary to live an independent life full of the complex interpersonal relationships that make life as fulfilling as it can be.

As noted, under the current constructs of a functional analysis of behavior, there is no identified purpose of "control." One of the main problems with trying to include control as an additional possible function of socially mediated behavior is that it is difficult, if not impossible, to define and measure. When a behavior intends on meeting with attention or escape, it is reasonably simple to identify if that behavior has been successful. It is also reasonably simple to find ways to stop the behavior from being successful. But what exactly is control and can you reliably measure when or if control has been achieved? Please keep in mind that the behavior intention I have labeled "control" is merely a catch all title for behaviors that are complex in nature and have multiple purposes all designed to maintain relational dominance. Control cannot be adequately defined and is too general to truly include in the science of behaviorism. However, this chapter holds importance, as there remains a need to explain and teach to the many behaviors that can be chosen by a child solely out of a desire to help him exert dominance or control in his interactions. Perhaps looking at these behaviors in terms of servicing the purpose of "winning" is more scientifically viable. I expect that behavior emitted as an attempt to "control," "dominate," or "win" will be more comprehensively studied in the coming years.

Although, the current tool for assessing the function of a behavior may be extremely helpful in developing program recommendations for many children and many behaviors it remains incomplete. There is still more that needs to be studied in regards to the purpose of behavior discussed in this chapter. For those of you who are looking for ways to work with control children with whom traditional functional analysis has not been effective in helping you earn instructional control, consider this chapter and including some of the above 7 rules for working with the control child in your program.

The following poem written by an individual living with autism named Brian Henson (bhenson@bfree.on.ca) adds another voice to the discussion of control serving as a generalized reinforcer for behavior.

From One Autistic:

by Brian Henson

Alone, but in control, the world is not intimidating...
it is serene; I just need someone else to experience
this serenity with me, ...again, to reiterate, without
trying to take control (by, for example, trying to make
it more serene) as the more they attempt to take
control the less serene it becomes, and more intimidating.
Without the external control, the serenity flows, by itself,
and the potential flows along with it, to reveal the hidden
talent, so far buried by the culture of control.

Summary of Chapter 7

When speaking of control as a reinforcer of behavior, I refer to a desire for power or dominance in an interaction or relationship. I believe that the desire to obtain or maintain control or dominance is responsible for many of the difficult to explain behaviors demonstrated in life (page 101).

In terms or their persistent behavioral objective of maintaining dominance or control in their relationships, I have affectionately identified children with a reflexive motivation to refuse all attempts at sharing control "Control Children" (page 104).

When a child is in control he is able to do exactly what he wants whenever he wants. This freedom from outside pressure will then motivate an even stronger desire to hold the dominant position and maintain control. For a strong control child this refusal to relinquish control will occur regardless of any immediate reinforcement that giving up control in the current situation might afford (page 104).

Many children with autism have an unusually strong desire to maintain a dominant position in their environment. They do not easily relinquish control nor are they easily dissuaded from reaffirming their position of power (page 105).

Children with autism often have real and pervasive sensitivities to their environment. Accepting these issues as unchangeable is counterproductive to the child's future. Without your help, these issues are reinforced and often become more intrusive and problematic over time (page 112).

Labeling and excusing your child's behavior choices becomes a self-fulfilling prophecy. Assuming a child cannot say a word or deal appropriately with a stimulus simply because he has not said a word or dealt appropriately with that stimulus may take the pressure off of you as a teacher but it does nothing beneficial for the child (page 113).

Rules for interacting with a control child

Rule 1: Remain calm and in control of your emotions. If you cannot, pretend to be calm or leave the interaction (page 114).

Rule 2: Whenever possible, work choice into your directions including choices about the order of activities and reinforce every difficult choice the child makes quickly and appropriately (page 114).

Rule 3: Know what behavior choices you want to reinforce and which choices you want extinguished. Offer more control as a reinforcer for choosing an appropriate behavior and do not allow the other behavior choices to be reinforced with any more control going to the child (page 115).

Rule 4: Whenever you see your child use an inappropriate behavior, consider him in an extinction situation until he makes a more appropriate choice (use prompts if necessary) (page 118).

Rule 5: Do not let "I don't care" Behavior stop your use of extinction (page 118).

Rule 6: Try to camouflage attempts to get your child to enjoy new things (page 120).

Rule 7: Always look after the safety of other students and siblings (page 120).

When you change your behavior because of your child's lack of interest, you reinforce the power of his refusal. Thus, your child will resort to that behavior when he wants to avoid something. By understanding "I don't care" behavior as one of the many extinction burst behaviors a child might attempt, you can extinguish it from your child's repertoire as well (page 119).

As your child's advocate, you should insist on knowing exactly what procedures will be used with your child. You should fully understand the purpose behind the use of any aversive techniques, as well as the possible alternatives, before giving your approval (page 123).

Chapter 8

DTT: The Nuts and Bolts of Teaching

Discrete Trial Teaching (DTT) is the primary teaching method used in the science of ABA/VB. Teaching sessions are composed of multiple series of these independent trials. A discrete trial always has a defined beginning and ending. Each trial begins with the presentation of a stimulus and includes some sort of consequence. The consequence that is most often used in DTT is reinforcement. But there is more to good teaching than just throwing reinforcers at a child. You need to know the best possible ways to reinforce and you need to reinforce with an overall goal in mind.

You need to reinforce with an overall goal in mind.

There are four main factors involved in reinforcer effectiveness. To successfully reinforce a behavior you will need to understand and adequately account for all four. These factors are immediacy, size, contingency, and satiation. The first factor, **immediacy,** indicates that for a reinforcer to be effective it should occur as soon after the behavior as possible, usually within three seconds of the completion of the skill. As a program grows over time and a child's communication skills develop, you can begin purposely to delay reinforcement without diminishing its effectiveness. However, in the early stages of teaching it is important to keep the time between the response and the presentation of the reinforcer as short as possible. Following a behavior with reinforcement immediately will ensure that the connection between the skill to be taught and the reinforcement used to build that skill remains clear and meaningful to the child.

The second factor involved in reinforcer effectiveness, **size**, refers to the reinforcing impact of the consequence. Reinforcers need to be large enough to overcome any competing desires. Attempting to give your child a ball to play with may work as a reinforcer for simple skills. However, the effectiveness of this reinforcement might diminish if the television is on or the skills become more difficult.

Reinforcement works! If it is not working in a specific situation, it is likely you have not considered the optimal levels of reinforcer immediacy, size, contingency, or satiation.

The third factor involved in reinforcer effectiveness is **contingency**. Reinforcement must be contingent on the skill you want to teach. Does the child only obtain reinforcement when he performs the desired skill or does he occasionally receive reinforcement even when he avoids demonstrating the skill?

The final important factor involved in effective reinforcement is **satiation**. If a child is overwhelmed with or bored by a reinforcer he is likely satiated with that reinforcer. The amount of work your boss could get you to do on a Saturday afternoon for $10 might be significantly different if you have no money than it would be if your bank account overflows. People seldom eat when their bellies are full and you cannot expect a reinforcing item or activity to be effective if a child has grown tired or satiated with that item or activity.

Understanding how the considerations of immediacy, size, contingency, and satiation influence the value and successful implementation of reinforcement is important to your ability to teach. The fact is that reinforcement as a tool to increase behavior choices works. If it is not working in a specific situation, it is likely you have not considered the optimal levels of reinforcer immediacy, size, contingency, or satiation.

In addition to knowing the most effective ways to reinforce your child for individual skills, you need to know that there is also an overall reinforcement progression that you will want to work through. A reinforcer is something that follows a behavior and increases the likelihood of that behavior recurring. Anything that your child desires could be a reinforcer. Something is considered a reinforcer based solely on the fact that it works. My wife finds many things reinforcing that I do not. She enjoys getting flowers and cards from friends, loves eating salads and finds running in the woods or at the beach to be a motivating activity. The list of items and activities that I find reinforcing is just as numerous but would not include flowers, salads, or long distance running. When working with children with autism we find that for many their list of reinforcers is smaller and much less diverse. There may only be a few things that your child enjoys. Food items and self-stimulation are the main reinforcers for many children with autism. Since it is the use of reinforcement that teaches and your child may have only a few items that serve as reinforcement, you do not have the luxury of attaching judgments to the items you use to teach. In the beginning, your teaching may need to be based on favorite foods including candies, chips, soft drinks or juice. You might use bouncing on a trampoline or swinging in a blanket. You may be forced to sit through endless re-showings of a favorite Teletubbies or Barney episode. The bottom line is that reinforcement is in the eye of the beholder and in many cases your only choice is to teach with what works, or not to teach.

The principle of pairing takes a major role in developing cooperation and reinforcer effectiveness.

The benefit of good teaching is that if you apply all the major principles of behavior comprehensively, your child will move forward reasonably quickly and your teaching will be able to change to match the new skills that your child learns. Pairing takes a major role in developing cooperation and reinforcer effectiveness. As discussed in the second step to instructional control (Chapter 5), it is imperative that you pair yourself with reinforcement so that your child will choose to spend his time working with you rather than playing alone. Pairing also works with reinforcement. If you only have three or four items that work as reinforcement for your child, you must pair other non-reinforcing (neutral) items or activities with those reinforcers. The principle of pairing states that by connecting a reinforcing item or activity with neutral items or activities, the reinforcing value of one item will transfer to the others. If you want to expand the types of items that are reinforcing to your child, you need to begin pairing non-reinforcing items together with things that you know he already enjoys such as food, music, or a favorite video. Maybe your child does not have a strong interest in soap bubbles. To create one, begin by introducing bubbles when your child is also enjoying music. The feeling of joy coming from listening to the music will begin to transfer to the experience of playing with the bubbles. Over time, the bubbles themselves may become a fun activity in which your child will participate even when there is no music involved. At this point you have just created a new reinforcing item that you can begin to use to teach.

If your child is only strongly motivated by food and drink items, you have no choice but to begin using food and drink items as reinforcement for good behavior choices. However, when teaching with food, you should pair yourself and other neutral activities such as tickling, swinging, and toys with the food item. This causes the neutral items to become reinforcing enough to teach with. Once you can teach with tickles, toys, and swings, you should shift your focus to pairing positive praise and phrases of approval with the food, toys, and tickles. Over time, the praise itself becomes reinforcing enough to teach with and the need for tangible reinforcers will decrease. Ultimately, the use of praise can be paired with the completion of tasks so that task completion itself becomes reinforcing. Our ultimate goal is to have a child who works hard to finish difficult tasks because the act of being successful is its own reward. Even as we move along this reinforcement progression, it is unlikely that we will ever stop using tangible or social reinforcers; however, the more you pair current reinforcers with more sophisticated items or activities the more your child will begin to work for these newer more appropriate forms of reinforcement.

Every interaction has three specific ingredients, which combine to create the ABC paradigm.

In addition to knowing the most effective ways to reinforce and the reinforcement progression, you also need to know how interactions work. Earlier in this book the terms antecedent, behavior, and consequence were mentioned. Every interaction has three specific ingredients that combine to create the ABC paradigm. The "A," "B," and "C" in ABC-paradigm stand for antecedent, behavior, and consequence.

An **antecedent** is anything that is present in the environment of a child *before* the behavior occurs. Antecedents in our life are always present and at any one time too numerous to count. For example, when sitting at the breakfast table, antecedents to possible behavior choices surround me. There may be a coffee pot on the table that could be the antecedent to me pouring a cup of coffee, a radio could be the antecedent to me turning on the radio, or a person entering the room could be my antecedent to saying "Good morning." As you can see the number of antecedents in our environment at any given time is immeasurable and constantly changing.

The **behavior** part of the ABC-paradigm is any measurable change observed in a person. Pouring coffee, turning the radio on, and wishing someone a good morning are all common breakfast behaviors. At this moment, you are probably exhibiting several common reading behaviors. You are likely holding this book. You may be flexing to support your body weight while sitting in a chair or lying in a bed. Fairly soon you will be turning a page. Hopefully, you are not yawning, but if you were that would also be considered a behavior. Other actions that would be considered behavior might surprise you. For example, scanning your eyes back and forth across the page is a behavior. Breathing out deeply when you read something funny is a behavior. Having an elevated heart rate when you read something that excites or scares you is also a behavior. Remember, any measurable change in a person would fall into the category of a behavior.

The final part of the ABC-paradigm is the **consequence**, which is anything that happens in the environment *after* the behavior has occurred. For example, having a cup of coffee ready to drink is the consequence of having poured the cup of coffee. Having music play could be the consequence of turning on the radio. Having someone smile at you is the possible consequence for having said "good morning." Antecedents, behaviors, and consequences are the main factors involved in every interaction. Knowing that the ABCs exist is nice; however, it is not until we know ethical and systematic ways to manipulate them that we can use these ingredients to teach.

The manipulation of the antecedent and the consequence to evoke a desired behavior is the basis of ABA/VB.

Many children with autism are only able to learn the skills for which they have a strong interest or desire. It is the systematic manipulation of antecedents and consequences that will give your child the strong desire he will need to learn the skills you need to teach him. The manipulation of the antecedent and the consequence to evoke a desired behavior is what ABA/VB is based on. The specific system used for manipulating these factors is called discrete trial teaching (DTT).

DTT is a system of teaching that has a defined beginning and ending. The beginning starts with a purposeful antecedent called a discriminative stimulus or S^D. The ending involves a purposeful consequence called a reinforcing stimulus or S^R. The only thing that makes an S^D(discriminative stimulus) different from any other commonplace antecedent is history. For an antecedent to be called an S^D for a behavior, it must have a history of evoking that behavior. The only difference between a consequence and an S^R (reinforcing stimulus) is also history. Once a consequence has developed a history of reinforcing a specific behavior, the consequence can be called an S^R for that behavior.

The following table illustrates how these terms work together:

Examples		Before Teaching		After Teaching
Coffee Pot	=	**Antecedent**	=	S^D
Pouring a cup	=	**Behavior**	=	**Response**
Cup of Coffee	=	**Consequence**	=	S^R

It is the discriminative stimulus (S^D) and the reinforcing stimulus (S^R) that you must develop and manipulate with every interaction you have with your child if you hope to teach him the skills that he lacks. This may seem complex in theory but in practice it is a simple process that anyone can learn to do consistently. In its simplest form, a discrete trial has three specific parts: First, you present the child with a discriminative stimulus (S^D); then you observe the response to the S^D made by the child and finally, you present the child with some form of consequence that is usually a reinforcing stimulus (S^R). Remember this is DTT (discrete trial teaching) in its simplest form. All teaching in ABA will have these three parts. At its basic level teaching through ABA/VB is this simple three-part exercise: present an S^D (discriminative stimulus), observe the child's response, and then present an S^R (reinforcing stimulus). The S^D signals the child that an S^R or reinforcer is available and the S^R acts as a reason the child will want to perform the desired behavior in the future.

In a more complex view, it is also possible that you could add a few more parts to this equation. In addition to the S^D, you may decide that a prompt is necessary to assist the child in finding the correct response. In some instances you may also want to add the process of recording data to the end of the trial. A more complete discrete trial might resemble the following.

Discrete Trial Teaching Procedure:

1. Present an S^D (discriminative stimulus) to your child while he is attending to you.

Add or remove something from your child's environment that you have found has a likelihood of evoking a desired behavior. Remember your child's environment only includes things that can affect his behavior. If your child is not attending and misses your S^D, his environment has not changed. This does not mean that your child must look at you before you present the S^D. This is far from true. Just be sure that your child is not walking out of the room or involved in a significant stereotypical behavior that would make him unlikely to notice your attempt at changing his environment with an S^D.

2. When appropriate, give your child a prompt that assists the discriminative stimulus (S^D) in evoking the desired response.

Prompting has always been used in teaching and in recent years has been an extremely hot topic of discussion. There are many benefits and pitfalls that can come with the use of prompts. Pointing to the area that the child can find the answer is a prompt. Physically moving the child to help him complete a skill is also a prompt. At this point just realize that in a discrete trial, prompts are optional and come attached to the S^D. However, we will detail the definition of a prompt and how one should best be used in Chapter 11.

3. Observe your child's behavior.

It is not uncommon for parents and professionals to present an S^D to a child and then fail to notice a behavior that should have been reinforced. Often when teaching a child to use a specific body movement as a sign to ask for something, the child will unexpectedly say the first sound to the item for which he is asking. If you are too focused on obtaining the appropriate sign, you may miss the opportunity to reinforce this unexpected surprise. Reinforcing a child's first attempt at using a sound can make a large difference in the speed with which a child moves to the next level of requesting. Regularly missing those opportunities may disrupt or delay a child's progress. Always watch for the unexpected surprise when teaching and be ready to reinforce it strongly when you see it.

4. Reinforce your child's correct response.

Children are constantly using behaviors that are appreciated and their parents, teachers, or therapists would like to see again. However, if you do not ensure that these behaviors are being followed with something that is likely to increase their use in the future (reinforcement), the chance of your child using these positive behaviors remains out of your control. Understanding how best to reinforce behavior, including immediacy, size, contingency, and satiation will help you offer successful teaching on a consistent basis. If your teaching is good, your child will spend most of his day being correct and the behaviors leading to this success will begin to occur more often. The more successful your child is during teaching, the more he will learn. Additionally, the more successful he feels, the more he will enjoy the learning process. Ensuring success is paramount in teaching children with autism. The many ways to ensure success in teaching through ABA/VB is detailed in Chapters 10 and 11.

5. Take data on the quality or correctness of your child's response as determined by your team.

Applied Behavior Analysis is a data driven science. It is the objective analysis of observable results that allows for the assessment of one's teaching choices and methods. The level of recommended data taking can range widely from analyst to analyst. Traditional ABA programs tend to take notes between every discrete trial. This data taking process can offer a wealth of information about the child's performance and progress. However, in the home teaching setting, copious note taking and keeping track of percentages correct can be as much a curse as it is a blessing. It is true that you can best decide how to teach based on the data collection of your past efforts, but data keeping can also disrupt the flow of your teaching and act as a barrier to the connection you are trying to build with your child. Working closely with parents I understand their need to minimize the unnecessary workload while maximizing their teaching effectiveness. Additionally, copious data taking can vastly increase the amount of time that passes between each of your discrete teaching trials. In ABA/VB it is recommended that you keep the inter-trial interval as short as possible. A short interval between teaching trials is important for keeping the reinforcement value of teaching high while limiting the value of outside reinforcement. Without knowing the specifics of the child you are trying to help, it is impossible to know what data will be beneficial to your team. However, the following recommendation applies to everyone. Develop a simple and effective way to take data on your child's progress but take only as much data as you need to best evaluate the effectiveness of your teaching and the progress of your child.

The VB approach to autism intervention recommends taking probe data. This is a process of probing or testing each skill once at the beginning of a teaching session and taking data on the child's performance. Then, when you are finished probing each skill once, your teaching can begin keeping your focus fully on your child from one discrete trial to the next. Probe data is then compiled and compared after teaching has concluded. Here is a final example to help clarify any questions you still have about the DTT (discrete trial teaching) process.

Develop a simple and effective way to take data on your child's progress.

S^D: Mom: says, "Touch your nose"

Prompt: Mom: helps by pointing to her own nose (when necessary)

Response: Child: demonstrates skill by touching his nose

S^R: Mom: reinforces the behavior by tickling the child

Data: Mom: checks the "touches nose with prompt" box on her

                         data sheet.

<u>Summary of Chapter 8:</u>

The fact is that reinforcement as a tool to increase behavior choices works. If it is not working in a specific situation, it is likely you have not considered the optimal levels of reinforcer immediacy, size, contingency, or satiation (page 130).

The manipulation of the antecedent and the consequence to evoke a desired behavior is what ABA/VB is based on. The specific system used for manipulating these factors is called discrete trial teaching (page 133).

<u>Discrete Trial Teaching Procedure:</u>

-   Present an S^D to your child while he is attending to you (page 135).

-   When appropriate, give your child a prompt that assists the discriminative stimulus (S^D) in evoking the desired response (page 135).

-   Observe your child's behavior (page 135).

-   Reinforce your child's correct response (page 136).

-   Take data on the quality or correctness of your child's response as determined beneficial by your team (page 136).

Develop a simple and effective way to take data on your child's progress but take only as much data as you need to best evaluate the effectiveness of your teaching and the progress of your child (page 137).

Chapter 9

Classifying Language through

Verbal Behavior

I have written a lot about ABA and I have been very careful always to attach VB to my recommendations. In the next several chapters I will begin demonstrating why using the principles of Applied Behavior Analysis without the procedural recommendations of Verbal Behavior will only give you a small part of what your child needs.

The term Verbal Behavior (VB) was coined by, B. F. Skinner, the father of modern behaviorism. Skinner used the study and research of others in the early 20th Century as the basis for his work developing the major principles of behavior. Since then, ABA has grown and developed over the years through the scientific application of his first book "The Behavior of Organisms" (published in 1938). This book was the beginning of the experimental analysis of behavior that was first applied to the deficits of autism by Dr. O. Ivar Lovaas, and moved forward with others in the field. However, it was not until Dr. Jack Michael, Western Michigan University, and his colleagues began studying and incorporating another of Skinner's books "Verbal Behavior" (published in 1957) into ABA programs that we started seeing the most impressive results. This later book was the first to take a behavioral look at the acquisition of language.

When first hearing the phrase "verbal behavior," many people tend to think that VB is merely an approach to teaching language. VB does deal with behavior that is specifically taught and has communicative intent; however, it has become much more. Technically, **Verbal Behavior** is any behavior that is established and maintained by reinforcement coming from another individual. By definition, VB is more than a language program. For example, teaching your child to talk would fall into the category of VB but so are teaching reading, writing and math. A stop sign you pass on the street could be considered a form of Verbal Behavior. Traffic signs are an antecedent and consequence contingency that is provided by the government to help us drive more safely. The sign itself is the antecedent to the behavior of stopping. Receiving a ticket when you choose not to stop when presented with the stop sign is a consequence the government applies to be sure you make the safer choice in the future.

ABA programs that are not based on Verbal Behavior break language acquisition into two categories: receptive and expressive. In most "older" forms of ABA, receptive language was traditionally taught first through intensive teaching methods while expressive language was expected to develop on its own. Consequently, many children with autism in these programs would develop a strong repertoire of receptive language skills but might never learn to talk. If these children did acquire spoken language, the level of functional speech often remained well below typical development. Thanks to progressing research, an increasing number of traditional ABA approaches are now focusing more effort on teaching the expressive side of language. However, the analysis of Verbal Behavior teaches us that language is more than just expressive or receptive. In fact, all language falls into any one of nine distinct categories. It is important to recognize that it is <u>function</u> and not <u>form</u> that defines these categories. Thus, its letters or sounds do not define a word. Rather, a word is defined by the intent that word suggests to the people who experience it in the context it is shared.

Even when examined in non-behavioral terms there is no rhyme or reason to the formation of words. For example, it could be argued that the word "cat" and the word "catch" are similar in their form. Both start with a c-a-t and both sound similar when spoken. However the functional meaning of these two words is different. Upon hearing the word "cat," one likely thinks of a small furry animal with whiskers. When hearing the word "catch," one likely thinks of a person snatching a ball out of the air, trying to reel in a fish, or maybe coming down with a cold. The point is that the words are defined by the images they conjure rather than the letters by which they are made. Actually there is no reason why words mean what they do. Understanding words is nothing more than a rote memorization exercise of experience. This can be confusing to a child with autism as it often is for many of us.

If I say the word "cow," you might be thinking of a large animal on a farm being milked. If that is the case, then the meaning of my word has been successful. But, if I asked you what color that cow is, some people will respond "white and black" and others will say "light brown." The image the word summons differs based on individual experience. Communication is by no means an exact exercise with linear rules. Do not underestimate the difficulty of understanding written and spoken language. Words only mean what they have been experienced to mean by the individual who has experienced them. In addition, definitions change based on how a word is used. For example, the word "will" may mean a future intention such as in, "I will do that" or it may be referring to your strong desire such as in "summon all of your will." It is also possible that the word is merely referring to a person's name. Most importantly, when the function of a word is examined behaviorally, one can find a series of implications important to the process of teaching language.

B.F. Skinner gave us many wonderful gifts with the development of Verbal Behavior and the Science of ABA. One of the most important was his creation of the Behavioral Classification of Language. Through his study, Skinner was able to organize all language into nine separate functions. For your child to be an effective communicator, he will need to be able to use each word he learns across most, if not all, of these functions.

For people with autism, the ability to generalize information and ideas is usually neither easy nor automatic. The skill of generalization can be practiced and improved like any other skill but in many cases this is an area of weakness that comes with autism. The fact that your child understands a word in one context does not mean that he can use it in other contexts. In the beginning stages of teaching words and their meanings, you will likely have to teach

Through his study, Skinner was able to organize all language into nine separate functions.

specific words across several different functions of language to give your child the full concept of the word. For example, can your child ask for a cup? Can he point to a cup when you ask him to? Can your child say, "cup" when one is pointed at or he is asked, "What is this?" Can he say, "cup" when you ask him to name something from which he can drink? Only being able to demonstrate "cup" in a few of these categories indicates that a broader understanding of the concept "cup" is still needed.

The first and easiest of the nine categories of language to teach is called manding. A mand is a request for items, activities, or information. A good example of a mand occurs when a child says "pretzel" when he wants you to give him a pretzel. However, there are different levels of mands. For example, a child is also manding if he shows you the sign language symbol for a pretzel or points to a pretzel in the hopes of you giving him one. The main factor in making those functions of that communication behavior a mand is not what the child does or says but rather the intention of the behavior. To be a mand, the child must actually desire to have the pretzel at the time the behavior occurs.

The second behavioral classification of language is motor imitation. Motor imitation is no different than it sounds. Any movement your child makes that is an attempt to copy or mimic an action he sees is a motor imitation. Motor imitation is an important skill for your child to have. If your child cannot imitate your movements, he will not be able to use sign language as a bridge to communication. He will be unable to copy mouth or tongue movements that will aid his ability to talk. It is likely that 80-90% of all learning behavior exhibited by a typical child age three or younger involves the use of motor imitation skills. It is the lack of this extremely important early developmental skill of motor imitation that causes children with autism to become delayed so quickly in so many different ways. A simple example of a motor imitation skill is saying "do this," and touching your head simultaneously. If your child can touch his head by hearing the words "do this," and seeing you touch your head, then he has demonstrated a motor imitation skill. More complex motor imitation skills might include copying sequences of actions or spontaneously copying the actions of a group of others. How many times have you missed a direction in school or at work and used your motor imitation skills to copy what you saw everyone else doing? Motor imitation is an extremely important skill in the development of using sign and non-verbal language and your child needs to learn how to use this category of language as well as every other category to be a fully functioning communicator.

The third classification of language is called verbal imitation. Verbal imitation is the ability to repeat exactly what you hear. If you say, "mama" and your child can repeat "mama," he has demonstrated a verbal imitation. Verbal imitation is also known as an echoic. Can your child echo sounds and words that he hears? For some, the ability to echo has become a major problem in a child's functional ability to communicate. The topic of echoing will be covered in Chapter 16. Suffice to say, verbal imitation is a natural and important part of learning language and remembering information. For example, when a friend tells you his phone number, you might choose to repeat it aloud to help you remember. This is an important functional use of verbal imitation and it helps you to put things into your long-term memory. Your child must learn to verbally imitate to learn to talk. Additionally it is the ability to echo that plays a large role in the acquisition of other parts of language.

Verbal imitation is the ability to repeat exactly what you hear.

Receptive language, the fourth classification of language, is the ability to follow instructions or to comply with requests. This classification includes the ability to identify items non-verbally. For example, if you were asked to hand someone a napkin, your ability to hear and correctly comply with the request is receptive language. You may remember receptive language as the main area of teaching in traditional ABA programs. Receptive language has many different levels, one of which is the ability to recognize and respond to one's name. Others include, identifying named common objects, following instructions in daily routine situations, and receptively identifying people in the environment. A more difficult level is the ability to correctly identify by pointing to a complete set of multi-colored semi-transparent mononucleides with similar properties to that of the representative sample. ;-)

Receptive language is the ability to follow instructions or to comply with requests.

The fifth classification of language is the tact. Tacting is the skill of verbally identifying objects, actions, and events in the environment. A common term that is substituted for tacting is labeling. If you point to a car and ask your child to identify the object and he responds "car," he can tact that object. Of course, if your child is non-vocal and he can use a sign for the word "car" this would also be considered tacting. Other examples of tacting include, labeling items using carrier phrases such as, "That is a ____," labeling with adjectives such as, "Look, a yellow bus," or labeling with prepositions such as, "The cat is

Tacting is the skill of verbally identifying objects, actions, and events in the environment.

in the tree." One of the more difficult skills to teach early learners is spontaneous vocal tacting. Typical children use this skill regularly by pointing out objects they find interesting to others. There is little that is more rewarding than watching a parent's face when his child spontaneously tacts something such as, "Look, daddy, an airplane," for the very first time.

A receptive identification of an item by its feature, function, or class is called an RFFC.

The sixth classification is called receptive by feature, function, and class (RFFC). As noted, receptive language is the ability to follow instructions or comply with requests. An RFFC is the ability receptively to identify specific items when given some description of its function, feature, or class. The ability to teach features, functions, and classes of items can be difficult as many objects have more than one of each. However, taking the time to teach many, if not all, of the common features, functions, and classes of items is extremely important. A child with a strong RFFC repertoire is much more likely to be a functional communicator. There are many RFFCs for the object "ball." For example, a ball could be identified as something round, red, or rubber (receptive by feature), something that you bounce, you roll, or that you play with (receptive by function), and sporting or playground equipment (receptive by class).

Intraverbals deal with answering questions or having conversations where words are controlled by the different words of others.

The seventh classification of language is called the intraverbal. Intraverbals deal with answering questions or having conversations where the words used are controlled by the different words of others. For example, someone asks "Where were you yesterday?" You respond by answering, "I was at work." Some of the first intraverbals taught in a Verbal Behavior program are the words of songs. If you can sing a song, stop at a certain point and your child can say (or preferably sing) the next word; he has just demonstrated an intraverbal skill. Saying, "ready, set" as an S^D (instruction) for your child to say "go!" is also an example of an early intraverbal. More advanced intraverbals include answering what, where, and why questions, answering questions about the future or past, and telling stories.

Language can also be classified as being textual or writing.

The final two classifications of language are simple to explain as most people experience them almost daily. The first is called textual. You are at this very minute engaged in the textual function of language. Textual language involves the reading of written words. The final classification of language is called writing. This means handwriting words and letters but also includes typing words that are spoken to you.

There is another important consideration that must be made when teaching children with autism the many functions of words. This is that the name of an object often describes more than just an individual object. When tacting (labeling) a car, your child needs to be able to demonstrate that he knows other cars are also cars. Can he also tact a picture of a car? Can he identify both your real car and a toy car as a car? Does he know that a bus is not a car? These are all questions of which you must be aware when teaching language to your child. Often you will finish the job of teaching a word to your child only to discover that he has a limited understanding of how to use the word. Your understanding of Verbal Behavior and the Behavioral Classification of Language will allow you to be more systematic in your approach to teaching language. It helps you to be more complete in the meanings you teach and it helps your child to become a more effective communicator.

For more detailed information on how to use Skinner's Behavioral Classification of Language in the context of an ABA/VB program I recommend "Teaching Language to Children with Autism and other Developmental Disabilities," written by Dr. Mark Sundberg and Dr. James Partington.

Summary of Chapter 9:

B.F. Skinner gave us many wonderful gifts when he developed Verbal Behavior and the Science of ABA. One of the most important was his creation of the Behavioral Classification of Language. Through his study, Skinner was able to organize all language into nine separate functions. For your child to be an effective communicator, he will need to be able to use each word he learns across most, if not all, of these functions (page 141).

The first and easiest of the nine categories of language to teach is called manding. A mand is a request for items, activities, or information (page 142).

The second behavioral classification of language is motor imitation. Motor imitation is no different than it sounds. Any movement your child makes that is an attempt to copy or mimic an action he sees is a motor imitation (page 142).

The third classification of language is called verbal imitation. Verbal imitation is the ability to repeat exactly what you hear. If you say, "mama" and your child can repeat "mama," he has demonstrated a verbal imitation (page 143).

Receptive language, the fourth classification of language, is the ability to follow instructions or to comply with requests. This classification includes the ability to identify items non-verbally. For example, if you were asked to hand someone a napkin, your ability to hear and correctly comply with the request is receptive language (page 143).

The fifth classification of language is the tact. Tacting is the skill of verbally identifying objects, actions, and events in the environment. A common term that is substituted for tacting is labeling. If you point to a car and ask your child to identify the object and he responds "car," he can tact that object. Of course, if your child is non-vocal and he can use a sign for the word "car" this would also be considered tacting (page 143).

The sixth classification is called receptive by feature, function, and class (RFFC). As noted, receptive language is the ability to follow instructions or comply with requests. An RFFC is the ability to receptively identify specific items when given some description of its function, feature, or class (page 143).

The seventh classification of language is called the intraverbal. Intraverbals deal with answering questions or having conversations where the words used are controlled by the different words of others. For example, someone asks "Where were you yesterday?" You respond by answering, "I was at work" (page 143).

The final two classifications of language are simple to explain as most people experience them almost daily. The first is called textual. You are at this very minute engaged in the textual function of language. Textual language involves the reading of written words. The final classification of language is called writing. This means handwriting words and letters but also includes typing words that are spoken to you (page 143).

For more detailed information on how to use Skinner's Behavioral Classification of Language in the context of an ABA/VB program I recommend "Teaching Language to Children with Autism and other Developmental Disabilities," written by Dr. Mark Sundberg and Dr. James Partington (page 144).

Chapter 10

EO: The Secret to Motivated Learning

with Verbal Behavior

Verbal Behavior has given us a better understanding of the functions and best teaching methodologies of language. However, the VB approach to ABA is more than merely teaching communicative intent. One of its most important advancements involves understanding how to capture and use a child's naturally occurring motivation to give him a <u>reason</u> to learn the skills you want to teach him. This motivation comes in the form of an **Establishing Operation (EO).** An EO is anything that temporarily alters the value of a reinforcer. If something makes a reinforcer more valuable to you, it has increased your motivation to use any behavior or perform any skill that is likely to help you obtain that reinforcer. A fundamental aspect of ABA is the effective use of reinforcement. Reinforcement is the consequence that will make a specific behavior more likely to reoccur. For more than 50 years, ABA programs have become increasingly better about evoking a skill or behavior from a child after the child has found that the successful completion of that skill will likely lead to some form of reinforcement. However, it is the application of VB techniques that teach us how to use the establishing operation to give the child a reason to attempt the skill from the beginning.

Although EO and motivation are not synonymous, motivation is a good substitute when looking for a word that explains how you will use establishing operations to help your child learn. Some behavior analysts prefer to concentrate only on the motivating power of an establishing operation (EO) and will use the term motivating operation (MO) instead. Whether you are working with a behavior analyst who uses the term EO or MO, you are still dealing with the concept of motivation. I will use the more traditional term EO to refer to the motivating conditions that drive a child to act.

Using reinforcement without consideration for motivation leaves you little choice but to force your child to experience the value of participation. For example, if you want to show your child that asking for a cookie will be reinforced with a cookie, but your child does not want the cookie at that time, your only choice is to force him to ask. However, if he wants a cookie at the time of the teaching lesson, he will be motivated to ask. This leaves you without a need to force his participation.

Motivation is a good substitute when looking for a word that explains how establishing operations (EO) work to help you teach your child.

If your current goal is to teach your child to remain seated in a chair during learning tasks, you should never physically force him to sit. Forcing a child to remain seated until skills can be prompted and reinforcement can be delivered is common practice in traditional ABA programs. However, when pushed, a person's natural reaction is to push back. Trying to force your child to stay in a chair during learning (escape extinction) will only increase the value of avoiding or escaping the chair. In addition, this type of forced or coerced interaction is counterproductive to a relationship of mutual respect and trust. Trust and respect is what you will need from your child if you are going to teach him to desire being more connected to the social world. Instead of forcing your child to remain seated, you should employ the seven steps of instructional control from Chapters 5 and 6 with the goal of making the choice of staying in his seat your child's most beneficial option. In other words, restrict all forms of reinforcement, assure that while he is seated his interaction with you is fun, offer large amounts of positive reinforcement for skills performed while seated, and refuse to allow access to any reinforcement when he chooses to leave his seat. When done appropriately and consistently, your child will begin choosing to stay in the chair for longer and longer periods of time. Eventually he may even begin calling you over to the chair for more learning fun.

If you want your child to demonstrate a skill or participate in an activity, it is your job to give him a reason. In the VB approach to ABA, it is preferred to make the desired skill or activity the most interesting and enjoyable option in the environment. Reinforcement and motivation (EO) can be looked at as reasons. When asked, "Why will your child want to engage in this behavior," your answer should indicate some form of reinforcement or EO. Remember, reinforcement is the reason your child will want to engage in a behavior again in the future. An EO (motivation) is why your child will want to attempt the skill this time. A good example from the Behavior Analysts, Inc. workshop "Teaching Children with Language Delays" presented in 2003 by Stacy Carroll, B.S., BCABA and Steven Ward, MA, BCBA involves teaching a person the skill of turning a thermostat. According to the principles of ABA, if I want to teach a child the behavior of turning a thermostat on the wall, I need to manipulate the antecedent or consequence to evoke this behavior. For instance, I need to put the child in a room, put a thermostat within reaching distance, and set the room in such a way so that when the thermostat is turned the child experiences some form of reinforcement. It is also important that many repetitions of this skill occur so that the consistent experience of receiving reinforcement after turning the thermostat causes the child to want independently to turn the thermostat in the future.

In traditional ABA programs skills are often removed from their general context and taught in an intensive table setting. Table teaching allows the child to get the necessary number of repetitions in a setting that is easy to control, where reinforcement can be easily delivered, and data can be easily taken. Many traditional ABA programs often try to identify an important reinforcer or two, often food, and use only those items as reinforcement for new behavior skills in this intensive setting. With these procedures to teaching in place, you might find an ABA consultant recommending that you place a thermostat on the table, tell the child to, "turn it," and when he does, reinforce him with a cookie or chip. The proven principles of behavior tell us that if chips and cookies are reinforcers for this child for skills such as turning a thermostat the child *will* learn this skill. The problem is that skills are often so far removed from there original EO that learning them in this environment seldom leads to independent use. Traditional ABA professionals consider antecedents solely as S^Ds; however, more correctly, antecedents are a combination of S^D (instruction) and EO (motivation). The main difference that a consultant versed in VB would likely bring to the equation is the use of a naturally occurring reinforcer for turning a thermostat -- warmth. When warmth is the reinforcer, you would then

If you want your child to demonstrate a skill or participate in an activity, it is your job to give him a meaningful reason.

just need to create an EO for warmth and the actual skill being taught becomes self-reinforcing. By simply leaving the thermostat where it is and adding cold air to the environment, you can easily create an EO for warmth. The colder the air in the room, the more involved your child will become in performing skills that lead to warmth. Not only will a child learn a skill faster when he is motivated to participate in the learning, but he will also learn the skill within the context of its general use.

The definition of an EO is anything that temporarily alters the value of reinforcement changing the frequency of behavior related to that reinforcement. If something makes a reinforcer more valuable to you, it has increased your motivation to use any behavior or perform any skill that is likely to help you obtain that reinforcer. A room being cold makes warmth more valuable to you and, therefore, increases the likelihood of your demonstrating behavior that your experience has shown might lead to warmth. Similarly, having no money in your pocket increases the perceived value of a nickel in the street making you more likely to pick it up. Feeling ill increases the value of feeling well thus, increasing your motivation to ingest a distasteful medicine. The consequence (heat) is the reason the child is more likely to turn a thermostat the next time he wants warmth. The EO (the room being cold) is the reason the child will desire to attempt the skill this time. Consideration concerning the EO for a skill is one of the main reasons why modern ABA is very good for teaching children with autism but ABA/VB is a better way to teach toward recovery.

EO: Anything that temporarily alters the value of reinforcement changing the frequency of behavior related to that reinforcement.

EOs come in many shapes and sizes. One of the most obvious motivations is thirst. Demonstrating how you can use thirst as an EO is a great way to explain the differences between traditional ABA programs and ABA/VB programs. In traditional ABA programs you may want to teach a child the word "water." This process would likely involve a therapist and child sitting at a table. The therapist presents the child with a cup of water or a picture of a cup of water and asks the child to "show me water." The repetitive practice of this skill is meant to lead the child to a receptive understanding of the word "water." To develop expressive language the therapist would point to the water or picture of water and tell the child to say "water." Once the child has consistently demonstrated the ability to point to water on request and say the word when asked, what is this, the concept of water would be considered mastered. Most often reinforcement for this behavior would be in the form of a candy, pretzel, or other preferred snack.

Teaching in an ABA/VB program would likely look very different. For starters, you would not teach receptive and expressive language. Rather you would use the nine classifications of language as detailed in Chapter 9. It is not until the word "water" is taught across these nine categories that you should consider the *concept* of water mastered. In addition, you would not try to teach the concept of "water" in a contrived situation with artificial reinforcement. You would instead start with the easiest form of the word to learn, the "mand." A mand is a request for items, actions, or information. The reason the mand is the easiest to teach is that it comes with a naturally occurring EO. If you want to teach "water" as a mand, you would be best served to use the EO of thirst. A child cannot learn to ask for something if he does not want the item at the moment he is asking for it. If he does not want the item, he can only learn to tact (label) it.

Thus, instead of sitting your child at a table, you could take him outside and play a game that involves running around and having fun. This is an example of pairing, the second step of instructional control. A by-product of pairing in this fashion would create your EO of thirst. Once you have created the EO (motivation) for water in your child, you only need to prepare a cup of water and wait for him to try to obtain it. When he does, you now have the optimal situation in which to teach. What you would teach your child depends on his current level of manding ability. It could be to say the word "water," make a sign for water, or it might be to use a full sentence to ask for his water. Regardless, you will want to use the water itself as the natural reinforcement for the successful completion of this skill. Outside of your teaching setting, the skill of asking for water will likely be followed by receiving water. Using this naturally occurring consequence as the reinforcer for your teaching will make the jump to maintained independent use of this skill easier for the child.

Looking at the results of these two approaches to teaching "water," you will see the obvious benefits of ABA/VB. In traditional ABA approaches the child would be able to say "water" when asked "what is this?" in the presence of water or a picture of a cup of water. Conversely, using the naturally occurring EO for water the child will learn how to ask for cup of water at a time when he actually wants water. Once the child can ask for water, it is time to begin teaching the other functions of language for that word. You could then teach it receptively asking "show me the water," as a tact (label), "what is that?" or as an RFFC (receptive by feature function or class) "what is something you drink?" The importance of a word is found in its function. Water has many functions, primarily to quench thirst. So, it would only make sense to teach the concept of water when your child has a desire for its function.

This chapter has offered you a simplified example of traditional ABA compared to ABA/VB. There is no "one way" to teach anything in either type of program. In fact, many traditional ABA services are now beginning to incorporate VB research and techniques into their programs. Others who claim to be VB specialists are merely doing traditional ABA while incorporating Skinner's behavioral classification of language. Although understanding the functional differences in language will undoubtedly improve the quality of their teaching, not understanding the value of EO and other VB research might leave them unable consistently to teach you how to teach your child toward recovery. The quality of your child's program will always be determined by the program decisions made by the person in charge. Do the best you can to become well versed in the procedures of ABA/VB so that you can be sure your child is getting the best possible teaching. For many years traditional ABA has been the most successful approach to autism intervention the world has ever seen. My intention is to demonstrate the differences and advancements of the VB approach to ABA. ABA is the basis for everything you should do with your child with autism or other learning delays. However, not applying the principles and teachings of VB to your ABA program will likely leave you with good but less than optimal outcomes.

Using temperature, thirst, or hunger as an EO (motivation) is only the beginning of understanding the multitude of ways ABA/VB consultants are now using EOs as teaching tools to speed the process of learning. The following is a partial list of other EOs that you can consider using as the reason your child will want to attempt a skill that you are trying to teach.

Establishing Operations (motivation) you can use to teach:

Restriction of Reinforcement: Control of reinforcement was the focus of step 1 of instructional control and an important part of teaching. It also helps serve as an EO (motivation) for learning. Not allowing your child to have free and easy access to his reinforcing items and activities makes those items more valuable to your child when you want to use them to teach.

By not applying the principles and teachings of VB to your ABA program you will likely find yourself with good but less than optimal outcomes.

Errorless Learning: Using a teaching system that ensures success will keep the skills you teach from becoming aversive or leading to escape activities. Whatever reinforcement you are using will have more value if your child also has the proper amount of assistance available to help him stay successful in the learning process. Errorless learning is an extremely important teaching procedure that will be discussed in Chapter 11.

Mixing and Varying Tasks: Intermixing between the types of tasks you teach will keep your child from becoming bored with the repetition of instruction. It will also encourage him to focus more completely on the instructions you are giving increasing the value of your teaching. Children can begin to see the patterns in repetitive teaching and will answer questions based on the pattern and not the question itself. Constantly mixing and varying your teaching targets will keep your child focused on the S^Ds and not on following the pattern of your teaching.

Alternating Task Difficulty: Intermixing easy skills with the more difficult keeps the average difficulty of your teaching low. When a learning activity is consistently hard, the value of the reinforcement you have available lessens. However, by mixing between easy and hard skills, you will increase the value of your reinforcement by giving your child an easier road to obtain that reinforcement.

Decreasing Inter-trial Intervals: Keeping your inter-trial interval short helps keep your child focused on the reinforcement you are offering and gives him less opportunity to find outside reinforcement that might lower the relative strength of the reinforcement you have available.

Fluency: Expecting and then differentially reinforcing quick and accurate responses keeps a child from being slow or incomplete in his response. It also encourages him to work harder to attend to your instructions and answer at a rate that will lead him to more and better things. Teaching a child to be fluent is an important consideration in autism intervention and expecting fluency as part of your normal teaching procedure will only help in this regard.

Free Samples: Giving a child a free sample of reinforcement can be useful in encouraging a higher interest in obtaining more of the item. The film industry knows that people are much more likely to go to a movie if they have seen the movie trailer on TV. Seeing a glow-in-the-dark ball with the lights off will increase a child's desire to obtain that ball and have the lights turned off. Tasting one salty chip is likely to increase the desire to ask for more chips. Tasting a salty chip can also be used to create an EO (motivation) for requesting water.

Response Effort: How easy does obtaining the reinforcement seem? When an item is or appears to be impossible to come by, I will spend less time trying. However, if I feel that I have a good chance of gaining access to the item, I will try harder. A person might be perfectly happy to walk to the corner drugstore for a candy bar. However, the value of that candy bar might be less if he has to drive downtown in rush hour traffic to find the store.

Turning the Tables: Pushing a child will often cause him to push back in the opposite direction. If you want a child to go in one direction, sometimes it is better to encourage him away from your target and let his desire to control the interaction lead him to choose the direction you want him to go. This process of turning the tables on autism is a concept that will be detailed in Chapter 16.

All of these are examples of EO that you should be using to improve the effectiveness of your teaching. They help you to teach because they become the reason why your child will *want* to perform your target skill. For a child to learn a new behavior in the fastest and most complete way, he will have to desire learning it. What is your child's reason for demonstrating a behavior is a question you must be able to answer. You will always be able to answer that question once you become a better teacher. Your answer will usually be something such as, "Because he wants the ball" or "Because he knows it is the only way he will get my attention" or "Because he knows that I will not give him a direction until he comes back and finishes this and without another direction, he will not be allowed to play with his cars." The answer "Because I said so" is never a reason why a child with autism will follow an instruction. "Because we held him down and forced him to participate" should never be the reason either. Through the VB approach to ABA there has developed some incredibly intricate ways to evoke a desire to learn. Effectively considering a child's EO (motivation) has removed the need for forcing a child to participate from the landscape of autism education. Understanding how to use the list above as well as many other forms of EO is imperative to good teaching.

Understanding EO (motivation) is the key to improving your teaching with VB. It is the combination of EO and reinforcement that will be the reason your child will desire to achieve the skill you want him to learn. By extending the use of EO and reinforcement into every interaction you have with your child, you can truly teach to all of the deficits caused by autism. By not incorporating EO, many traditional ABA programs often fail when attempting to teach relationship development skills. However, when EO is considered while teaching to social relationship development targets, you can give your child the same desire for social contact, reciprocal communication, and experience sharing that exists in each of us. Understanding ABA/VB helps you to understand the reasons why your child would want to use these skills and gives you a structure by which to teach to these and other important goals in a systematic way.

One of the most recognizable behavior deficits that a child with autism might demonstrate is a lack of normalized eye contact. There have been techniques and strategies designed to develop eye contact since people began applying ABA to autism. If you have had any experience in older forms of ABA, you might have been advised to tell your child to "Look at me" and then offer him a piece of candy when he does. Another older ABA procedure used to evoke eye contact is to hold a reinforcer between your eyes and wait for your child to look at it before you deliver it. Both of these programs would likely help to build eye contact in the teaching setting they are introduced. But neither is a good approach in educating toward recovery. Neither of these approaches takes into consideration the natural EO for eye contact. That EO (motivation) is attention. The reason that we all use eye contact is that it has consistently proved to earn us better attention from those with whom it was desired. If you ever get a chance to participate in a Knospe-ABA workshop, you will see video after video of children making great eye contact with people in their environment. With VB we achieve this without ever once asking a child to look at us. In fact, Knospe-ABA does not have a specific program for eye contact at all. What we have found is that by following the seven steps of instructional control and interacting with a child in a way that he can understand, the desire to have our attention is a natural by product. This newly gained desire (EO) to gain the attention of those around him encourages a child to make behavioral choices to gain and maintain that attention. One behavior that naturally evokes attention from others is eye contact. If you do not agree that eye contact is a powerful tool

ABA/VB helps you to understand the reasons why your child would want to use the skills you want to teach him.

Instead of telling your child to look at you, give him an EO for eye contact.

to gain attention, try putting this book down, walk to the nearest person, and make long sustained eye contact with him. You will most likely gain his attention in the form of a verbal remark almost immediately. When you want someone's attention you look into his eyes. You also speak loudly and clearly. When your child is taught the benefit of having your attention and you can make specific decisions on how and when he is able to obtain it, your child will naturally begin using attention gaining behavior in consistent and appropriate ways. Instead of telling your child to look at you, give him an EO for eye contact. If you teach him to desire your attention through ABA/VB, he will choose to make eye contact with you to earn and keep your attention the same as everyone else.

Summary of Chapter 10:

Although EO and motivation are not synonymous, motivation is a good substitute when looking for a word that explains how you will use establishing operations to help your child learn (page 150).

If you want your child to demonstrate a skill or participate in an activity, it is your job to give him a reason. In the VB approach to ABA, it is preferred to make the desired skill or activity the most interesting and enjoyable option in the environment. Reinforcement and motivation (EO) can be looked at as reasons. When asked, "Why will your child want to engage in this behavior," your answer should indicate some form of reinforcement or EO (page 150).

The definition of an EO is anything that temporarily alters the value of reinforcement changing the frequency of behavior related to that reinforcement. If something makes a reinforcer more valuable to you, it has increased your motivation to use any behavior or perform any skill that is likely to help you obtain that reinforcer (page 152).

ABA is the basis for everything you should do with your child with autism or other learning delays. However, not applying the principles and teachings of VB to your ABA program will likely leave you with good but less than optimal outcomes (page 154).

Understanding EO (motivation) is the key to improving your teaching with VB. It is the combination of EO and reinforcement that will be the reason your child will desire to achieve the skill you want him to learn (page 157).

Instead of telling your child to look at you, give him an EO for eye contact. If you teach him to desire your attention through ABA/VB, he will choose to make eye contact with you to earn and keep your attention the same as everyone else (page 158).

Establishing Operations (motivation) you can use to teach (page 154):

Restriction of Reinforcement

Errorless Learning

Mixing and Varying Tasks

Alternating Task Difficulty

Decreasing Inter-trial Intervals

Fluency

Free Samples

Response Effort

Turning the Tables

Chapter 11

Errorless Learning: The Art of

Most-to-Least Prompting

Chapter 8 discussed discrete trial teaching (DTT). Next is a quick example of what the DTT procedure looks like.

S^D (instruction):	Teacher: "What is that?"
Prompt:	Teacher: "Puppy." or "PUH." (optional)
Response:	Child: "Puppy."
S^R (reinforcement):	Teacher: "Great Job" while tickling child.
Data:	Teacher: puts mark in data box. (optional)

The purpose of this chapter is to discuss prompting, the second part of the DTT procedure. A practical definition for a prompt is anything added to an S^D (instruction) to help your child make a desired response. Prompts come in many forms and are used by people every day in every way. When someone asks you the direction to the restroom, you might respond "It's in the Southwest corner of the building." However, pointing in that direction at the same time makes it easier for the person to find his way. Pointing to the restroom is a prompt that assists the S^D, "It's in the Southwest corner of the building." It makes the process of following your direction easier. Although arguably different, prompts can act as EOs. They are included in the antecedent and by changing the difficulty level of the task at hand can temporarily change the value of the reinforcer. Prompts make reinforcement more valuable by making it easier to obtain. Here is a real-world example of a prompt acting like an EO.

When you go to the grocery store, you usually plan to buy specific items. You may even take a list of items you need to prompt your purchases. Stores use a scientific approach to stocking their shelves. The most prized locations are those shelves that display items at eye level. Studies show that people are more likely to purchase items that are easily located. Have you ever noticed that most major brands are generally prominently placed? Product placement is so important and influential that many major chain stores charge a slotting fee for prominent product placement. This eye-level placement is called a positional prompt. Positional prompts decrease the workload necessary to perform a skill and, in turn, increase the reinforcement value of performing that skill. In other words, the same amount of benefit becomes more worthwhile when the amount of effort necessary to earn it is reduced. Positional prompts are such a powerful aid that companies pay large sums of money for the right to have the best positions in the store.

There are nine different types of prompts in two distinct categories with which you should be familiar. To be your child's best teacher, you need to know how and when to use each.

The primary purpose of a prompt is to help ensure success. Each different type of prompt offers a slightly different level of help. Some are stronger and more supportive than others. The two categories of prompts are physical and verbal. The largest or most supportive physical prompt you can use is a **full-physical prompt**. That is a physical manipulation of the body to complete the task. For example, a full-physical prompt occurs when you teach your child to write by placing a pencil in his hand, holding it in place and guiding his hand as he writes.

A **partial-physical prompt** is slightly less supportive. In this case, you would place the pencil in his hand and hold it until he makes the movement of writing the line independently. A partial-physical prompt is defined as a partial manipulation of the body to complete a task. Another example of a partial-physical prompt could be a gentle push from the elbows to help your child to touch his head. For this to be a partial physical prompt, you need to let go of his arms at some point and allow your child to complete the skill independently.

Less supportive than a partial-physical prompt is an imitative or model prompt. **Imitative prompts** are visual demonstrations for your child to copy. For example, you wave while asking your child to wave goodbye. More so than the partial and full physical prompts the imitative prompt requires an independent behavior to be performed by the child to fulfill the request.

The gesture prompt is even less supportive. **Gesture prompts** are defined as pointing or cueing a child where to look or how to find the answer. Pointing to the bathroom in the Southwest corner of the building is a gesture prompt. Tapping near an item you would like your child to select or looking at the correct answer are also examples of gesture prompts as they clue your child where to locate the answer.

Positional prompts are the least supportive of the physical prompts. When you move your body or an object in relation to your child, you are using position to affect what you want him to do. For example, you hold up a pen and a cup and direct your child to, "Touch the cup." Then, you hold the cup closer to your child to indicate that it is the correct answer.

Prompt fading is the process of giving a certain amount of initial support and then systematically reducing that support.

You must also understand the concept of prompt fading before you can effectively use prompts to teach. Fading is the process of giving a certain amount of initial support and then systematically reducing that support in a way that allows your child to remain successful while becoming increasingly more independent. Whenever you need to use a physical prompt, you should use as strong or as supportive of a physical prompt as necessary to help your child be successful. For example, you may need to start with a full-physical prompt and quickly fade to a partial-physical prompt. When your child is performing well with only partial-physical help, you can then start using a gesture prompt or possibly a positional prompt. Ultimately, you will fade out every type of prompt until your child is able to do the skill without help. The process of fading to increasingly less supportive prompts allows a child to become increasingly more independent at demonstrating a skill or new behavior.

Sometimes you will need to work with verbal prompts. There are two major types of verbal prompts, echoic and instructional. Echoic prompts are usually used when you need to help a child to find a verbal answer such as in the question "What is this?" As with physical prompts, verbal prompts should be faded. Start with a **full-echoic prompt** such as saying the whole word you want your child to repeat. For example, "What is this? Ball!" and your child repeats the word "Ball." A full-echo prompt does supply the child with the correct answer, but it should not be looked upon as a failed attempt; rather it should be considered a prompted success. Once your child can answer the question "What is this" with the full-echoic prompt "Ball," you begin asking, "What is this? Ba!" This is called a **partial-echoic prompt**. You can even fade within a prompt. For example, you might use the partial echoic prompt "ba" and later fade to the partial echoic prompt "b."

Verbal prompts can also be instructional. Instructional prompts are usually used when you want your child independently to remember to do something. For example, before going to bed you want your child to remember to wash his hands or put away a toy. In these instances you will want to use direct and indirect verbal prompts. However, it should be noted that all prompts can be used in many different situations and combined depending on the skill being taught. The **direct verbal prompt** is the most supportive instructional prompt. "Wash your hands" and "Pick up your toys" are examples of direct verbal prompts that could be appropriate for the S^D "What are you supposed to be doing?" As with all prompts, this verbal assistance should be faded. For example, instead of directing your child to wash his hands, you might say, "It is something we do in the bathroom" or "It makes you clean for dinner?" This is called an **indirect verbal prompt**.

Mastering the art of prompting and prompt fading is essential to effective teaching.

Mastering the art of prompting and prompt fading is essential to effective teaching. It is a fluid process that may differ from one instructional program to another. Additionally, how one should prompt and fade can differ from one target goal to the next within a program. Some skills may be more difficult for a child to learn and, consequently, require more prompting. Your child may find other skills intrinsically motivating and, therefore, will require less prompting. Knowing exactly what prompts to use and when to fade from one prompt to the next is an inexact science that relies on experience and direct observation of the child. Early learners may need a series of faded physical prompts to master the skill of basic motor imitation. When teaching a child to imitate a simple motor movement such as touching his head it is usually best to start with a full-physical prompt. The process begins by giving the child the S^D (a demonstration of the skill of head touching and the words "Do this"). Then give the child a full-physical prompt (take the child's hands and move them until they touch his head). Be sure to reinforce this prompted success. For many children with autism, one prompted trial is not enough to lead the child to independent ability in the skill. In subsequent trials, continue giving the child a full-physical prompt and reinforce his success until you begin to feel him helping you move his hands through the proper motion. This is when you should attempt to fade to a partial-physical prompt (moving the child's hands toward his head and then letting go before completion of the skill). If the child is unable to complete the skill, quickly help him to be successful by full-physical prompt and try again. If the child is able to successfully finish the skill without your help, you can reinforce this partial-physically prompted response to encourage future success. Once the child is consistently touching his head with a partial-physical prompt, fade to a less supportive, partial-physical prompt. Instead of moving the child's hands toward his head, you might try giving him a slight push at his elbows. When he has shown that the skill is easy to achieve with a push from the elbows, perhaps just touching his elbows will be enough to cue independent use of this motor imitation skill. Once you have successfully faded all supports the child will have learned his first independent motor imitation.

The VB approach to ABA recommends teaching with most-to-least prompting.

Starting with more supportive prompts and fading to less supportive ones is called most-to-least prompting. The VB approach to ABA recommends teaching with most-to-least prompting. Although it is true that many people learn from their mistakes, the study of VB shows us that mistakes are not a necessary ingredient of learning. During their formal education most teachers are taught to prompt children as little as possible to allow them the greatest opportunity to be independent. Teachers often start with indirect instructional prompts such as, "It starts with the letter c." If the child cannot find the answer, the teacher then moves up to more supportive prompting methods such as a partial-echo prompt "cle." If that doesn't help, the next step is to move to more supportive prompts such as the full-echoic prompt "cleaning." This approach is called least-to-most prompting. With least-to-most prompting, the child often is left to struggle toward the correct answer while being incorrect several times before receiving the help he needs to be successful.

Teaching a child to participate in an activity is only worthwhile if you can also ensure that the child will want to participate in that activity in the future.

There is more involved in learning than independently demonstrating a skill. Special consideration must be made for how the child will feel about the skill, teacher, and learning in general. Teaching a child to participate in an activity is only worthwhile if you can also ensure that the child will want to participate in that activity in the future. Understanding VB is the equivalent to understanding motivation. Which learning process is going to keep your child most motivated to participate? With least-to-most prompting your child might be incorrect four times before being given enough prompting necessary to be correct once. Will your child remain engaged long enough to achieve success? With most-to-least prompting, he would be prompted to success four straight times possibly receiving reinforcement for each prompted response. The prompt would have been systematically faded until he could do it independently. Your child learned the skill just as quickly but also the learning process itself is successful and reinforcing. A person tends to prefer things in his life that meet with success and reinforcement. Gaining important learning and behavior skills is no different. If it is easy and reinforcing, your child will want to be part of it. If it is difficult and unsuccessful, he will look for ways to escape.

To return to the statement at the beginning of this section: although many people learn from their mistakes, people do not need to make mistakes in order to learn. Sometimes it is the accumulation of mistakes or the fear of making mistakes that causes people to avoid a situation rather than learn from it.

For this reason ABA/VB recommends teaching with errorless learning. **Errorless learning** is the process of always adding enough of a prompt to your S^D to keep a child successful, but systematically reducing the amount of prompt used to help the child become more independent over time. Teaching with errorless learning means using a most-to-least prompting procedure and is a more natural approach to teaching novel skills. For example, as an infant you were completely incapable of survival on your own. Your parents or caregivers saw to your basic needs while at the same time teaching you to meet those needs independently. As they fed you, they also taught you to feed yourself. Initially, they likely poured milk into a bottle for you, put on a nipple, turned it upside down, and then held it for you while you drank. Then, as you acquired better motor skills, your parents moved to the next step. They held the bottle with you as you turned it upside down. Then they faded more assistance until you could grasp the bottle on your own. Later you were encouraged to drink the milk from a glass without the nipple. As you became more secure in your skills, your parents began to allow you to pour your own milk and eventually drink it completely independently. To teach you to drink, your parents used errorless learning. If parents typically used least-to-most prompting, there would be a

Sometimes it is the accumulation of mistakes or the fear of making mistakes that causes people to avoid a situation rather than learn from it.

Errorless Learning is the process of always adding enough prompt to your S^D to keep a child successful but systematically reducing the amount of prompt used to help the child become more independent over time.

multitude of thirsty babies and even more spilled milk. Most-to-least prompting is how all people learn. No one is put into a car, given the keys, and told to learn from their mistakes. Imagine stepping up to play baseball for the first time with a 90-mile an hour fastball coming at you. Nobody is asked to pick up a bike and try to ride it for a while before being given help. The process of learning to ride a bike starts with three wheels. Then you move to a two-wheel bicycle with training wheels. After that, the training wheels are taken off but your mom or dad runs up and down the driveway with you before eventually letting go. Finally, you ride the bike independently. The literature is filled with examples of how this natural and sensible prompting method works to the benefit of the learner. But it is ultimately your decision to choose which method of prompting makes the most sense to you.

Prompts are helpers that assist your child in finding the correct answer. But to be effective, you must have a plan for fading the prompts you use. The danger of inadvertent prompting entails the use of prompts of which you are unaware. Do not allow prompts to become barriers to independence. How many times have you said "Stand up" and waved your arms in an upward motion at the same time? How many times have you inadvertently tipped your child off to the correct response by looking directly to the object you asked him to select? How many times have you said "Put it on the table" and pointed in the direction of the table? These prompts are natural and not usually a problem. However, if you are trying to teach your child what the words "Stand up" mean, or what a table is, these inadvertent prompts could prevent your child from true independence in these skills.

Do not allow inadvertent prompts to become barriers to independence.

Prompts support effective and positive instruction. It is important to know how and when to use prompts but it is just as important to know the best way to fade them. Not fading prompts quickly enough can create prompt dependence. Fading them too quickly may lead to incorrect answers and decreased motivation to participate. Becoming a good teacher to your child requires becoming adept at teaching with errorless learning procedures that employ most-to-least prompting and prompt fading.

Summary of Chapter 11:

There are nine different types of prompts in two distinct categories with which you should be familiar. To be your child's best teacher, you need to know how and when to use each (page 162).

Physical Prompts

Full-Physical Prompts

Partial-Physical Prompts

Imitative Prompts

Gesture Prompts

Positional Prompts

Verbal Prompts

Full-Echoic Prompts

Partial-Echoic Prompts

Direct Verbal Prompts

Indirect Verbal Prompts

Prompt Fading is the process of giving a certain amount of initial support and then systematically reducing that support in a way that allows your child to remain successful while becoming increasingly more independent (page 163).

The VB approach to ABA recommends teaching with most-to-least prompting (page 165).

There is more involved in learning than independently demonstrating a skill. Special consideration must be made for how the child will feel about the skill, teacher, and learning in general. Teaching a child to participate in an activity is only worthwhile if you can also ensure that the child will want to participate in that activity in the future (page 165).

Sometimes it is the accumulation of mistakes or the fear of making mistakes that causes people to avoid a situation rather than learn from it (page 166).

Errorless learning is the process of always adding enough of a prompt to your S^D to keep a child successful but systematically reducing the amount of prompt used to help the child become more independent over time. Errorless teaching is a most-to-least prompting procedure and is a more natural approach to teaching novel skills (page 166).

Prompts support effective and positive instruction. It is important to know how and when to use prompts but it is just as important to know the best way to fade them. Not fading prompts quickly enough can create prompt dependence. Fading them too quickly may lead to incorrect answers and decreased motivation to participate. Becoming a good teacher to your child requires becoming adept at the use of most-to-least prompting and prompt fading (page 167).

Chapter 12

Give Your Teaching Life

There have been far too many improvements made to ABA through the implementation of VB than can ever be mentioned here. However, in previous chapters, we have described two major advancements: Establishing Operation (EO) and the Behavioral Classification of Language. Here is a quick review of Skinner's nine behavioral classifications of Language.

1. A mand is a request for items, activities, or information.

2. A motor imitation is any movement your child makes that is an attempt to copy or mimic an action he sees.

3. A verbal imitation is the ability to repeat exactly what you hear.

4. Receptive language is the ability to follow instructions or to comply with requests.

5. A tact is verbally identifying objects, actions, and events in the environment.

6. An RFFC is the ability to receptively identify specific items when given some description of its function, feature, or class.

7. Intraverbals are responses where the words used are controlled by the different words of others.

8. Textual language involves the reading of written words.

9. Writing is handwriting or typing words and letters that are spoken to you.

Another improvement, the recognition of the importance of three different types of teaching, is just as revolutionary. If you have any experience with older forms of ABA that do not include the advancements of VB, you likely have a picture in your mind of a therapist and a child sitting at opposite sides of a table in a special room used only for teaching. You likely imagine the therapist with his legs wrapped around the child's chair legs to keep him bound in while repeatedly delivering the same instructions. The walls would most probably be bare to limit the amount of distraction in the room and this teaching would likely include the use of only one or two strong edible reinforcers. Fortunately, the practice of ABA has moved beyond that limited view of teaching through the addition of VB techniques. It is now understood that you need to expand rather than limit a child's experiences. The last thing you want to do with a child who might have flexibility and control issues is to hold him to a rigid teaching routine.

Teaching should be far more than a room in which the child learns or a table at which he works and a set of materials that he uses.

Teaching should be far more than a room in which the child learns or a table at which he works and a set of materials that he uses. For children with autism, this kind of structured teaching setting becomes a velvet coffin. Velvet in that, children may learn to perform many skills on command, but still a coffin in that for many children it will kill any real chance at recovery. Children with autism tend to feel safe with routines. Many prefer to know what is coming next and given the choice they like to order everything that they do. Most aspects of the TEACCH program such as the use of left-to-right learning stations and visual schedules use the child's desire for order and consistency to manage a child's behavior. However, progress is often only made within this rigid setting when the child is in his learning room, at his learning table, sitting with his learning therapist, and wearing his learning socks. Thus, the child becomes attached to the specifics of learning rather than to the skills you want him to master or the desire to learn in general. What happens if the learning therapist becomes ill or quits? Even worse, what happens if the child loses one of his learning socks? I know that this might sound like I am joking, but I have met a family who actually allowed their child to have a pair of learning socks which he always wore in the teaching room. Imagine the problems that can arise when you allow your child to believe that there is only one certain way he is expected to learn.

In addition to supporting the families of children recently diagnosed with autism, I am often asked to assist families and organizations throughout the world who want to convert ongoing ABA and TEACCH programs into ABA/VB programs. In this capacity, I normally meet children that possess many more skills than those who have not experienced an intensive teaching environment. However, the problems caused by the management techniques of many TEACCH programs, and the procedural recommendations of traditional ABA approaches are often glaring. Children in programs that do not incorporate the latest research in VB tend to have relatively strong receptive language and motor imitation repertoires but demonstrate only a limited supply of mands, tacts, and intraverbals. These children often engage in avoidance or escape behavior as a result of the constant use of discrete trial teaching without the benefit of pairing procedures. A strong reliance on escape extinction leaves many of the children who do sit and participate only a minimal desire to achieve. The overuse of negative reinforcement procedures causes children to gain skills but perform them solely out of a desire to be left alone. Parent participation is often minimal or non-existent. Many children work without a playful connection to their therapists as therapists often use inter-trial breaks and reinforcement time to write data notations instead of building a relationship with the child or gaining child interest. Eye contact and other important social skills become prompt dependent. Often these children use rote or rehearsed language or social behavior. Generalization of everyday skills is often delayed or unlikely because teaching is relegated to a specific setting or station. Consequently, there is often a major disparity between what these children can do at the teaching station and what they will do outside the teaching setting. Many cannot handle slight changes in their daily routines or can work only under the instruction of a few specific people. These children may have the ability to answer many questions but offer few in return. Generally, many children in TEACCH and traditional ABA programs are not having as much fun as they will need to have to genuinely desire the learning process. Teaching skills to a child with autism is not good enough if the methods being used also isolate the child or the skills do not generalize to independent use. Changing to an ABA program based on the VB approach is apt to correct most if not all of these common problems.

The following quote is from the mother of a child who recently changed from a traditional ABA program to a program featuring Verbal Behavior.

I have a boy with autism who will be four next month. After a Vince Carbone workshop here in Phoenix, I got all fired up about ABA/VB and hired a BCBA to help get a home program going. We have three fantastic ABA tutors who my son was beginning to dislike because they took him upstairs, away from his two favorite things (TV and computer) to sit at a table and do Lovaas-style ABA. We had been doing traditional ABA since Johnny's diagnosis almost two years ago and it has helped, but he was starting to really resist our attempts to teach him and was having meltdowns of protest when his therapists arrived.

We have only had two six-hour consultations with our BCBA so far and things have really changed. She identified three top motivators to become Johnny's first mands. These mands were for "Movie" (his baby Einstein DVD's), "Computer" (playhousedisney.com) and "milk" (his bottle of hazelnut milk). She taught him two of these signs in one day and three days later, we had him signing correctly for all three! On her second visit, four weeks later, we added "bubbles," "open," and "chip" and he got those almost immediately.

He had previous experience with PECS in his autism-only preschool, but had no experience with signing. Now, he is fiddling with his hands all the time, trying to make them ask for things. It's great! He is drunk with power, being able to ask for things and get them whenever he wants. And he loves to see his therapists arrive every day now. He's been liberated from his therapy room and everything about our household has been changed. It has been hardest on me, because he used to be tucked up in his therapy room for the majority of the day with the therapists. Now, he is all over the place and his little sister and I have no peace anymore. I can't get anything done, but the results speak for themselves. (Kim Bowman)

Life is change; nothing living remains stagnant. A child who does well only when sitting in a specific chair will not make an adequate adjustment when he begins learning in school. In fact, you are creating a situation fraught with new problems and, worse, you are setting your child up for failure. The last thing you want to do is try to convince your child's teacher that your child could learn more if you were allowed to bring your kitchen table into the classroom. You need to build flexibility into everything that you do with your child. From the beginning refuse to let your child slip into routines that are difficult or time consuming for you to continue or change. Take a lesson from the half-hour bedtime ritual discussed in Chapter 3. The need for this type of routine develops from a desire to control and not a need for the routine itself. These routines may begin as sensory or flexibility preferences but it is your willingness to placate them that creates opportunities for your child to wield control over his environment and everyone in it. You need to be carefully reinforcing your child's appropriate attempts at earning control in his environment and limiting his access to it through this type of controlling ritual. By doing so, you will find that these rituals and routines never take hold to begin with. Then your child will begin to learn strategies to overcome his sensory concerns instead of using these issues as a tool to gain control.

Chapter 1 shared the story of a little boy named Aaron that our school district special education team was not successful at including in a general education classroom. Aaron was a strong control child. Without the ABA/VB procedures that are now available, the district had no real system in place to help him succeed. The prevailing belief at the time was that Aaron, and others like him, had sensory issues that made them unable to respond normally in certain situations. Reportedly, Aaron had many of these sensory "needs" that our special education staff was expected to appease. We were encouraged by well-meaning professionals to give Aaron a rubber padded seat so that he could feel his body better in his chair. We were given large rubber therapy bands to put around the legs of his chair so that he would have something to push his legs against when he was in need of sensory input. We were asked to allow Aaron to chew gum in class because he seemed calmer when allowed to do so at home. We were asked to make a safe comfortable place under a table to which he could retire when his senses were overloaded. We were asked to allow him to

A child who only does well while sitting in a specific chair will not make an adequate adjustment when he begins learning in school.

use a pen instead of a pencil because he did not like the way that the pencil sounded on the paper. All of these allowances were called modifications or accommodations for Aaron's sensory needs. Although there are often times when making modifications and accommodations for children with disabilities is appropriate, in Aaron's case we were seldom doing anything except submitting to his control. The more we were willing to make allowances for Aaron's behavior the more controlling his behavior became. The more we modified our expectations to meet his sensory "needs" the more his needs multiplied. Eventually we even asked permission of Aaron's teacher to allow him to write a fictional name he had adopted on all of his desk and homework. Allowing Aaron to convince us that he needed constant modification and accommodation, kept Aaron in control. It kept him from learning better behavior skills and eventually the school district felt it had no choice but to remove him from school.

Instead of reinforcing a child's desire to control, create a consistent motivation and reinforce the child's attempts to relate in a more acceptable way.

We fail children when we accept their difficulties as unchangeable rather than working to help them overcome these difficulties. Instead of reinforcing a child's desire to control, create a consistent motivation and reinforce the child's attempts to relate to the environment in a more acceptable way. If you keep in mind that your child might be overly susceptible to falling into rigid routines, you can plan to keep that from happening to begin with. This type of forethought is always much easier than trying to break these rituals once you have allowed them to take root. To avoid rituals from forming, it is important consistently to teach your child in different ways. Use many different instructions as S^Ds. Teach on the floor. Take a different route home from school. Some days put on his socks and then shoes and on some days put on one sock and one shoe before putting on the other sock and shoe. Notice when you are being pushed into repetition by your child. Don't let your child's desire to control your interaction become a strengthened ritual. Stop rituals from forming and be careful not to allow sensory preferences become sensory demands. If your child already has many of these ritualistic behavioral insistences, you will need to refer to Chapters 5 and 6 and use the Seven Steps to Instructional Control to help him reduce or eliminate these rituals in safe and effective ways.

Stop ritualistic behavior from forming and be careful not to allow sensory preferences become sensory demands.

There are important reasons to teach in different settings that have nothing to do with your child becoming mired in ritualistic patterns. Adhering to

VB principles, teaching is categorized into three specific and important types. Depending on where your child is in the learning process, he will likely need one type of teaching in greater measure than the others. However, as his skills and teaching goals change, so will the percentage of time he will need to spend engaged with these different types of teaching.

The three types of teaching in which you must become well versed are Natural Environment Teaching (NET or teaching in the NET), Intensive Trial Teaching (ITT), and Incidental or "On-the-Move" Teaching (OTM). These three teaching types use the same basic discrete trial teaching format as discussed in Chapter 8. The biggest misconception about these three different types of teaching is that the difference between them has to do with the location in which they occur. It is not the location that makes one style of teaching intensive and another natural but rather it is the type of target you are teaching and its relationship to the child that differentiates them.

What makes a teaching session ITT has nothing to do with the fact that you might be sitting at a table. Instead, ITT involves the chosen target behavior to which you are teaching. In ITT settings, you are teaching to targets that are artificially introduced into your child's environment. Good examples of this include, but are not limited to, teaching with picture cards, paper cutting practice, or requiring your child to touch his head. These items are considered ITT because they are target goals that you have set for your child and introduced even though he has no internal desire or interest in performing them. ITT is an extremely important type of teaching for your child to learn to accept because most school curriculum is taught without having first earned the child's motivation. However, it is not the only method as some traditional ABA providers might lead you to believe.

NET (natural environment teaching) can be done anywhere including the kitchen, the bathroom, the playroom, the car, or even at the table. What makes a teaching session NET is that the targets you are working on are skills your child is naturally interested in performing. For example, singing a song or asking for a cookie would be considered NET even if the teaching occurs while your child is wearing his learning socks. Another way to look at the difference between these two types of teaching is that NET uses the child's naturally occurring EO (motivation) and ITT involves teaching your child skills without concern for his interests by using some form of artificial EO. Because ITT (intensive trial teaching) means that your child does not have a naturally

The three types of teaching in which you must become well versed are NET, ITT, and OTM.

occurring motivation, it becomes imperative that your child's participation in the skill be contrived and maintained through the effective use of prompts and other EOs.

OTM (on-the-move) teaching is done at the spur of the moment whenever and wherever you happen to be. Also called incidental, this kind of teaching can occur on your way to the store, in your car, or even sitting at your dinner table. Anytime your child shows an interest in something you can take that opportunity to teach. If the teaching involves targets that were not planned by you in advance and they happen, based on your child's natural motivation, you are using OTM. For example, when your child stops to look at a butterfly and you say "That is called a butterfly...can you say butterfly?" this is called OTM teaching. NET and OTM teaching are similar as both are based on using items the child is naturally interested in learning. The main difference is that in NET, although you are teaching naturally motivating targets, these targets have been planned in advance. When teaching in the NET, you may need to design many of your teaching opportunities. For example, if you know you want to teach the word cookie, you might choose to place a bag of cookies on the shelf just out of your child's reach. Then in the natural environment when your child reaches for the cookies, it gives you a chance to teach him a better way to ask. In OTM teaching, you are taking an unplanned teaching moment based on the introduction of an unplanned teaching target. Whenever you happen to be with your child and he demonstrates a motivation for something you did not plan for, you can still use that motivation to teach. It is just considered OTM teaching.

The following example will illustrate the difference in the three types of teaching. While you are taking a walk with your child through the woods, you might engage in any or all three types of teaching along the way. You could use ITT to quiz your child on the names of different types of trees and flowers. You might tell him to receptively identify objects around you. You might ask him to do gross motor movements on the different objects that you see. If you have planned these target goals and they are not something in which your child is naturally interested, this teaching would be considered ITT. At the same time, if you know your child loves insects and you want to teach him the names of insects, this would be considered teaching in the NET. You might point out different insects along the way and when your child runs over to look, you could ask him to identify what he sees. If you are teaching prepositions, you can use this EO for insects to ask whether the insect is in the branch, over the branch, or on the branch. In this natural environment teaching (NET) format, you might even prompt your child to ask you to identify the type of insect he is looking at. This would be considered a manding skill. Manding (requesting) is always best taught in the natural environment or on-the-move. If a child is not naturally motivated to have an item, you cannot teach him to ask for it.

Incidental teaching (OTM) could also be done during this walk. Perhaps while you were teaching about insects and having your child perform motor movements along the way, you see that a tree has fallen over the path. You may not have planned to teach about lightning or life and death, but because of your child's interest in this fallen tree, you might take the opportunity to address these unplanned targets. If your early learner is motivated to play with leaves from this tree, you could use this opportunity to teach him a new mand using the sign language gesture for "leaf." This would be considered OTM teaching. As you can see the type of teaching you are engaged in relies solely on whether the targets were planned or not and whether there is a naturally occurring EO (motivation).

Manding is always best taught in NET or on-the-move. If a child is not naturally motivated to have an item, you cannot teach him to ask for it.

The true benefit of knowing that there is more than one type of teaching is that you no longer need to feel tied to the rote table teaching of traditional ABA. Now, in addition to using EO to make intensive trial teaching more palatable, you may also teach in the natural environment and on-the-move to give your teaching life.

Although ITT is the teaching of traditional ABA, it is actually NET and OTM teaching that is the easiest to engage your child in. Because, NET and OTM are based on your child's interests and motivations, most of your work is already done for you. Once you have his motivation it is easy to apply DTT (discrete trial teaching) procedures to a positive result. However, in ITT there is no naturally occurring motivation. This causes teaching in ITT to be more difficult to maintain. It is in intensive trial teaching (ITT) situations where your understanding and use of the Establishing Operation (EO) becomes most important.

Teaching in all three settings supports the idea that your child, like the rest of us, is constantly learning and capable of gaining skills from myriad settings and through a variety of different means. Thus, your child will understand that learning is not relegated to a specific place or time. Instead, he will begin to accept following directions and giving full effort regardless of where he is or what he is doing. This variety also eliminates your child's tendency to avoid teaching situations. Once teaching becomes part of his normal daily interactions and not just something that occurs in the teaching room for a few hours a day, your child will accept teaching as part of his life. To win your tug-o-war with autism's never-resting grip, teaching must be a part of every interaction you have with your child. Because teaching can take place anywhere and at any time, you are helping your child to not only learn skills, but to understand the larger world by creating experiences for him to develop more natural and varied interests.

Motivation is everything for a child with autism and knowing how to teach in the NET and OTM means knowing how to find, capture, and teach to your child's naturally occurring motivation. These two teaching types, along with a more flexible view of ITT, give the necessary techniques for you to help your child develop into a life-long learner.

You may need help in understanding and using these teaching types in the most effective way. Although manding is usually best taught in NET, vocal imitation is almost always taught in ITT. Having this kind of information available to you through the consultation of a qualified and experienced service provider is invaluable. ABA/VB has the potential to be more than you might have imagined. It should not be stale, rote, memorization followed by reinforcement. It should be fluid and ever-changing. It should include your child's natural motivation. Occasionally learning targets should come as a surprise to both the learner and teacher. There is no such thing as a learning opportunity. There are only learning experiences. If your child is not learning something positive with every interaction in which he is engaged, he is likely learning something you would rather he not learn. You need to be well versed in the three types of teaching - NET, ITT, and OTM - so you can take better advantage of the learning interactions you are having with your child at all points of his day.

Motivation is everything for a child with autism and knowing how to teach in the NET and OTM means knowing how to find, capture, and teach to your child's naturally occurring motivation.

Summary of Chapter 12:

We fail children when we accept their difficulties as unchangeable rather than working to help them overcome these difficulties. Instead of reinforcing a child's desire to control, create a consistent motivation and reinforce the child's attempts to relate to the environment in a more acceptable way (page 176).

Don't let your child's desire to control your interaction become a strengthened ritual. Stop rituals from forming and be careful not to allow sensory preferences become sensory demands (page 176).

The three types of teaching in which you must become well versed are Natural Environment Teaching (NET or teaching in the NET), Intensive Trial Teaching (ITT), and Incidental or "On-the-Move" Teaching (OTM) (page 177).

Because ITT (intensive trial teaching) means that your child does not have a naturally occurring motivation, it becomes imperative that your child's participation in the skill be contrived and maintained through the effective use of prompts and other EOs (page 177).

Manding (requesting) is always best taught in the natural environment or on the move. If a child is not naturally motivated to have an item, you cannot teach him to ask for it (page 179).

The true benefit of knowing that there is more than one type of teaching is that you no longer need to feel tied to the rote table teaching of traditional ABA. Now, in addition to using EO to make intensive trial teaching more palatable, you may also teach in the natural environment and on-the-move to give your teaching life (page 179).

Motivation is everything for a child with autism and knowing how to teach in the NET and OTM means knowing how to find, capture, and teach to your child's naturally occurring motivation. These two teaching types, along with a more flexible view of ITT, give the necessary techniques for you to help your child develop into a life-long learner (page 180).

Chapter 13

Teach Your Child Functional

Speech with Verbal Behavior

Many of the children with autism that I meet make very few sounds. Others make babbling noises most of the day. Some can say the first sounds of words and others can use one-word sentences. Still others are able to speak in full sentences but often not in a fully functional way. The Verbal Behavior approach to ABA has brought us many amazing techniques and strategies to help children gain all kinds of skills. However, the philosophy behind teaching children to speak is where this approach to education excels.

All parents look forward to the day when they can have a conversation with their child. However, for parents of children with autism, complex and meaningful conversation with their child may seem an impossible dream. Yet, considering all that is involved in the process of conversing, it is a wonder any of us have mastered the skill.

To have a conversation with someone, you need the ability to produce a variety of complex sounds. You need to be able to order your thoughts, gauge what you want to say, and balance what you want to impart with what your partner might be most interested in hearing. Then, you need to compile those thoughts in a package of specifically ordered words. You need to know how to ask questions as well as answer them. You need to be able to name items, describe them, recall past experiences, and consider future events. You may also manipulate your body language and vocal tone in a way that helps you to convey your meaning effectively. All of this needs to be accomplished in milliseconds and only partly describes the expressive half of the battle. At the same time, you need to be able to understand the meaning of words and their order, read body language, facial expressions, and voice inflections. You must also understand the decision-making factors involved in taking turns while assessing the effect your words have on your partner. Teaching children to engage in such a complicated flow of exchanged thoughts and ideas seems impossible under the most ideal circumstances. And, yet, most of us have mastered the basics of this complicated interaction by age five.

Breaking down complex concepts into manageable chunks and teaching these chunks in developmentally appropriate order is the basic teaching philosophy of ABA/VB.

However, if we can pinpoint and teach to all of the individual skills needed to communicate in an orderly fashion, we will always make some sort of progress toward our ultimate goal of complex conversation. For some children we have to break each of these individual skills down into even smaller pieces before the concepts are clear and simple enough for them to learn. Breaking down complex concepts into manageable chunks and teaching these chunks in a developmentally appropriate order educates toward recovery. It is also the basic teaching philosophy of ABA/VB.

The ability to communicate is learned and it is based on the reinforcing activities of others. Our first language is the cry. Infants learn quickly that their cries will result in some form of response. Depending on volume and/or voracity, these cries might be used as cues by the parents to pick up the baby and rock or bounce him in their arms. When certain types of cries gain desired results, these types of cries increase at times when the baby wants that result again. It is not a fluke that most mothers can begin to differentiate between cries of hunger, exhaustion, diaper change, and pain. When the baby makes noises that are not cries, mom and dad get excited, repeat those noises, and make funny faces. This non-cry noise making by baby, leading to attention and other forms of reinforcement from mom and dad, increases baby's continued noise making. Eventually these sounds are shaped into usable forms. For example, mom uses the word "bottle" when giving baby his bottle. Eventually, baby begins to use the word "ba," which is the sound he is capable of making closest to the word "bottle. "ba" becomes "ba-ba" which becomes "bottle," which becomes "I want a bottle." Baby has learned that if he continues to make a specific sound, he will be able to obtain a specific object. Baby also learns that by repeating certain sounds such as "mama" and "papa," he gains the attention of his parents.

For whatever reason, many children with autism stop responding in the same way to this daily social interaction. This does not mean that his parents have failed to communicate appropriately with their child. It most certainly does not mean that the parents have ignored their child. Most of the parents of children with autism are loving and attentive. In fact, as a group these parents are remarkably committed to their children's advancement. However, because their child is predisposed to the behavior deficits of autism, these parents must learn something no other parent is expected to know--how to directly teach communication. Because most of us, including children with other disabilities, learn to speak without any direct teaching, there has been little research done over the past several hundred years based on how to best teach speaking. What work that has been done has focused on articulation of words and not communicative intent. Consequently, parents of children with autism are confused and frustrated by their failure to teach this seemingly simple basic skill to their offspring. However, in just the past twenty to thirty years or so, there has been much done in this area especially related to the science of VB.

When given appropriate language intervention through VB at an early age, many children with autism can be taught effective communication without losing ground on their peers. When this special need is not discovered until much later in the child's life, the same teaching is necessary to teach the same skills but now must be accomplished after several years of language deficit has occurred. In recent years, the push for early diagnosis in the United States has made great strides. This work of early identification and intervention must continue throughout the world because it is one of the best weapons available to avoid unnecessary communication delays in our children. However, regardless of current deficit, children who do not learn to speak naturally can be taught to vocally communicate through appropriate behavior analysis and the application of VB. This teaching often needs to be systematic and intensive. It involves the use of motivation (EO) and reinforcement (S^R) and it needs the help of a friend. That friend is called augmentative communication. Sign language is the form of augmentative communication most often used in the Verbal Behavior approach to autism intervention.

When given appropriate language intervention at an early age, many children with autism can be taught effective communication without losing ground on their peers.

The most basic level of language involves understanding the concept of "if I do something, I get something; if I do something else, I get something else." This is at the root of all communication and it is the first concept that our team at Knospe-ABA needs to teach many of the children we help. Remember all forms of communication have a function. If you recall Skinner's behavioral classification of language, you will see that "doing something in order to get something" would be considered a mand. A mand is the ability to request items, activities and information that you want. "If I do something, I get something" falls into this category. For instance, if I say, please get me some water, I will probably receive water. If I point to a piece of gum on the table and say gum, I will most likely be given some gum to chew. This is a very basic concept of which many children with autism may not have developed an understanding on their own. Not only is it important to break conversation down into its categories to teach manding, but it is also important to separate manding into levels and teach them one at a time.

There are several versions of the levels of manding that you can work from. Here is the one that I have developed for Knospe-ABA:

Manding Levels

1. **Crying to get a wanted item.**
2. **Crying near a wanted item.**
3. **Taking someone's hand to the wanted item.**
4. **Pointing to the wanted item.**
5. **Using augmentative communication (sign language) to get a wanted item.**
6. **Asking for the wanted item with a partial word or sound.**
7. **Asking for the wanted items with a full word.**
8. **Asking for the wanted item using a carrier phrase.**
9. **Asking for the wanted item using describing words.**
10. **Having a discussion about the wanted item as a way to convince someone to give it to you.**

Regardless of how old your child is or how advanced his language has naturally become, he will be somewhere on this manding hierarchy. Many children only have the ability to cry or tantrum when they want something. Others have managed to get over the part of their learning barrier that allows them to point to or pull their parents to an object that they want. Regardless of where your child may be on this list of manding levels, there are now proven behavioral strategies that you can learn to move him forward.

The very first step in teaching children to speak is to start by getting this simple idea of "If I do something, I get something; if I do something else, I get something else" across to them. If your child is capable of echoing your speech, you can easily give him words to echo and then reinforce his use of these different words with different items that he wants. This will begin to give him the concept of <u>doing</u> becomes <u>getting</u>. However, if your child is unable to echo words, you need a preliminary step to use as a bridge to spoken language. This bridge comes in the form of an augmentative communication system. In most cases when working with a non-vocal child, sign language is the best bridge to use.

Sign Language is an augmentative communication system based on the exchange of mutually understood body movements.

Sign language is an augmentative communication system based on the exchange of mutually understood body movements. It is impossible to use full-physical prompts to force a person to speak. Thus, it is impossible to reinforce talking in a non-vocal child. Since only behavior that is reinforced increases, this is where society's ability to teach spoken language to non-vocal children with autism traditionally stalled. Through Verbal Behavior, it is possible to mix motivation and reinforcement in ways that solve this problem. When a child is not naturally vocal, you need to create a stronger EO (motivation) for communication. The only way to create an EO for communication is to reinforce communication. The reason sign language is a good bridge to spoken language is that it gives you a form of communication that is easily prompted and, therefore, easily reinforced.

Sign language is the best way to teach the power of communication to a nonvocal child.

Because you can physically prompt and reinforce the use of sign language, when a person does not have the ability to echo words, then sign language is the best way to teach him the power of communication. Begin by manipulating the environment so that there are items that your child is likely to want and for which he will mand (request). Keep these objects just out of his reach. Wait until the motivation for one of the items grows to the point that he tries to reach for it. At that point, intercept his reach and demonstrate a simple modified sign of your choosing for him to imitate. Then, redirect his reach by physically prompting him to make the same sign himself. Immediately, reinforce the completion of this sign by giving the child the item he wanted. If he then reaches for a different item, give a model prompt and then redirect him to make a different sign. Once completed, reinforce the making of that sign by giving the item he desired. Given enough repetitions, this procedure is effective with every child with whom I have worked. But, because the use of sign language is only meant as a bridge to spoken language, be sure to pair this teaching process with the spoken word for the item at least three times with every trial. Say the word you want your child to eventually learn one time when you give the child a model prompt, once again when you physically prompt him to make the sign, and a third time when you reinforce with the item. Once your child becomes familiar with the procedure, his desire to obtain the item will motivate him to help you speed the sign making process along. The first step toward independent signing is to offer you his hands so that you can prompt him to make the sign faster. Eventually you will begin to feel him helping you make the movement when you physically prompt him. When this occurs, it is time to begin using partial-physical prompts so the child can do more of the sign alone. Remember with partial-physical prompts, you will begin to help him make the sign but will allow him to complete the skill alone.

Some children begin independently imitating the model prompt without physical help after only a few trials. Others may take months to get to this point. Regardless of how long it takes a child to begin imitating your sign independently, you need to begin the process of teaching him to use his signs spontaneously. Spontaneous language is often delayed in children with autism. The path from prompted mand to spontaneous mand can be slow. One way to accelerate this process is to avoid asking "What do you want?" before prompting the sign. "What do you want?" is actually an indirect verbal prompt that your child will come to depend on. This dependence can significantly delay the transition to spontaneous signing. Instead, wait until your child demonstrates a desire either with his reach, eyes, or sounds. Then begin your sign language teaching process repeating only the word for the mand three times.

Example: The beginning language teaching procedure for a non-vocal child learning to use a sign language mand for "cookie."

Child: Reaches for a cookie

Mom: Intercepts child's reach and gives model prompt for the cookie sign while saying the word "cookie" clearly.

Mom: Uses a full-physical prompt to help the child make the cookie sign while once again saying "cookie" clearly.

Mom: Then reinforces the child with the cookie while saying "cookie" a third time.

As a rule, only ask "What do you want?" when you do not know what the child is asking for at the time. If you are aware of the child's desire, begin your mand teaching by saying just the name of the item you want the child to learn.

When you are ready to move your child from prompted mands to spontaneous ones, you must begin to wait longer *before* giving the sign for your child to imitate. The increased waiting time will give your child an increased EO (motivation) to find a way to gain access to the item sooner. This increased EO will likely cause him to begin skipping straight to the part of the process where he makes the sign himself. When this happens, it is a very important teaching moment that you should reinforce strongly.

The first rule when teaching sign languge manding is to teach to your child's motivation.

There are many ways to make the process of teaching signs easy for your child, as there are also many ways of making it difficult for him. Do not try this technique at home without first doing more research or obtaining the guidance of a qualified behavior analyst. The first rule when teaching sign manding is to teach to your child's motivation. Teach signs for favorite food and drink items as well as toys or activities that he loves such as trampoline, swings, or video. Always teach very specific terms such as juice, milk, and water instead of general terms such as drink or thirsty. Avoid teaching a child to make signs for specific people and stay away from requests such as more, I want, yes, no, and please, until your child's manding repertoire is large. Requests such as more and thirsty have non-specific or flexible meanings that will counteract your attempts to simplify the process of communication. It does your child absolutely no good to walk around the house making the sign for "more, more, more" when you have no idea of what he wants more of. Additionally, if your child learns yes and no as his first signs, you will spend your entire day holding up item after item for him to affirm or refuse and he will have no EO (motivation) to learn to ask for those items independently. Another sign you should avoid teaching in the beginning is toilet. Teaching a child to use this sign will be extremely difficult unless your child is highly motivated to use the toilet <u>and</u> you are willing to wait for him to make the sign before you allow him access to go.

Always teach more than one sign at a time, particularly in the beginning. If not, you run the risk of the first sign you teach becoming the universal sign for "I want." At Knospe-ABA we usually try to teach approximately five different signs at a time. However, depending on the child we may start with as few as three or as many as ten or more. Finally, protect against scrolling. **Scrolling** is the process of running through all of one's known signs in an attempt to more quickly get to the reinforcement. This is a common problem, but one that is easily remedied. Be consistent about stopping your child when he begins to scroll and prompt him to repeat the manding process from the beginning. The added time it takes to gain reinforcement after scrolling will give your child the motivation necessary to focus more intently on making the correct sign the first time. Reinforcement should only follow a correct sign when it comes without scrolling.

Reinforcement should only follow a correct sign when it comes without scrolling.

While teaching your child to communicate with sign language, it is important to remember that his signs are only meant to act as a bridge to spoken language. Do not let your desire to teach sign language cause you to accidentally extinguish your child's natural attempts at using sounds. Once the concept of manding becomes clear to a child, he may naturally begin making sounds along with or in place of his signs. Regardless of the correctness of the sign used by your child, it is important that you reinforce these vocal attempts immediately and intensely when they occur. This will give your child every reason to attempt to use vocal sounds with his signs in the future. However, unless your child makes immediate progress using differing sounds for each of his mands, the need for further instruction using sign language will remain.

For children who do not naturally begin to try to echo our vocal prompts, verbal imitation becomes a separate area of important instruction. At the same time you are teaching your child to mand for items with sign language, you need to begin working on verbal imitation. Teaching your child to imitate verbal sounds is often difficult in the beginning. For many children, however, once they understand what you are looking for, their ability to imitate sounds can rapidly increase. The procedure for teaching a child to imitate verbally includes engaging your child in a very exciting and reinforcing activity. Then, when your child is at his most motivated to continue, stop the interaction and make a sound for him to imitate. In the beginning you want to reinforce any vocal attempt your child makes. You do this by quickly starting the fun activity again. Eventually after making this sound and reinforcing any sound in return, you can begin to hold out for increasingly better approximations of the sound for which you are asking. As your child shows the ability to match your sound, begin to change the sound you use as an S^D (instruction). Then begin to reinforce only when your child makes the right sound for the right S^D. Exactly what sounds you should begin teaching your child is still up for debate. A good speech pathologist in your area should be able to tell you which sounds are developmentally easier than others. The goal of all teaching in ABA/VB is for your child to be successful most of the time. If it appears that verbal imitation will be an extremely difficult skill for a child, try to begin with a sound that you know he makes frequently. Your first goal will only be to get him to make that preferred sound on request.

In the beginning of teaching verbal imitation, you want to reinforce any vocal attempt your child makes.

The way that you request a verbal imitation may differ depending on the child. In some cases it is best to use only the word or sound you want the child to imitate as your S^D. For example, you could look the child directly in the face and clearly say "ball" for him to imitate. For other children it may make more sense to use the word "say" in your request such as, "Say ball." The problem with using the word "say" is that many children get stuck trying to echo the word "say" as well as the actual sound you want imitated. Conversely, the problem that can arise when you do not use the word "say" in your S^D is that some children will begin imitating everything that you say to them. This can become an issue when you begin teaching skills such as receptive language and the child is not listening to the direction you are giving but rather trying to echo what you say. It is not uncommon to ask a child who is learning to verbally imitate "What is this?" and have him answer "What is this."

At Knospe-ABA we prefer to teach children to echo words without using the word "say" in the S^D. However, there are two additional considerations that we make to keep this approach as effective as possible. First, we develop a clear and simple way to differentiate our verbal imitation S^Ds from our other S^Ds. Making eye contact, when possible, and using a slightly exaggerated pronunciation and rhythm can become a signal to the child that you are looking for an imitative response rather than another type of response. Additionally, you can refuse to allow non-verbal imitation responses to be reinforced when your child also echoes the S^D. We have found that it is sometimes better to teach an understanding of the word "say" as a signal that an echo response is desired when children are older, have better receptive language repertoires, or are over-echoic. This may be a difficult and time-consuming differentiation to teach, but when successful it can drastically increase the rate at which the child learns both verbal imitation and other responses.

Although verbal imitation and manding should be included in your teaching, they should not be taught at the same time. When teaching a verbal imitation you can teach with any combination of sounds you choose. However, when teaching a child to mand for a specific item, you should only use the word for the item that you want your child to learn to mand. In other words, teach manding in the natural environment (NET) only when your child wants to gain access to something and teach verbal imitation with intensive trial teaching (ITT), using other motivation to evoke responses.

After a child is able to demonstrate enough different sounds and can use sign language spontaneously and consistently to ask for 15 or more different items or activities, you can begin the process of moving him to vocal manding with partial words or sounds (manding level six). Teaching a child to mand spontaneously involves waiting longer before prompting your child. Conversely, teaching a child to begin using sounds as mands is accomplished by waiting longer before you deliver reinforcement. Once your child begins expecting reinforcement to follow his spontaneous sign language requests, you can begin to wait after the sign is made for some form of vocal mand. This is best done by holding the reinforcer in view of your child and saying the name of the item for the child to echo. Because you have been working on verbal imitation separately, your child should begin to realize what you are trying to accomplish and may try to make the sound. As is the case with teaching verbal imitation, you start by reinforcing *any* sound your child makes and eventually begin to shape the quality and complexity of that sound over time. The sounds will improve as you continue carefully to withhold the reinforcer until your child pronounces better approximations of the target word.

Although verbal imitation and manding should be included in your teaching, they should not be taught at the same time.

Once your child is able to approximate or say a single word to ask for his favorite things, the need to use sign language is lost and your child will naturally stop using the signs. However, these signs often act as helpers for the child when he has a difficult time remembering a word. Once a child can ask for things with words (manding) and imitate sounds (verbal imitation), this newly gained ability can be used to teach many other parts of language such as tacts (labels), intraverbals (answers to questions), and FFC's (language regarding feature, function, or class). Teaching from the echo is usually done with the transfer procedure discussed in Chapter 14.

The strength of ABA/VB is that it designs or captures a child's naturally occurring motivation to have and do things and then uses this incentive to teach increasingly more complex ways to request items or activities.

Example: Teaching sign language as a bridge to spoken language for the mand "cookie."

Step 1

Child: Reaches for a cookie

Mom: Intercepts child's reach and gives model prompt for the cookie sign while saying the word "cookie" clearly.

Mom: Uses a *full-physical* prompt to help the child make the cookie sign while once again saying "cookie" clearly.

Mom: Then reinforces the child with the cookie while saying "cookie" a third time.

When you feel the child helping you physically prompt him, move to Step 2.

Step 2

Child: Reaches for a cookie.

Mom: Intercepts child's reach and gives model prompt for the cookie sign while saying the word "cookie" clearly.

Mom: Uses a *Partial-physical* prompt to help the child make the cookie sign while once again saying "cookie" clearly.

Mom: Then reinforces the child with the cookie while saying "cookie" a third time.

When you feel that your child is ready to make the sign without physical assistance move to Step 3.

Step 3

Child: Reaches for a cookie.

Mom: Intercepts child's reach and gives model prompt for the cookie sign while saying the word "cookie" clearly.

Mom: Waits for child to make cookie sign *without* prompt (prompting only when absolutely necessary).

Child: Makes sign for "cookie" independently.

Mom: Says cookie when the child completes sign alone.

Mom: Then reinforces the child with the cookie while saying "cookie" a third time.

When the child is consistent about making the sign independently after a model prompt, it is time to begin working on spontaneous manding with the sign in Step 4.

Step 4

Child: Reaches for a cookie.

Mom: Intercepts child's reach and asks "cookie?" or says "Oh, you want a cookie"; then waits expectantly for the child to make the sign spontaneously.

Child: Option 1 - If child does not make sign after a reasonable wait, mom should finish this trial the same as Step 3.

Option 2 – If the child makes sign for cookie spontaneously, mom will say something like, "Cookie! Of course you can have a cookie!"

Mom: Then reinforces the child with cookie while saying "Here is your cookie" and celebrating with further praise such as "Good job asking me for a cookie"

When the child is consistently asking for cookie spontaneously, you need to begin to teach him to ask for cookies when they are not currently present in the environment. This can be done by removing the cookies between trials either behind your back, under the table, or in a box or cabinet. Then wait for (and if necessary prompt) the sign. When the sign is made, bring the cookies out of their hiding place and reinforce.

Once the child is spontaneously asking for cookie regardless of if cookies are present, you can then begin working on vocal manding. Please remember that in addition to Steps 1 through 4, you should also be working on verbal imitation for simple sounds and eventually focusing on sounds that will be useful as the beginning sounds to the child's favorite mands.

Step 5

Child:	Spontaneously makes the sign for cookie.
Mom:	Says "cookie?" or asks "Oh, you want a cookie" and holds the cookie in front of the child and gives him a verbal imitation prompt "cookie" and waits expectantly for the child to make any sound.
Child:	Option 1 - If child does not make sound after a reasonable wait, mom should reinforce with a small piece of the cookie.
	Option 2 – If the child makes any sound, mom will say something such as "Cookie! Of course you can have a cookie!"
Mom:	Then reinforces the child with a full cookie (or more) while saying "Here is your cookie" and celebrating with further praise such as "I knew you could do it!"

Once your child is making the sign and any sound to mand for cookie, you can begin to wait longer for a more appropriate sound for the word cookie such as the "k" sound. Obviously this is only possible if your child has been making the "k" sound in verbal imitation. Once "k" is easy for your child, begin waiting longer for the "kuh" sound and then "kuh-e" and then "cookie," and eventually "I want a cookie," etc.

The process of holding a cookie in front a child and waiting for him to say "k" is what most parents and teachers try to do with a non-vocal child. However, this procedure is not normally going to be enough without having done each of the earlier steps first. Creating an EO (motivation) for communication through sign language and teaching verbal imitation when you have a child's strong desire to participate are prerequisites that cannot be overlooked. Once you have a child's motivation and have used errorless learning (Chapter 11) to prompt him to success with one type of request, you can begin to put that type of request on extinction (Chapter 6). This will cause the child to extinction burst. When guided correctly, these extinction-burst behavior choices will eventually include some form of appropriate response from the next level of manding. Since it is only the reinforcement of new behavior choices that will increase the use of those choices again in the future, you must be ready to reinforce this new more advanced level of requesting when it occurs.

The VB approach to language acquisition has helped many older children and even young adults begin speaking for the very first time. However, for some children, having a strong motivation to speak is not enough. There are possible reasons that a child with a strong motivation and many practice trials may remain unable to put complex sounds together. However, there are many excellent speech and language programs that when paired with ABA/VB can make even the most delayed language learner capable of speech. A few that are notable include Nancy Kaufman's, Kaufman Speech Praxis Treatment Approach found at *www.kidspeech.com*, Sara Rosenfeld-Johnson's, Talk Tools Oral Motor Program found at *www.talktoolstm.com*, Deborah Hayden's, Prompts for Restructuring Oral Muscular Phonetic Targets (PROMPT) found at *www.promptinstitute.com*, and Deborah Beckman's, Beckman Oral Motor Therapy found at *www.Beckmanoralmotor.com*. Additionally, Tamara Kaspar and Nancy Kaufman have teamed up to develop a box of cards teaching to the deficits of autism and apraxia called the K&K Sign and Say Verbal Behavior Kit. This kit can be found at the Northern Speech Services Inc. website, *www.nss-nrs.com* and offers a great combination of pictures and word progressions to help children improve their speech.

Regardless of past difficulties, do not give up on your child's ability to speak.

Do not give up on your child's ability to speak. Regardless of past difficulties, there are now many excellent speech programs available that paired with a good ABA/VB approach could be the help that your child needs to learn to talk.

Summary of Chapter 13

Breaking down complex concepts into manageable chunks and teaching these chunks in a developmentally appropriate order educates toward recovery. It is also the basic teaching philosophy of ABA/VB (page 184).

Sign language is the form of augmentative communication most often used in the Verbal Behavior approach to autism intervention (page 185).

The very first step in teaching children to speak is to start by getting this simple idea of "If I do something, I get something; if I do something else, I get something else" across to them (page 187).

Sign language is an augmentative communication system based on the exchange of mutually understood body movements (page 187).

Because you can physically prompt and reinforce the use of sign language, when a person does not have the ability to echo words, then sign language is the best way to teach him the power of communication (page 187).

As a rule, only ask "What do you want?" when you do not know what the child is asking for at the time. If you are aware of the child's desire, begin your mand teaching by saying just the name of the item you want the child to learn (page 189).

There are many ways to make the process of teaching signs easy for your child, as there are also many ways of making it difficult for him. Do not try this technique at home without first doing more research or obtaining the guidance of a qualified behavior analyst (page 189).

Reinforcement should only follow a correct sign when it comes without scrolling (page 190).

Although verbal imitation and manding should be included in your teaching, they should not be taught at the same time. When teaching a verbal imitation you can teach with any combination of sounds you choose. However, when teaching a child to mand for a specific item, you should only use the word for the item that you want your child to learn to mand (page 190).

Teaching a child to mand spontaneously involves waiting longer before prompting your child. Conversely, teaching a child to begin using sounds as mands is accomplished by waiting longer before you deliver reinforcement (page 190).

The strength of ABA/VB is that it designs or captures a child's naturally occurring motivation to have and do things and then uses this incentive to teach increasingly more complex ways to request items or activities (page 191).

Do not give up on your child's ability to speak. Regardless of past difficulties, there are now many excellent speech programs available that paired with a good ABA/VB approach could be the help that your child needs to learn to talk (page 195).

Chapter 14

General Teaching Procedures of

Verbal Behavior

It is important that you are appropriately prepared to teach before you attempt any intervention with your child. In addition to reading this book, I recommend that parents join ABA/VB and autism Internet groups, study the books, and view the DVDs that I have recommended and detailed at the end of this book, and seek the guidance of a BCBA who is trained in VB. You must also be well versed in a variety of important teaching procedures. It is the use of these general teaching procedures based on the principles of behavior that will offer your child his most accelerated learning across many different skills.

Transfer procedures should be a part of any good teaching program. **Transfer procedures** can be used in many different ways and for a variety of skills. The idea of the transfer procedure is simple, however remembering to apply it to your teaching is sometimes less so. A transfer procedure is the process of transferring a response from a known S^D (instruction) to a new S^D. For example, if you are asked to name the first president of the United States, you might be able to respond "Washington." Once it is known that the S^D "Who was the first president of the U.S?" has gained reliable control over your response "Washington," that control can be transferred to other S^Ds. It might be transferred to the name of the famous bridge in New York, or to the seat of the U.S. government, or the middle name of the man who invented the peanut. To do so, one only has to pair the original S^D "Who was the first president" and its response "Washington" with a new S^D. Here is an example more specific to early learners with autism. Assume that you have taught your child how to touch his head when you say the words "Do this" while touching your head. That means that the response of your child touching his head is under the control of that S^D. By pairing that response with a different S^D that expects the same answer, you can transfer the control from the "Do this" S^D to the new S^D. Often this is done with the use of prompt. The following is a transfer procedure from the S^D "Do this" (motor Imitation) to the S^D "Touch your head" (receptive Language).

Therapist: "Do this." (touches head).

Child: Touches head.

Therapist: "Good job!"

Therapist: "Touch your head." (touches head).

Child: Touches head.

Therapist: "Way to go!"

Therapist: "Touch your head." (No model prompt).

Child: Touches head.

Therapist: "Right on; good job."

Your child begins with a simple motor imitation marked by the S^D "Do this." Next you will transfer that response to the receptive language S^D of "Touch your head." This is just one of the many ways that you can use a transfer procedure to enhance the rate at which a child can learn new skills. Why start from scratch teaching every new skill when you can pair a new skill with responses your child can already give?

Here are a few more examples. The first transfers a tact intraverbal such as "What is a ___" into a fill-in intraverbal such as "A ___ is a ???." In this example a child can answer a simple question such as "What is a dog" with the answer "An animal," but does not currently do fill-in statements such as "A dog is an ___."

Therapist:	"What is a dog?"
Child:	"An animal."
Therapist:	"Good job!" "A dog is an _____." (waits).
Child:	Does not answer.
Therapist:	Prompts "A dog is an aaaan."
Child:	"Animal."
Therapist:	Excellent, a dog is an _____." (waits).
Child:	"Animal."
Therapist:	"That is correct; a dog is an animal, good job buddy."
Therapist:	"What is a cat?"

This next example transfers from a receptive language identification of a common object (coffee cup) to a receptive language identification of a common object by feature function or class.

Therapist:	"Show me the coffee cup."
Child:	Touches coffee cup.
Therapist:	"Good job!"
Therapist:	"Show me what has a handle." (feature).
Child:	Does not know answer.
Therapist:	Prompts by pointing to coffee cup.
Child:	Touches coffee cup.
Therapist:	"That's right; a coffee cup has a handle!"
Therapist:	"What has a handle?" (no prompt).
Child:	Touches coffee cup.
Therapist:	"Excellent. Now show me what holds coffee?" (function).
Child:	Points to coffee cup.
Therapist:	"Yes, show me what you can drink coffee from?"
Child:	Points to coffee cup.
Therapist:	"Way to go!"

A transfer procedure allows a child to give the same response to changing S^Ds to expand the number of skills the child can perform correctly. Transfer procedures are extremely useful and whenever possible should be used for teaching new skills. The transfer procedure works quickly because the child already knows the answer but he is learning how to apply it to other questions. By pairing that answer with the other questions and using appropriate prompting you can expand the use of that answer for him in quick and meaningful ways.

Another method, correction procedure, should be used whenever your child makes an incorrect response. **Correction procedure** harks back to the basic beliefs of VB. A child needs to be correct as much as possible so that the free flow of reinforced learning fun can continue unabated. However, when a child is wrong, it is not useful to offer reinforcement because that would increase the likelihood of the child being wrong the next time. But it is important to avoid using the word "no" or other aversive forms of punishment when a child is wrong because their application takes the enjoyment out of the process, frustrates the child, and increases the value of escape. The best way to avoid any of these pitfalls when your child has made an incorrect response is to use a common correction procedure. This procedure recognizes that your child's errors are due to a lack of experience and likely a result of your teaching mistakes. If you are appropriately using errorless learning, you will be prompting your child to success and prompt fading as he is ready for more independence (Chapter 11). If your child makes a mistake during errorless learning, it is likely that you faded your prompt before your child is ready to respond without it. In this case it is now you who must do the work to help remedy this situation.

There are two types of correction procedures recommended at Knospe-ABA. The first is designed to help your child when he is incorrect during natural environment or on-the-move teaching. When teaching on-the-move or in the NET, your teaching is based on your child's motivation. Therefore he will most likely be invested in finding the correct answer. Whenever your child is incorrect in the natural environment, quickly repeat the S^D; this time, with the amount of prompt he needs to be correct. It is important that you give enough of a prompt so that your child is correct, allowing you to reinforce that correct response. This keeps the positive flow of reinforcement strong. However, teaching is not finished at this point and it is important that you do not end here. Because your teaching goal is to evoke the correct response without the prompt,

Transfer procedures are extremely useful and whenever possible should be used for teaching new skills.

you need to restate the original S^D a third time without the added prompt. Since your child has just given the correct response and that response was reinforced, he will likely be able supply the correct response again. In the natural teaching environment this is often the best way to correct a mistake and move on with your teaching.

Here is an example of a three-step natural environment correction procedure:

Trial 1 -   Mom: "Bring me a cup."

              Child: Brings a plate.

Trial 2 -   Mom: Restate S^D "Bring me a cup." (points to the cup).

              Child: Brings the cup (with help of prompt).

Trial 3 -   Mom: Restates S^D "bring me another cup." (without prompt).

              Child: Brings another cup.

              Mom: Reinforces this correct response.

There is a more complete correction procedure that is normally recommended for use during intensive trial teaching. ITT is teaching that takes place without your child's natural motivation therefore requiring more support. This correction procedure begins the same way but includes two additional steps. Whenever your child is incorrect in intensive trial teaching repeat the S^D again, with the amount of prompt needed to evoke a correct response. Then restate the S^D a third time without the added prompt. To make sure that your child has learned the correct answer and is not just offering you a delayed echo of the last response, you should then do an easy distracter trial or two. A distracter trial is any easy skill that will take your child's mind off the last response for a few seconds. Then after the distracter trial(s), you once again give the original S^D to see if your child has retained the target response beyond the distraction. If so, reinforce this independent correct response more heavily than the previous prompted trials, as this is an important positive learning moment. If your child is once again incorrect, you need to start the correction procedure from the beginning. The goal of any correction procedure is to show your child that a response was not correct without punishing his effort when he gives an incorrect answer. In turn, correction procedures use prompts and prompt fading to help teach independent correct responding. The added benefit of a correction procedure is that it always ends with reinforcement, maintaining the child's perception that the teaching process is worthwhile and fun.

This five-step formal ITT correction procedure is a more complete way to reinforce your child's learning after a mistake. In many cases it is advisable to use this longer procedure in NET as well. However, when using this longer correction procedure in NET or on-the-move teaching is too cumbersome or dismantling to the overall interaction, it is possible to make the correction by using the three-step NET correction procedure instead.

Here is a good example of a full five-step ITT correction procedure for an early leaner making an error in receptive language:

A correction procedure always ends with reinforcement, maintaining the child's perception that the teaching process is worthwhile and fun.

Trial 1 -	Mom: "Touch head."
	Child: Touches nose.
Trial 2 -	Mom: Restate S^D "Touch head." (prompts correct response).
	Child: Touches Head (with help of prompt).
Trial 3 -	Mom: Restates S^D "Touch head." (with less or no prompt).
	Child: Touches Head.

Distracter trial 4 – (Mom presents different S^D to which the child responds).

Trial 5 - Mom: Restates Original S^D.

- If child touches his head, then reinforce and move on.

- If child is incorrect again, go back to trial two and repeat.

- Always end by reinforcing the best possible response you can obtain.

Frequently, learning a language is fraught with many small misunderstandings. So many in fact that using a single correction procedure on an error in the natural environment is likely insufficient to affect your child's future responding. It is important that you make a note of each error that needs a correction procedure in the natural environment. Then you can add that skill to your daily teaching list. With enough repetition, you can permanently remove these misunderstandings from your child's future language use one after another.

Applying a correction procedure to incorrect responses is the best way that you can end every skill with reinforcement without reinforcing mistakes or frustrating the child when he is incorrect. The correction procedure is important in helping keep learning a preferred activity for your child. Here is an example of a correction procedure for an advanced learner making an error in preposition use.

Trial 1 -   Mom: "Where did you put the ball?"

Child: "I put it over the table."

Trial 2 -   Mom: "Where did you put the ball?..I put it <u>on</u> the table." (echo prompt).

Child: "I put it on the table"

Mom: "That's right you put it <u>on</u> the table."

Trial 3 -   Mom: "Where did you put the ball?"

Child: "On the table."

Mom: "Wow, you learn so fast." (makes note to practice

words "over" and "on").

Distracter trial 4 – (Mom presents one or more different easy S^Ds to which the child responds correctly).

Trial 5 -   Mom: "Where did I just put the pen?"

Child: "On the Table."

Mom: "Yes, I did just put the pen <u>on</u> the table. You are

really paying attention!" (tickles child for added

reinforcement).

Transfer and correction procedures are tried and true verbal behavior techniques with much study and evidence supporting their use. I have personally developed and regularly use the two procedures that follow, "The Teaching Arc" and "Mini-consequences," based on my experience and application of basic behavioral principles. Our consultants are using these techniques to the benefit of hundreds of children worldwide. However, at this point there is a need for more research and data to support their use by others. Consider this fact before deciding to incorporate these procedures into your teaching.

The **Teaching Arc** is based on the concept of Instructional Control. It is often taught that to earn instructional control, you start with pure pairing and then slowly begin to add in a few easy instructions that your child will not mind following. This shows your child that following directions is easy and fun and something that he likes to do. Then when your directions become more difficult, you already established an idea in your child that direction following is fun and worthwhile. This should help him negotiate the more difficult skills. Nobody enjoys doing particularly difficult work; however, as a rugby player I learned that pain, sweat, and effort are easily compensated with a positive result. In addition, the organization of a workday can have a big impact on someone's feelings about his work. If you consistently have all of your least favorite or most difficult tasks given to you at the end of the day, you will likely spend the night dreading going back to work in the morning. However, try setting up your day so that it always starts the morning with light easy work. Then move into your more difficult tasks in the middle of the day. Finally, spend the last few hours involved in your most enjoyable work activities. Consequently, you will likely go home upbeat. You will feel better about your job, and in turn, you will be more willing to return, knowing that an easy morning will be waiting for you. At Knospe-ABA, we teach families to set up each of their Intensive Trial Teaching (ITT) sessions in this same format. I call this format a "Teaching Arc." A teaching arc is designed to make learning as fun and reinforcing as possible. A teaching arc always starts and ends with "pairing."

A Teaching Arc always starts and ends with "pairing."

1. Start by pairing with your child. This means getting involved in some fun reinforcing activity in which he wants your participation. In the beginning, avoid directions or S^Ds. Your goal is strictly to get him laughing and enjoying being with you.

2. Begin to incorporate a few small and easy S^Ds into the play. Make them things that your child is most likely to do without thinking. Many times skills that you know your child has recently mastered work well here. Be sure to reward those responses appropriately with more or better play.

3. Begin your teaching and remember to mix easy and difficult demands while reinforcing with the fun activity.

4. Begin to ease off difficult demands <u>before</u> your child becomes bored or tired with the activity and begin using a higher ratio of easy S^Ds and more pairing.

5. Always finish the activity with a period of pairing alone.

6. Try to be the one who leaves the activity while your child is still enjoying it; always leave him wanting more.

It is important to use a teaching arc whenever you teach because it eases your child into learning and leaves him with a memory of the teaching process as fun and something he wants to do again. You should use teaching arcs with each reinforcing setting and across whole teaching sessions. When done appropriately, a teaching arc can be a strong EO for teaching in general. If you start a teaching interaction with fun and finish with fun, regardless of the level of difficulty in the middle, your child will want to come back for more. One of our early goals with a child is to help families develop a large repertoire of reinforcing teaching activities. These are all activities that the child likes and is willing to work for. Often video watching, swinging, jumping on a trampoline, playing with soap bubbles, and dancing to music are a part of that list. When a parent or therapist begins to work with a child, he should allow the child to choose a desirable activity from this list. Once the six-part teaching arc has been completed, the parent or therapist should tell the child that it is time to do something else and allow the child to choose a new activity. As the parent or therapist joins the child in this activity a new teaching arc begins. Once the process is established, you will find that your child spends his time happily moving from one motivated learning setting to another.

Experience has led Knospe-ABA to another concept: **Mini-consequences.** This concept is particularly successful when supporting the learning behavior of control children. Simply, the concept allows for small demonstrations of potential consequences, organized in a set of ever-worsening conditions. Mini-consequences work because they help ensure your child's immediate realization that he is on the correct or incorrect path to getting what he wants. Once you have given an S^D to your child, every movement or behavior he demonstrates can be considered closer to, or farther away from, the response you seek. A small movement or gesture on your part will cue your child as to whether his behavior choices will get him closer or father from what he wants. This can only be accomplished by making his every movement or behavior contingent on getting him visibly closer or farther from his desired reinforcement. For example, your child has been given the S^D, "Touch the cup." There are many behavior choices that would be considered moves in the right direction to fulfilling that instruction. Looking at the objects on the table, moving forward in his seat, reaching for one of the objects, and pointing his finger at one of the objects are positive movements that indicate that your child is well on his way to appropriately responding to your S^D. Conversely, hitting himself on the head, grabbing at the reinforcer, not moving, laughing, or vocally challenging your authority show that he is headed in the wrong direction to fulfilling the instruction. These incorrect or inappropriate behavior choices should be met with immediate indications that he is now farther away from what he wants. Depending on the teaching setting and the reinforcer, any one of many mini-consequences could accomplish this task. In the example of the S^D "Touch the cup," if the reinforcer being used is a plate of grapes, the first mini-consequence could be putting your hand on top of the plate to block his access and view. If he notices this and makes a better choice, you should then remove your hand. If he continues to make incompatible choices to the response you are looking for, you could slide the plate to the other side of the table. If he notices this and chooses a better movement, you can slide the plate back. Sometimes the next step might be to put the plate behind your back or hold it up and away from him. If he chooses further inappropriate behavior, you can then remove the grapes to a counter out of reach and eventually a cabinet out of sight.

Mini-consequences are a negative punishment procedure. Negative punishment is anything that is removed from a child's environment that reduces future use of the behavior that preceded it. At the end of Chapter 6, it is suggested that positive reinforcement, extinction, and negative punishment all teach a child toward recovery. In addition to having their desired effect on a behavior, these forms of consequence also increase a child's motivation to engage in further interaction with the source of the consequence. The benefit of mini-consequences is that they allow you to demonstrate dissatisfaction with a behavior choice without giving any type of attention or positive reinforcement. It also does not put you into a corner by completely dismantling the teaching setting with one quick consequence. It has been my experience that the intelligent use of mini-consequences is one of the most effective tools available for quickly addressing problem behaviors or inappropriate choices made during teaching. More importantly, it addresses these issues without compromising the teaching setting as a whole.

Mini-consequences are also an important part of the seven steps to instructional control. Chapters 5 and 6 discuss the use of adult attention as a method of showing a child he is getting closer or farther away from what he wants, this is a form of the mini-consequences procedure. If your child needs you to help him obtain his favorite toy, every step you take toward the toy is a positive or reinforcing mini-consequence. Conversely, every step you take away from the toy is a negative or punishing mini-consequence. This is the reason, for instructional control purposes, it is recommended that you become very good at reading your child's behavior. Then you can quickly change your body movement and direction as a clear and immediate statement of whether your child is on the correct or incorrect path to getting what he desires. When your child is asking you appropriately for a toy, you should walk toward the toy to show him that this is a behavior choice that you are appreciating. However, if he makes an inappropriate choice such as raising his voice, hitting himself, or stomping his foot, immediately stop your forward progress as a mini-consequence. If he continues on the wrong path, you can take a few steps back or even turn away. Then when he stops the inappropriate response, you can continue toward the toy once again. For children with autism, this type of clear and immediate response is an extremely effective way to build skills and reduce inappropriate behavior.

By using mini-consequences, every teaching trial becomes more consistently effective in motivating correct responding.

By using mini-consequences, every teaching trial becomes more consistently effective in motivating correct responding. This occurs because every inappropriate movement of the child is met with the potential reinforcement immediately becoming visibly more difficult to attain. When you use mini-consequences consistently with your child, you will find that you can begin to signal the upcoming worsening set of conditions (mini-consequences) with a facial expression or minor vocal sound. Often, all that it takes is a special look from the parent or teacher to alert the child that a set of mini-consequences is on its way if his current behavior path continues. This type of situation is known in the science of VB as a reflexive-EO. Having been sufficiently paired with mini-consequences, a specific look or facial expression can evoke a reflex motivation in your child to engage in any behavior that will change or abolish this upcoming set of conditions. In other words, knowing that a specific facial expression will consistently lead to a mini-consequence removal procedure, the presentation of that expression will become an automatic EO (motivation) for your child to stop his current behavior choice. Additionally, using facial expressions as signals to environmental conditions teaches children the importance of attending to and interpreting non-verbal communication.

Correction procedures and mini-consequences are similar in that they are implemented when a child is not successfully demonstrating a skill you are attempting to teach. The way that you can decipher which procedure is best for a given situation depends on your analysis of the reason for your child's lack of success. Choose a correction procedure when you feel that your child is giving an appropriate amount of effort but is unsuccessful because he lacks experience or ability. Mini-consequences are a better option when you believe that your child has had sufficient experience but uses insufficient effort or incorrect choices as a means of escape or establishing control.

These are only a few of the many strategies and techniques one needs to become a good teacher. However, correctly implementing these four procedures at appropriate times will greatly improve the quality of your teaching. Using transfer procedures, correction procedures, a teaching arc, and mini-consequences consistently will drastically increase the effectiveness of your teaching and in turn decrease the number of trials it takes your child to learn any new skill.

Summary of Chapter 14

A transfer procedure allows a child to give the same response to changing S^Ds to expand the number of skills the child can perform correctly. Transfer procedures are extremely useful and whenever possible should be used for teaching new skills (page 204).

Applying a correction procedure to incorrect responses is the best way that you can end every skill with reinforcement without reinforcing mistakes or frustrating the child when he is incorrect. The correction procedure is important in helping keep learning a preferred activity for your child (page 207).

It is important to use a teaching arc whenever you teach because it eases your child into learning and leaves him with a memory of the teaching process as fun and something he wants to do again (page 209).

By using mini-consequences, every teaching trial becomes more consistently effective in motivating correct responding. This occurs because every inappropriate movement of the child is met with the potential reinforcement immediately becoming visibly more difficult to attain (page 211).

Choose a correction procedure when you feel that your child is giving an appropriate amount of effort but is unsuccessful because he lacks experience or ability. Mini-consequences are a better option when you believe that your child has had sufficient experience but uses insufficient effort or incorrect choices as a means of establishing control (page 212).

Using transfer procedures, correction procedures, a teaching arc, and mini-consequences consistently will drastically increase the effectiveness of your teaching and in turn decrease the number of trials it takes your child to learn any new skill (page 212).

Chapter 15

Changing your Child's View on

Toilet Training

Even under the best of circumstances, toilet training can be problematic. For many families of children with autism, successful toilet training may seem an impossible dream. However, there are many different programs designed to help families through this transition. I have found helpful the toilet training program in "A Work in Progress" by Ron Leaf and John McEachin. Information is also available on myriad other programs that can be found by accessing parent networks throughout the Internet. I have seen a great number of these "potty" programs work for many different children. However, it is not uncommon to see young adults with autism older than age 13 wearing diapers. Why do some children make this transition easily while others seem utterly to refuse? More importantly, why do some programs work for certain children and not for others? The toilet training program you choose will not make or break the diaper routine. If you have truly earned instructional control with your child, any one of the most popular toilet training programs will likely work for you. However, if you have not effectively earned instructional control or have not been able to maintain it, you might find it difficult to achieve success with any program.

It is not recommended that you start a toilet training program at the beginning stages of an ABA/VB program.

If you have tried and failed with a variety of programs, it could be that you have not earned instructional control with your child or were not applying the principles of ABA/VB correctly. This will often cause the entire act of using the toilet to become aversive stimuli where the mere mention of toilets, potty, or flushing can send your child into a tantrum. The program that I offer here was designed to reverse this sort of negative pairing. It should work in all cases and is especially recommended for children who are the most resistant to learning this skill. However, it is not magic and it will not work without instructional control. It is designed to teach your child that going into the bathroom can be a fun and rewarding experience, one they would want to do again. If your child already sees toilet training as a strong aversive, I recommend re-reading Chapters 5 and 6. Then, once you have earned better instructional control with your child, use the following program to remove the negative feelings your child associates with using the toilet.

It is not recommended that you start a toilet training program at the beginning stages of an ABA/VB program. Toilet training can be difficult for the child and the family. A well-rounded ABA/VB program needs to be in place for you to have the best chance at a quick and painless process for all. This program should include a strong pairing element and you should be well out of the beginning instructional control phase. It is also important that you do not try to start toilet training before your child is developmentally ready. Consult your local physician to see if there are any strong indications that your child is not developmentally ready to begin a toilet training process.

Finally, before beginning the program, be sure to have a special ultimate prize reinforcer. Make it available to your child only when he successfully voids in the toilet. This reinforcer should not be given to the child for any other reason and should be the most prized reward your child has.

Part 1 - Levels

The goal of the program is to help your child move through the levels of acceptance for toileting listed below. When ready to start your toileting program, your child will be at one of the following levels.

1. Your child willingly goes into the bathroom upon request.
2. Your child willingly sits on the toilet with clothes on (optional).
3. Your child willingly takes pants down at the toilet upon request.
4. Your child willingly takes pants down and sits on the toilet for one second upon request.
5. Your child willingly takes pants down and sits on the toilet for 10 seconds upon request.
6. Your child willingly takes pants down and sits on the toilet for 30 seconds upon request.
7. Your child willingly takes pants down and sits on the toilet for one minute upon request.
8. Your child willingly takes pants down and sits on the toilet for five minutes upon request.
9. Your child willingly takes pants down and sits on the toilet for up to 10 minutes.
10. Your child willingly takes pants down, sits on the toilet, and voids upon request.

* Your child self-initiates going to the bathroom and voids without help... Hurrah!!!

Find out which of the levels your child is at by asking him to (A) come into the bathroom, (B) take down his pants, (C) sit on the toilet, and (D) void. Be sure to make this process reinforcing with music, singing, or other reinforcement. A toileting song can be used effectively for this process. The "It's Potty Time!" series of DVDs is particularly helpful as it offers a number of songs that can be later translated into action. Once you know which level your child has achieved, begin reinforcing him to the next level. In addition to the fun activities you will engage in during the process, reinforce with a strong tangible reinforcer when your child is successful at hitting the goal for the next level.

If your child is at level 1, meaning he will go in the bathroom but will not sit on the toilet with clothes still on, you would then ask him to come into the bathroom, and sit on the toilet with his clothes on. If he shows any hesitation, physically prompt him and then immediately reinforce the activity. Be sure to make it fun and "worth it" for your child. Repeat this process on the regular schedule detailed in part 2 until your child can perform the next level skill without any prompts or hesitation. Then begin prompting toward level 3.

If your child is at level 2, meaning he will sit on the toilet with clothes on but will not pull pants down at the toilet, you would ask your child to come into the bathroom and take his pants down. If he shows any hesitation, physically prompt him and then immediately reinforce the activity. Be sure to make it fun and "worth it" for your child. Repeat this process on the regular schedule detailed in part 2 until your child can perform the next level skill without any prompts or hesitation. Then begin prompting toward level 4.

Keep your reinforcement value high! Make every trip to the bathroom fun and do not let it become routine or boring.

If your child is at level 3, ask him to take down his pants and sit on the toilet. If he shows any hesitation, physically prompt him and then immediately reinforce the activity. Be sure to make it fun and "worth it" for your child. Repeat this process on the regular schedule detailed in part 2 until your child can perform the next level skill without any prompts or hesitation. Then begin prompting toward level 5.

At level 4, ask your child to take down his pants and sit on the toilet and stay there. After 10 seconds of sitting you would reinforce your child as before. If he gets up or leaves the toilet, you would not reinforce the behavior in any way. On the next visit you would then reinforce after only 1 second, building back up to 10 as soon as your child is able. Remember to keep your reinforcement value high! Make every trip to the bathroom fun and do not let it become routine or boring.

If your child is at levels 5 through 10, gradually increase the amount of time your child must remain on the toilet before he is rewarded. If your child gets up before reaching the goal time, no reinforcement is given and on the next visit your child should be reinforced at the previous levels reinforcement time. All of this is done regardless of whether or not your child ever voids in the toilet. At level 10, meaning he will sit on the toilet with his pants down for 10 minutes but does not void, begin only to reinforce non-voiding trips to the toilet with small amounts of reinforcement.

If your child is consistently refusing to participate or let you prompt him, allow him to leave the room. However, you are now in an extinction situation. Your child's behavior is not one you would like to see again so you cannot reinforce it. According to Step 7 of instructional control, although you allow your child to escape the instruction, he should not be given access to any outside reinforcement until he chooses to return and allows you to prompt him. Once in extinction, respond to any request with a reassuring "Of course you can, but first come to the toilet with me." Once he chooses to return, repeat your original S^D and reinforce appropriately.

The first time your child voids in the toilet, immediately bring out the giant reinforcer that your child only will get when he has appropriately voided. This reinforcer should not be used for any other teaching. It could be a very special video, a run through the sprinklers, trip to McDonald's, or whatever your child will see as the ultimate prize. This reinforcer should be decided on by you before beginning your program and should reflect your child's interest.

Part 2 – The regular schedule

In the beginning, your child needs to be put onto a regular bathroom schedule of 45 minutes. This means that you should set a timer that goes off every three-quarters of an hour during the day. When the timer goes off, you should stop whatever you are doing and cue your child to go to the bathroom and perform whatever level skill he is currently working on. After your child demonstrates two consecutive days without any accidents, move forward to the next longer interlude.

The time-spans you should use are

45 minutes

60 minutes

90 minutes

120 minutes

180 minutes

Once your child is on a three-hour schedule and can go two days without an accident, he should be self-initiating. If any time during the process your child self-initiates, he should be given the special grand prize reinforcement. After all, this is your ultimate goal.

Schedules are only used to keep *you* aware of the time and not in any way designed for your child. The best possible way to get your child to void in the toilet the first time is catch him when he needs to go. So, if at any time you see that your child is ready or looks like he might be about to void, immediately prompt him to go to the bathroom and implement part one. Then start your timer over from there. Do not be afraid to abandon the schedule once your child has begun voiding in the toilet. Now, the challenge becomes catching your child when he needs to go.

Part 3 – Accidents

The first two parts of this program are based on positive reinforcement for appropriate behaviors. Part three is designed to speed the process by taking any possible enjoyment out of accidents. This part is designed to eliminate reinforcement after the behavior of having an accident. It is not meant to be an aversive punishment procedure.

If at anytime during the process your child has an accident, take him immediately to the toilet and continue with your normal procedure. However, instead of following the procedure with reinforcement, take your child out of the bathroom to another area of the house and have him clean himself with a washcloth and towel. This should not be a painful experience for your child but should be one that he is not excited about repeating. Do not put him in the tub or offer any other reinforcing activities. The time following an accident should not be reinforcing in any way.

Any time your child has an accident, consider decreasing the time interval between bathroom visits. For example if you are on a 120-minute schedule and your child has an accident, move back to the 90-minute schedule.

Part 4 – Other important considerations

1. Do not allow your child to wear diapers at anytime during the toilet training process once he passes level two.

2. Keep your child's fluid intake high so that the opportunities to reinforce voiding in the toilet come as frequently as possible.

3. Consider running the water while your child is on the toilet.

4. Be prepared to give your ultimate prize reinforcer. The value of voiding in the toilet can only be taught when voiding is reinforced. In the beginning, any amount of void should be immediately and heavily reinforced with the ultimate prize.

5. Decide if you want to administer the program day and night or only in the daytime. If you choose to keep diapers on at night while running the program during the day, you will keep the bed dry during the early phases of instruction, but this will add an additional step to your teaching process. This choice will often depend on the needs of the individual family or child.

6. In the beginning, try not to differentiate between urination and bowel movement. Consider both voids and reinforce both strongly.

7. Consider your family and local society's view on boys either standing or sitting to urinate. It is often better to begin with all voiding in a seated position. However, additional considerations need to be made for boys concerning standing and using urinals.

8. Only teach your child a specific word (or sign) to request the toilet _after_ your child begins to self-initiate. Having a word or sign to mand (request) the toilet would be beneficial when your child cannot have open access to the bathroom, but can also become an added step that makes the skill more difficult for your child to master.

9. If your child does not find the act of cleaning up after himself a sufficient consequence for accidents, consider other consequences that will make voiding in the toilet a more valued choice. However, be creative and avoid presenting aversive stimuli whenever possible. Removal of outside reinforcement opportunities for a period of time after an accident might be an appropriate answer.

Toilet Independence Program

Once your child is using the toilet consistently, it is time to help teach him how to use it independently. To teach your child to enjoy the toileting process, you reinforced his toileting behavior while he was in the bathroom. Now, you need to delay the reinforcement until after he is finished. There are generally two ways that your child will now go to the toilet.

1. When he tells you that he has to go.
2. When you notice and tell him that he needs to go

Accompany your child to the toilet when he tells you he has to use it. However, instead of going into the bathroom with him, stop at the open door and give your prompts and encouragement from there. Do not reinforce until after he has finished. Once this is easy for him to deal with, close the door halfway but continue to look in and give directions and encouragement. The next step is to close the door but remain very vocal outside the door as he goes. Wait for him to open the door before you check on him. If he comes to the door without completing the task (for example, without flushing or washing his hands), remind him of what he forgot to do and send him back to the bathroom. Close the door and wait again. The final step is to slowly fade away your directions and encouragement. Then begin to move away from the door so that he does not see you immediately upon leaving the room. However, reinforce his behavior every time he is successful without your help.

When you are still the one who notices that your child needs to use the toilet, begin to gradually fade the prompts needed to get him to go on his own. Do not say, "Do you need to go to the toilet?" Instead, stop any reinforcing activity and look at him and ask, "Is there something you need to do?" Once he goes to the toilet, continue with the same delayed reinforcement procedure as in the first part of this toilet independence plan.

Children with autism can be taught to use the toilet in much the same way any other child learns this skill. The difference is that it may take you significantly longer to achieve the goal of independence. However, do not give up. Ultimately, by first earning instructional control and patiently following these steps, you and your child will be successful.

Summary of Chapter 15

The toilet training program you choose will not make or break the diaper routine. If you have truly earned instructional control with your child, any one of the most popular toilet training programs will likely work for you. However, if you have not effectively earned instructional control or have not been able to maintain it, you might find it difficult to achieve success with any program (page 215).

Remember to keep your reinforcement value high! Make every trip to the bathroom fun and do not let it become routine or boring (page 218).

Children with autism can be taught to use the toilet in much the same way any other child learns this skill. The difference is that it may take you significantly longer to achieve the goal of independence. However, do not give up. Ultimately, by first earning instructional control and patiently following these steps, you and your child will be successful (page 222).

Chapter 16

Knowing What to Teach

I designed this book as a guide to teach parents, teachers, and therapists <u>why</u> and <u>how</u> to use ABA/VB to teach children with autism or other related disorders. In doing so, I have included very little concerning <u>what</u> to teach. When it comes to children with autism, the range of skills that could be delayed or missing is so overwhelming that no single book could possibly cover them all. In addition, I do not have much to add in this arena as the tireless work of specialized autism curriculum development has already been done and is available in many different forms through a variety of sources. Several of these sources are detailed below.

My goal for this Chapter is to alert you that there are programs and procedures available to teach to *all* of your child's specific learning deficits. It is important that you know what these programs look like and how you can benefit from them. Once you begin to study your child and the best techniques available for teaching, many of you will begin to invent your own specific styles and program combinations to fit your child's specific needs. However, regardless of how good a teacher you become, you will always need outside ideas and assistance. There are five formal sources that I have found to be of the most useful benefit when deciding on what to teach a child.

There are programs and procedures available to teach to all of your child's specific learning deficits.

The first two books were written in the 1990s and offer basic ABA curriculums as well as a way to apply these learning programs to learners at different levels of learning. The first, edited by Catherine Maurice, Green, & Luce, is called "Behavioral Interventions for Young Children with Autism." The second, edited by Ron Leaf and John McEachin is called "A Work in Progress." Both books are listed in the reference guide at the end of this book and are required reading for teachers, therapists, and families in search of a better way of teaching children. Both books are especially helpful to those who are unable to find BCBA support and will need to develop ABA programs on their own. In her book, Maurice begins by objectively comparing many of the available methods of autism therapy and education. This leads to a conclusion and explanation of why ABA is the best available choice. In addition, the book comes complete with a suggested teaching curriculum. The Leaf and McEachin book is one of the very best available explanations of how the principles of ABA work. It also includes a helpful curriculum. An important perspective on teaching can be found in the preface of this second book:

> *This book has been more than 20 years in the making and it is still not finished. We consider it a work in progress. Even as these words are being written, one of our talented staff or a dedicated parent is out there somewhere thinking of a new and clever way to teach an important skill to an autistic child...*

> *This is not a cookbook and should not be treated as such. Every autistic child is different and the program needs to be tailored accordingly...*

> *One must proceed with flexibility and learn from the child. We want people to feel comfortable developing and trying out new teaching programs. As long as you are guided by the data, you will not go far astray. That is the beauty of Applied Behavior Analysis. (Leaf/McEachin)*

I find these statements to be the most beneficial way to look at any suggested curriculum for teaching any child. Although both books were written before the major developments of Verbal Behavior, "A Work in Progress" and "Behavioral Interventions for Young Children with Autism" are worthwhile books to help you understand the benefit and application of the basic principles of ABA.

The best and most complete curriculum available for teaching individuals with disabilities can be developed with the help of the "Assessment of Basic Language and Learning Skills – Revised™ (ABLLS-R™)." The ABLLS-R™ was developed by Dr. James Partington, PhD, and Dr. Mark Sundberg, PhD, in the 1990's and was revised by Partington in 2006. The ABLLS-R™ is organized into 25 different categories of language that takes into account Skinner's behavioral classification of language. It covers the learning areas of cooperation and reinforcer effectiveness, visual performance, receptive language, motor imitation, verbal imitation, manding, tacting, intraverbals, spontaneous vocalizations, syntax and grammar, play and leisure, social interaction, group instruction, classroom routines, generalized responding, reading, math, writing, spelling, dressing, eating, grooming, toileting, gross motor skills, and fine motor skills. This assessment tool is the most complete list of skills presented in a developmental sequence available to assess young children with autism. The ABLLS-R™ offers a clear way of deciphering exactly what skills your child is missing and which skills are next in line for you to teach. The assessment does not come complete with programs to teach these individual skills, but that is where an experienced BCBA who has training and experience teaching to the ABLLS-R™ can help.

The best and most complete curriculum available for teaching individuals with disabilities can be developed with the help of the ABLLS-R.™

If a BCBA is unavailable to you, there is a series of DVD's that have been developed to show you how to teach to many of the goals of the ABLLS-R.™ The "Intensive Teaching Series" was developed by behavior analysts, Holly Kibbe and Cherish Richards of Establishing Operations Inc. (*www.establishingoperationsinc.com*).

ABA and even ABA/VB can be learned and used by parents, teachers, and therapists willing to study the data and information available. In my consulting, I often find that children as young as age five can begin effectively to use the principles and practices of good teaching with their siblings with autism. You too can learn to teach with ABA/VB. It only takes the confidence that comes with knowing that you are your child's true expert. But as that expert, it is important that you bring in the experience of trained professionals to help. Ideally, your program should include the oversight of a BCBA, and everyone who is part of the child's daily environment. Your program also needs to be ruled by the principles of behavior and, the main curriculum guidance of the ABLLS-R.™ Although good teaching should extend well beyond the goals of this assessment, the ABLLS-R™ is the skills guide for the curriculum that we have developed and use at Knospe-ABA and it has fast become the world's most popular tool for selecting teaching goals for children with autism. In fact, you can now buy a complete set of teaching tools that will allow you to administer the ABLLS-R™ assessment and teach all of its skills in one easy-to-transport bag. This product was conceived and produced by Pam Dollins, a verbal behavior consultant who was, at the time of its development, working for the Carbone Clinic in New York. Pam knew the benefit of teaching to the ABLLS-R™ but was frustrated by the difficulty and expense of locating all of the materials needed to do so. The ABLLS kit itself is fairly expensive but remarkably less so than it would cost you to purchase the materials individually. These kits may be found at *www.vbteachingtools.com*. It is not recommended that everyone buy a kit. In fact, many good ABA/VB consultants and school classrooms throughout the world now have them. But if you are going to be the person responsible for administering and teaching to the ABLLS-R,™ it is an investment you might want to consider.

Another valuable resource associated with teaching to the ABLLS-R™ is the book "Language Targets to Teach a Child to Communicate" written by Diana Luckevich. Diana's book can be found at *www.talkingwords.com* and offers lists of language goals in a format that also serves as a data collection tool. This resource contains over 5,000 language targets organized into 190 categories. It includes common vocabulary, word associations, features, functions, phrases, questions, and conversation topics that you can use to help your child achieve his ABLLS-R™ goals.

The ABLLS-R™ itself, as well as the verbal behavior companion guide called "Teaching Language to Children with Autism or other Developmental Disabilities," can currently be purchased through many websites including *www.behavioranalysts.com*. This same website can connect you with the VB and ABLLS-R™ training workshops of Behavior Analysts Inc. Having this assessment at your disposal will help you to track what skills your child needs to learn while relieving some of the expense of having to pay others to administer it for you.

In addition to assessment and program development, the ABLLS-R™ is also an excellent tool for demonstrating the progress of your program. It allows you to show exactly what skills your child has learned from one administration to the next. Aside from good video documentation, it is the most useful record of progress you can have to convince your local insurance or government agencies to begin or continue paying for your program and service costs. One of the main reasons that the science of ABA has been so slow to grow in public awareness is that it is difficult to discern which children will make slow and steady progress with its teaching from those who will make immediate remarkable progress toward recovery. Often when these best cases occur, they happen so fast and unexpectedly that there is little documentation of the change. If you have a child with autism, you might consider enlisting someone to document your child's behavior right now. That means videotaping the many different ways that autism is affecting your child and family. Save and catalog these tapes by date. Update your videos monthly when you begin to teach. This will be the best evidence to your insurance companies, government agencies, schools, and the world of the true benefits of ABA/VB. As more people begin to do this, an increasing number of cases of autism recovery can be reliably demonstrated. This will make life easier for the next generation of parents trying to find help in their fight against the effects of autism.

There are at least two other program curriculums that I have found to be extremely beneficial in teaching toward recovery. The first can be found in a book by Sabrina Freeman Ph.D. and Lorelei Dake, B.A., entitled, "Teach Me Language: A Language Manual for Children with Autism, Asperger's Syndrome and Related Developmental Disorders," published by SKF books. This book is filled with great target goals and teaching ideas in several important categories including social language, general knowledge, grammar and syntax, advanced language development, and academics/language based concepts. This book is an excellent additional curriculum to the ABLLS-R™ for advanced language learners. It is filled with many good programs and sample drill sheets.

The second of these two additional programs is called Relational Development Intervention (RDI™). This concept was developed and is taught by Steven E. Gutstein Ph.D. Dr. Gutstein's conceptual work can be found in the book "Solving the Relationship Puzzle," Jessica Kingsley Publishers. RDI™ is a social relationship development program that is designed to teach the concept of experience sharing. The premise of the RDI™ program is that there are two main types of social interactions: instrumental social interactions and experience sharing. Dr. Gutstein believes that instrumental social interactions tend to occur naturally and often in complex ways among children with autism. However, he theorizes that autism's main social deficits come in the form of the child's inability to learn how to engage in experience sharing. His RDI™ program labels and breaks down the many levels of experience sharing and offers strategies designed to teach them to individuals with Autism Spectrum Disorder. The goal of this program is to help a child gain the important missing pieces that allow him to truly understand the shared benefit of being with others. The program is designed to give children with autism the tools needed to make real and lasting friendships. Similar to the curriculum in the other books mentioned above, RDI™ is for some children a useful curriculum supplement best taught within the context of a good ABA/VB program. There is now an excellent resource for parents and therapists looking to incorporate RDI™ goals and concepts into their ABA/VB programs. It is in the form of a Yahoo group and is called "ABAplusRDI." This Internet community is one of the few places that choose not to see ABA/VB and RDI™ as competition. Instead it encourages an intellectual dissection of the important curriculum ideas of RDI™ and discusses how to apply them within a good ABA/VB context. I detail the benefits and potential problems involved in developing a dual program involving ABA/VB and RDI™ in Chapter 20.

Using any of the curriculums listed in this chapter without a strong understanding of the principles of behavior will help you develop only a small piece of the overall picture.

Using any of the curriculums listed in this chapter without a strong understanding of the principles of behavior will help you develop only a small piece of the overall picture. In addition to the formal curriculum options mentioned above, there are two other important sources available to help you find target goals for your child's program. The first is your child's school. Whether in pre-school, kindergarten, first grade, or high school, there will be specific skills that your child's teachers and therapists are going to identify as important for your child. However, they may not always have the time or knowledge of how to help your child achieve these goals. Knowing what goals are important to your child's teacher and addressing them in your home program will help your child to be more successful at school. Additionally, you need to look at your daily life interactions for hints about what you should be teaching. What specific skills do you see your child missing in his daily routine? What misunderstanding and mistakes are you constantly correcting? Take note of these errors and turn them into teaching goals that you can address comprehensively in your program.

To go back to an earlier analogy, each of these curriculum options is a box of specialized tools. Using Sign Language, PECS, Floortime, RDI,™ The ABLLS-R,™ Teach Me Language, or any other programs or curriculums available is only being able to apply one set of tools to one set of needs your child may have. To truly help a child recover from the effects of autism, you need to become the expert on your child and use the principles of ABA/VB to teach to what he needs from all of these varied programs and curriculums. To be a master craftsmen capable of building a unique and independent structure, you need to be able to go to the right toolbox and pull out the right tool at the right time. Then you need to use the principles of motivation and reinforcement to make those tools work for you.

Summary of Chapter 16

My goal for this Chapter is to alert you that there are programs and procedures available to teach to *all* of your child's specific learning deficits. It is important that you know what these programs look like and how you can benefit from them (page 225).

The first two books were written in the 1990s and offer basic ABA curriculums as well as a way to apply these learning programs to learners at different levels of learning. The first, edited by Catherine Maurice, Green, & Luce, is called "Behavioral Interventions for Young Children with Autism." The second, written by Ron Leaf and John McEachin is called "A Work in Progress" (page 227).

The best and most complete curriculum available for teaching individuals with disabilities can be developed by using the "Assessment of Basic Language and Learning Skills – Revised™ (ABLLS)." The ABLLS-R™ was developed by Dr. James Partington, PhD, and Dr. Mark Sundberg, PhD, in the 1990's and was revised in 2006 (page 227).

In addition to assessment and program development, the ABLLS is also an excellent tool for demonstrating the progress of your program. It allows you to show exactly what skills your child has learned from one administration to the next. Aside from good video documentation, it is the most useful record of progress you can have to convince your local insurance or government agencies to begin or continue paying for your program and service costs (page 228).

There are at least two other program curriculums that I have found to be extremely beneficial in teaching toward recovery. The first can be found in a book by Sabrina Freeman Ph.D. and Lorelei Dake, B.A., entitled, "Teach Me Language: A Language Manual for Children with Autism, Asperger's Syndrome and Related Developmental Disorders," published by SKF books (page 229).

The second of these two additional programs is called Relational Development Intervention (RDI™). This concept was developed and is taught by Steven E. Gutstein Ph.D. Dr. Gutstein's seminal work can be found in the book "Solving the Relationship Puzzle," Jessica Kingsley Publishers. RDI™ is a social relationship development program that is designed to teach the concept of experience sharing (page 229).

Using any of the curriculums listed in this chapter without a strong understanding of the principles of behavior will help you develop only a small piece of the overall picture (page 230).

Additionally, you need to look at your daily life interactions for hints about what you should be teaching. What specific skills do you see your child missing in his daily routine? What misunderstanding and mistakes are you constantly correcting? Take note of these errors and turn them into teaching goals that you can address comprehensively in your program (page 230).

Chapter 17

Turn the Table on Autism

Learning how to use ABA/VB allows you to turn the table on autism. It is by understanding these two sciences that you can transform your child's worst enemies into his best friends. All of the things that you currently consider the most difficult or undesirable parts of interacting with your child with autism can become your strongest teaching tools. However, this is only true once you start consistently applying the principles of ABA/VB to his daily interactions. You can use the reinforcing techniques of Applied Behavior Analysis and the motivational strategies of Verbal Behavior to convert your child's barriers to doorways.

You can use the reinforcing techniques of ABA and the motivational strategies of VB to convert your child's barriers to doorways.

For many years being "echoic," has been considered a negative attribute of people with autism. As a young teacher I knew many children and young adults who were only able to repeat things they heard. One such person was Tony. Tony is a boy I worked with who had almost no functional language. If I asked "Do you want to play basketball?" he would repeat back to me "basskeball, basskeball, basskeball." Although he could approximate the word "basketball," he was unable to respond in either the affirmative or negative and would repeat the word "basskeball" whether or not he wanted to play. However, thanks to the advancements of ABA/VB, children who are only capable of echoing other's words are no longer considered as being unable to talk. In fact, the ability to echo is an early important step in learning to speak. Echoing, or verbal imitation, is one of the nine classifications of language and an important part of speech that all people use. My wife and I moved to Germany from one of the most beautiful places in the world, Hermosa Beach, California, to begin helping the children of Europe through the use of ABA/VB. We settled in the little farm town of Hespe. As uncomplicated as Hespe is, it is by no means a tourist attraction. Most people do not know where Hespe is on a map and many others have never heard of it. But the people who do know Hespe will often tell me what they think of it with an echo. After answering the question "Where do you live?" with the answer "Hespe," these people often look at me with their most sympathetic face, take a deep breath, and sigh "Hespe." In this case an echo was used by the person to tell me that they felt sorry for me. Have you ever noticed that people will repeat an address or telephone number you have just given them? They do this to make sure that you know they correctly understood the information they just received. This is also a functional use of an echo. Echoing behavior is a natural part of everyday speech and not something that needs to be avoided. When a teacher or doctor says that your child is only echoic, I wonder if this person realizes how lucky you are. If your child were non-vocal, you might have to spend weeks, months, or even years teaching him to become echoic before moving on to more advanced language.

When it comes to functional language, children who are naturally echoic have a head start.

When it comes to learning functional language, children who are naturally echoic have a head start. The proper procedure for transferring an echo into other functions of language such as a mand or a tact is not as complicated as it may first appear. However, to be able to teach this skill you need the help of many different concepts presented in this book. You need to have established good instructional control with your child (see Chapters 5 and 6). You need to know how to use the discrete trial teaching system (see Chapter 8). It is important to understand how and when to use reinforcement and EO effectively as discussed in Chapter 10. You need to be able to use errorless learning with prompting and prompt fading illustrated in Chapter 11 and how to use a simple transfer procedure covered in Chapter 14. Finally, you need to know the different functions of language such as a verbal imitation, a mand, and a tact that was detailed in Chapter 9.

When attempting to convert a child's echo into a tact, it is important that he be able to imitate what you say when directed. The goal of the echo-to-tact transfer procedure is for your child to be able to correctly tact (label) by answering a question such as "What is this" in the presence of the stimulus without echoing the question. Begin the procedure by presenting your child with the S^D and a full-echoic prompt. For example, "What is this? ball!" If your child is very verbal and can echo a whole sentence you might hear him repeat "What is this ball." This obviously is not transferring anything so, in this case you need to be more careful with differentiating between your S^D and your prompt. You might ask quietly, "What is this?" and then in a louder voice, say "ball!" Another way is to ask "What is this?" and wait until your child is about to echo. Then interrupt his echo with the word "ball!" This usually cuts off the first echo and causes him to echo just the last word "ball." The goal of this part of the transfer procedure is for your child to differentiate between the S^D (what is this?) and the echo prompt (ball). Once you have been working with your child for some time and have had some practice, you can usually figure out how to best present the S^D and prompt to evoke the correct response. After you are able to get the echo response you want, reinforcing it will make it more likely to occur during the next repetition. After several trials of reinforced responding, you will have a child who can now say "ball" after you give him the S^D "What is this?" paired with the full-echo prompt "ball!"

The next step is to fade from the full-echo to a partial-echo prompt and let your child transfer the response "ball" from a highly prompted response to a lower one. The way this works is by giving your child the S^D and prompt, "What is this? ball." and as soon as your child responds correctly, quickly repeat the S^D but only giving the partial-echo prompt "b." The goal is to get your child to transfer the response from the S^D and full-echo (ball) to the S^D and partial-echo (b). Once this has been reinforced enough times that it has sufficiently transferred, you can begin to fade from the prompted S^D to a completely unprompted one. At this point, your child will respond "ball." When you ask the question, "What is this" in the presence of a ball or picture of a ball. You will not immediately obtain the proper response. However, with enough repetitions your child will begin to respond independently.

Here is how an echo-to-tact transfer for the question "What is this?" might look in a teaching dialogue:

Therapist: "What is this? BALL!"

Child: "Ball."

Therapist: "Yes. What is this? B____?"

Child: "B."

Therapist: "What is this? Ba__?"

Child: "Ball."

Therapist   "Excellent, it is a ball" "One more time, what is this?"

Child: "Ball."

Therapist: (throws a party in celebration)

Those of you who are paying close attention might have noticed that I threw a quick correction procedure from Chapter 14 into this last example as well. Can you identify it?

Motivation and reinforcement are the keys to teaching any skill. In addition to the skill of teaching the answer "ball" to the question "What is this?" you have to realize that this is only a start. You will need to begin transferring other echoes into tacts until your child begins to understand labeling as a concept and can start to develop new tacts on his own. The same strategy holds true for transferring an echo into a mand. The only difference is that the S^D changes from something such as "What is this?" to "What do you want?" But, because a mand is a request for something, you want only to teach it when your child actually desires the item in question.

Another way that you can use an echo as a bridge to higher levels of communication occurs when you want to teach your child to mand for attention. It is difficult to teach an early learner that problematic behavior such as yelling, crying, or hitting is not the best way to obtain mom's attention. One of the best techniques available for teaching this skill comes from the Carbone Clinic in New York. The procedure usually includes two people working with the child. One person serves as motivation and reinforcement while the other supports the child with appropriate prompts. As is the case with all skills you will teach in ABA/VB, frame the lesson with fun. For example, mom, dad, and child are playing with a spinning top and laughing. Suddenly mom stops the interaction and gives the top to dad who turns away. In this instance, mom is prompter. When the child wants the spinning top, mom prompts with the word "daddy." As soon as the child repeats "daddy," dad immediately turns around and reinforces the child by praising the child and spinning the top again. The "daddy" prompt should be faded after several trials. Over time, the child will learn that he need not cry or scream for attention when a simple spoken, "mommy" or "daddy" will get him the attention he wants. Notice that the use of this procedure is completely dependent on the child first being able to echo the correct response.

Here is how an echo-to-mand transfer for attention might look in three distinct steps:

Step 1:

Mom: Takes spinning top and hands it to dad who turns his back.

Child: Begins to whine or reach for the top.

Mom: Gives full-echo prompt "daddy."

Child: Echoes "daddy."

Dad: Turns around and reinforces child.

When the child demonstrates that he knows what is expected of him, you can move to Step 2.

Step 2:

Mom: Takes spinning top and hands it to dad who turns his back.

Child: Looks to mom for a prompt.

Mom: Gives partial-echo prompt "da____."

Child: "Daddy!"

Dad: Turns around and reinforces child.

When the child is able to say "daddy" consistently with only a partial-echo prompt, you should move to Step 3.

Step 3:

Mom:	Takes spinning top and hands it to dad who turns his back.
Child:	Looks to mom for a prompt.
Mom:	Waits with an expectant look (gestures to dad if necessary).
Child:	"Daddy!"
Dad:	Turns around and reinforces child.

With many trials of an echo-to-mand procedure in many situations with many different items, a child who can echo mommy or daddy can easily be taught to use those responses to mand (request) for parental attention.

It should be noted that the above example teaches a child to request attention solely as a means to gain other preferred items. Once this goal has been achieved, it is advisable to teach applications of this program that are social in nature such as "Mommy, look what I did!" or "Dad, look an airplane."

A child who can echo mommy or daddy can easily be taught to use those responses to request parental attention.

Reinterpreting the power of the echo is only one of many ways that ABA/VB can turn your child's learning "problems" into your best teaching tools. Self-stimulating behavior, also known as ritualistic behavior, a tic, stim, or stimming has been one of the most recognizable characteristics of autism since the diagnosis has existed. Flapping hands, staring at lights or moving objects, perseveration, rocking, bouncing, and making vocal noises are all examples of stim behaivors. For many parents the thought is "The faster I can get rid of the stims the less my child will stand out in a crowd." While this may be true, the process of eradicating stims has not been met with a lot of success. In many cases, your best attempts will merely reinforce this stimming behavior. If you are successful in removing a stim without satisfying the desire that caused it, you will find another stereotypical behavior has taken its place.

Self-stimulating behavior should be seen as a desire your child has and a tool that you can use to teach.

Thanks to the advances of ABA/VB, self-stimulating behavior is no longer looked at as something to be eliminated. Instead, it is seen as a desire your child has and a tool that can be used to teach. For example, your child likes to stare at, into, or through shiny objects. You can choose to pull him away from these objects. This will likely make opportunities to be with the objects more valuable to your child. A better choice would be to gather as many shiny objects as you can find, put them into a bag, and use them to motivate and reinforce important learning behavior. You can teach your non-vocal child to make a sign for "open" to get into a bag or box of shiny objects. You can teach your early learner to make the sounds "EEEE" "AAAA" "OOOO" and "UUUU" for a chance to spend some time with the shiny things. If your child is ready to learn how to read, you can give him a shining object for every new word he learns. The benefits of using stims to teach are two fold. First and foremost, it works! Your child is desperately motivated to perform these stims. It is our thoughtful use of this desperate motivation that is our best weapon against the pull of autism. The second benefit is the principle of pairing. The principle of pairing states that when two objects or activities are paired together, the value of one begins to wear off on the value of the other. This generally works in both directions. The reinforcing value of the stims wear off on the teaching process making all of the factors involved - attention, focus, eye contact, and following directions - among others, more desirable to your child because they are paired with strong reinforcement. Conversely, the difficulty involved in the work being done will also begin to deplete the reinforcing value of the stim. Over time, the stim becomes less reinforcing naturally from the constant pairing with work.

There are many ways that you can use your child's self-stimulatory behavior to your teaching benefit. Children who love spinning objects will work for spinning tops, spinning plates, spinning CDs, and time with a spinning washing machine. It does not matter if it is an object, a song, or an activity; if the child knows he can obtain his desire by achieving a goal, he will work toward that goal. Many children demonstrate a strong desire to keep things in order. When this is the case, giving a child a half finished puzzle or blocks that need to be arranged is a great way to build motivation to work on any kind of skill. For many children, there is no limit to the list of stims and perseverations that they find interesting. When looked at for their teaching value, the possibilities are also limitless. There is currently an excellent website based in Germany that specializes in autism teaching materials which can be found at *www.pro-aba.com*. This website may have the largest collection of reinforcing "stim-toys" available in one place. If finding toys that act as reinforcement for your child's behavior is difficult, this website is a great resource.

Children use self-stimulation behaviors because they fulfill some form of desire that is not being filled another way. As you begin to teach your child other more interesting ways to enjoy the world, the desire to spend time engaged in stims will begin to fade. However, if you focus on reducing stimming, you will find that the stimming in most cases gets worse. If you are successful in

As you begin to teach your child other more interesting ways to enjoy the world, the desire to spend time engaged in "stim" behavior will begin to fade.

eliminating a stim through some form of punishment procedure, but do so without satisfying its corresponding desire with an appropriate behavior, often another more disruptive stim will take its place. Do not try to hide or bury self-stimulatory behavior. Instead, reduce its value by using it to teach. Then watch as the new reinforcing skills you teach him take over more of his daily activity. By consistently pairing stimming behavior with a less reinforcing item, you can increase the reinforcing value of that item while decreasing the value of the stim. Thus, by using stims to teach your child to do puzzles, look at books, play catch, or ask questions, you will find these new activities filling more of your child's day while the stims become less pervasive and problematic.

By consistently pairing stimming behavior with a less reinforcing item, you can increase the reinforcing value of that item while decreasing the value of the stim.

One of the biggest ways that ABA/VB has been able to turn an enemy into a friend is with the dreaded extinction burst. Extinction is the act of purposely not reinforcing a behavior that has been reinforced in the past (Chapter 6). The use of extinction is extremely beneficial in reducing inappropriate behavior but is also filled with peril. The biggest of these perils is the tendency of parents to relent and reinforce during an extinction burst. The extinction burst is the period during which your child will use more severe behavior in an attempt to get what he wants before choosing the new, more appropriate choice you are trying to teach him. Whenever parents use extinction to reduce a behavior, they must be ready to ride out the extinction burst wherever it might take them. When families begin the process of implementing an ABA/VB program, the extinction burst is always the prime enemy. Nobody likes to watch a child scream, cry, hit himself or others. These are sometimes the behavior choices made by children who are no longer being given reinforcement for inappropriate behavior. Many families cannot believe how far their child is willing to go before finally choosing a better way. But as much as you may learn to hate the extinction burst, it will become your very best friend once instructional control has been earned.

To best help your child to fully recover from autism, you must always be genuinely happy with any and all progress that he makes. However, you must never be satisfied with what you achieve until your child is functioning independently. Be happy that your child will make the sign for music instead of throwing a tantrum, but do not be satisfied until he can independently and correctly ask for music. To teach this you will be relying on your old rival the extinction burst. Once your child consistently and spontaneously makes the sign for "music," put his use of this sign on extinction. Yes, you have spent hours, days, weeks, or sometimes even months teaching the sign for music. But now that the sign is strong in your child's repertoire, it is no longer progress and you want to stop reinforcing it. Instead of reinforcing the sign for music, use it as a signal to begin holding your hand on the radio button, look at your child, and very clearly two to three times say the word, "music." If you put the sign for music on extinction in this way, your child will go into a period of extinction burst. Just as he did with inappropriate behaviors in the past, he will likely begin to increase the intensity of his manding behavior to get what he wants. Maybe he begins repeatedly to make the sign for "music." Maybe he will try to take your hand to have you make the sign with him. Because you are presenting the word "music" in the same way you present verbal imitation S^Ds, he might even use this extinction burst EO (motivation) to try to say the word "music." and a sound will come out. When he does, reinforce that sound by immediately turning on the music no matter what that sound is. Once you know that you can consistently obtain a sound with the sign when he wants to hear music, begin putting the use of any sound on extinction and reinforce only when his extinction burst causes him to make the "m" sound with his sign. When you begin to get the "m" sound consistently, put it on extinction and begin looking for the "mu" sound. Eventually you will lose the need for signs altogether when you start to get the word "music" and then the words "have music." and then "May I have music," and then "May I have the music on please?" until eventually your child will ask "May I please have my favorite music with that little boy who sings like a crocodile?" Although the extinction burst is difficult during the initial instructional control process, the stronger your child's extinction burst, the easier it will be for you to later use it to teach him important language and learning skills. It is your ability to understand and turn the table on your child's use of a strong extinction burst that will allow him to make progress toward the ultimate goal of recovery. Before you have instructional control, the extinction burst can make teaching difficult. However, once you have turned the table on autism you will embrace the extinction burst as an indispensable teaching tool.

Once you have turned the table on autism you will embrace the extinction burst as an indispensable teaching tool.

Although you should celebrate every success along the way, it is important that you do not relent in your teaching efforts until your child is fully capable. It can be a long and arduous journey for you and your child, but it is the best way your child can achieve a full, independent life. Unfortunately, there is no shortage of children with autism who have no friends and adults with autism who cannot hold a job. The number of extremely intelligent individuals with autism living in institutions around the world is at best unfortunate. Most are there because parents have been forced by a lack of assistance and information to give up on their expectations. Being satisfied with "good enough" is never good enough for your child. The goal of any parent is to prepare an adult who can live independently in the world. This goal is no different for parents of children with autism. For many it may take longer and the road may be rockier. For some this ultimate goal may never be reached, but even then, finding the right type of information and assistance and working toward independence should always be your ultimate goal.

Always be happy with any progress your child makes. Every skill your child learns is a reason to celebrate (and you should). Just be sure that you are always prepared to help your child address his next challenge. You can do this by consistently pouring on the motivation and offering the reinforcement that he will need to get over increasingly more difficult parts of the sand wall that surround him.

Every skill your child learns is a reason to celebrate. Just be sure that you are always prepared to help your child address his next challenge.

The following turn of the table shows just how powerful a tool ABA/VB can be when understood and used to its full potential. Aside from the seven steps to instructional control and strategies for teaching the control child, this might be the most important aspect of what this book has to offer. This final turn of the table is often the reversal that traditional ABA programs using high levels of negative reinforcement, positive punishment, and escape extinction are unable to make. The final turn of the table is this: if you want your child to learn everything he can as fast as he can, his desire to learn from you must be greater than your desire to teach him. Wow! The last sentence offers such a bold statement that it deserves to be repeated again, this time in bold letters. **If you want your child to learn everything he can as fast as he can, his desire to learn from you must be greater than your desire to teach him.**

The problem with this statement is not getting parents to agree with it. After all, if your child with autism could desire to learn more than you currently desire to teach him, how could he fail? Most children with autism have the ability to learn close to 100% of what they are genuinely motivated to know or do. Think about your own child's abilities in his areas of strong interest. Unfortunately, depending on the individual and how he is affected, it could be estimated that a child with autism's inherent motivation usually only covers 2% to 40% of what he will need to reach recovery. Just imagine if you could get your child to genuinely desire to learn 80%, 90%, or even 100% of the things you want to teach him. It is only then that the sky becomes the limit and recovery becomes a reasonable goal. To achieve this, every interaction needs to result in reinforcement of your child's choices to follow directions and meet you half way in your relationship. Right now you are likely doing more than 95% of the work it takes for the two of you to keep an interaction going. As long as you are willing to maintain this ratio, your child will never learn the skills necessary to develop positive relationships. Why will he use appropriate volume, voice clarity, eye contact, levity, non-verbal games, and other forms of positive social interaction if you are perfectly willing to do all of the work involved in keeping an interaction going? If at any point your child is not holding up his end of an interaction, it is usually best to turn and walk away. Put his unwillingness to participate appropriately on extinction. Then allow the extinction burst that follows to help him find new and more complex ways to gain back your attention and the free flow of reinforcement and pairing that comes with it. Your choice to walk away and "mean it" will become his EO for reciprocal communication and increasingly more complex relationship development skills.

Often parents and therapists are so concerned about keeping the child in a learning situation that they inadvertently give the child complete control until the situation barely resembles teaching. The child is playing games with the instructor, ignoring difficult instructions, intentionally making mistakes, laughing, and only participating to a level with which he is comfortable or willing. Since the child is consistently threatening to leave the teaching setting the only skills being taught are the ones the parent, teacher, or therapist learns as he struggles to keep the child engaged. How much do you think you can teach a child when he is allowed to wield this much control? Compare that to the amount you could teach your child if he was truly engaged in motivated learning. Instead of trying to convince or hold your child in captive teaching, it is always better to use the seven steps to instructional control and the other procedures outlined in this book. Then, when your child attempts to control a teaching setting by not participating to the level you want, you can actually choose to send him away. If his receptive language is good, tell him he is done and that there is no more playing with mom. If he is an early learner, pick him up and turn him away. Give him a gentle push away from the interaction to show him that he has lost the right to participate in your learning activity. Of course losing access to the learning activity also means that he loses all of your

Your choice to walk away and "mean it" will become your child's EO for reciprocal communication and increasingly more complex relationship development skills.

reinforcing fun and games that comes with it. When you have all the pieces in place and you are confident enough to do this, you will see a child who begins to use his "autistic-like" controlling desires to force you to let him back into the teaching setting. As long as you are convincing, he will actually begin to believe that he wants to learn from you more than you want to teach him. Then, when he demonstrates a good behavior choice or two, allow him to return and resume all the teaching fun. However, if his behavior begins to lag, use your mini-consequences from Chapter 14 to show him that you are not afraid to once again send him packing. Do not sell children with autism short. Believe that they have a desire to learn what you want to teach them but they must first surmount the extremely high parts of the learning wall that stand between them and their future. By combining the strategies of VB with the principles of ABA families are learning how to teach.

It is possible to follow all of the seven steps to instructional control and still have difficulty keeping your child involved in motivated learning to the degree you will need to help him find his true potential. Even if you follow the first six steps of instructional control to make learning as fun and reinforcing as possible and you use Step 7 to reduce inappropriate choices, you still might not see the extinction time decrease sufficiently enough to teach as much as you would like. When extinction burst time is not decreasing, it is usually that you have not fully grasped the final turn of the table--if you want your child to learn everything he can as fast as he can, his desire to learn from you must be greater than your desire to teach him.

Knospe-ABA has supported the education of a little boy with autism named Manny for almost two years. Although Manny had been identified by our team as a strong control child with few initial skills, his progress in our program has been described by his mother as "excellent." Manny grew from having no interest in participating with his mom or others in his environment to having several favorite therapists. Additionally, there is now nothing more reinforcing to Manny than time spent pairing with his mom. Manny was taught to mand (request) and tact (label) with sign language for more than 30 of his favorite items. He had even begun using initial sounds for these words and was starting to find his way to full words as requests. Manny's receptive language, visual performance, and imitation skills have vastly improved. Additionally, he is now identifying and labeling letters and numbers. By most standards, he is doing great; however, there was always something about Manny's program that did not seem optimal. It was difficult to decipher what that something was. But there were times when Manny's inappropriate behavior and the length of his extinction periods began to increase while his behavior acquisition slowed. This behavior could easily be misidentified as moods or bad days, but it became increasingly apparent that procedurally something was wrong.

Through the observation of teaching video it was discovered that although mom and the therapists were going through the motions of extinction, they were not convincing Manny to change his behavior. In fact, what was supposed to be an extinction procedure had, in Manny's eyes, become an extinction game. His mother's desire for Manny to learn set the bar so high that Manny could never hope to want to learn more than she wanted to teach. Thus, as soon as he moved into an extinction situation, mom and her therapists focused all their energy on trying to convince him to come back. Although she was not allowing him reinforcing items or activities during extinction, her obvious desire to get him back to teaching was still reinforcing his choice to avoid it. One of the tricks our team had taught mom to use to motivate Manny, was to continue playing with his reinforcing items during extinction to keep his interest in those items high. However, it was never convincing to Manny that mom was willing happily to enjoy the activity without him. Instead, it was obvious that she was only trying to convince him to come back to teaching. Additionally, mom and the therapists would constantly talk about the items that Manny was not allowed to have during extinction. For some children these techniques will build motivation in the child to participate and shorten the length of an extinction burst. However for Manny, these behaviors were seen as direct challenges and in effect acted as reinforcement that maintained his use of avoidance behavior.

The family's attempts at using extinction became an extinction game that Manny played better than they did.

By trying to convince Manny to make a better choice instead of truly moving on and allowing him to make the decision himself, mom and the therapists were sabotaging the extinction process. To Manny, each attempt to build his motivation was seen as a challenge that he would try to meet with more refusal. Each time, mom pulled out a toy to play with or talked about an item Manny could not have, he knew that he was involved in a game and that mom was only interested in getting him back to teaching. Not only did Manny move further away from learning but he even began to enjoy mom's attempts at extinction. The problem was that Manny's mom and therapists still allowed him to control the situation albeit in a different way. Their attempts at using extinction became an extinction game that Manny played better than they did. At times he would get back to work immediately to get what he wanted only to jump immediately back into another extinction situation and other times what he wanted was to see how his extinction burst behaviors were controlling the rest of the house.

To truly turn the tables on autism you have to convince your child that you honestly do not care whether or not he participates in learning. That is the only way he will begin to care enough to actively convince you to teach him. For Manny, the important missing ingredient in what was an otherwise solid program was for the team to genuinely grasp that he must want to learn more than they wanted to teach him. Since Manny was willing and able to turn their attempts at using extinction into a game at which he was superior, the best way for the team to win was not to play. We eventually gained full instructional control by having the team use Manny's inappropriate choice making as a reason to leave the room, start some housework, read a book, make program notes, or use the phone. Once Manny, a strong control child, saw that his chances to exert control were effectively lost as soon as he stopped participating appropriately, he instead began working longer and harder so that he could extend his opportunities to control. Without this turn of the table, Manny's program was good but still far from optimal.

Here is a review of the seven steps of instructional control.

1. Control the restriction and access to all forms of reinforcement in your child's environment.
2. Pair yourself with reinforcement making the process of being with you more fun to your child than being alone.
3. Demonstrate that you are willing to always do what you say and say what you mean.
4. Show your child that you will give him access to his reinforcers whenever he follows a direction.
5. Know what reinforces your child the most.
6. Reinforce every positive interaction working toward an increasing variable ratio of rienforcement.
7. Show your child that when he does not follow a direction you will not allow him access to reinforcement.

To truly turn the table on autism you have to convince your child that you honestly do not care whether or not he participates in learning.

If you follow these steps consistently and comprehensively, your child will follow directions because he knows it is the fastest and easiest way to get what he wants (step 4). You can always give him what he wants when he has earned it (step 5). If he chooses not to participate in the way that you expect, he will not receive any reinforcement from you (step 7) and if he leaves your teaching setting there will be nothing else fun for him to do (step 1). If you say, "I will go upstairs if you do not sit down," he knows that you mean what you say (step 3). Most importantly, because you pair yourself with reinforcement most of the time, your child will rather spend time with you than allow you to leave. (step 2).

When you have all of these steps sufficiently in place, you will have filled all the cracks in the bottom of your child's sand wall. There will be no way to obtain reinforcement without surmounting that wall with you. Then you can pour in all the motivation you want to help lift him up to the top of the wall. You can offer your S^Ds and prompts and every time he receives reinforcement (S^R), he will drag back in over that wall making it easier to climb the next time.

Now, throw some of the procedures of ABA/VB into the mix. If you use errorless learning, your child will usually be correct keeping reinforcement levels high. If you use a teaching arc, you will always start off with play and leave your child wanting more. If you mix and vary your instructions, your child will not become bored with the tasks you give him. If you mix easy with difficult tasks, the average difficulty level of work will never become too high. If you use mini-consequences, your child will always know immediately if he steps off the correct path and his motivation to succeed will increase as he gets closer to completing the skill.

When you earn and maintain instructional control, use the principles of ABA, and include the procedures of VB, you will have all the ingredients you need to teach your child everything he is capable of learning at the fastest possible rate. You will be able to decide what level of effort is acceptable learning behavior. You can decide how fast, how loud, how clear, or how appropriate your child should perform a skill. You can help him always to be successful at meeting this ever-growing expectation and you can reinforce his decision-making when he does. If your child falls below your level of expectation because of inability, you can use a correction procedure to teach the correct answer without damaging your teaching relationship. If he does not

ABA/VB gives you all the ingredients you need to teach your child everything he is capable of learning at the fastest possible rate.

perform to expectation because of effort or choice, you can use mini-consequences or, if necessary, choose to pick up your teaching and walk away. Remember, he wants to be with you having fun (step 2). He wants the fastest and easiest way to his reinforcers (step 4). He wants access to his favorite things (step 1). Having full knowledge of these desires allows you to stay poised in a strong teaching position while developing a reciprocal relationship based on giving and sharing control.

When you follow these steps, you will find that your child wants to learn to the extent that you will be the one who suggests a break. You will need to find or hire help because there will never be enough time for you to teach your child as much as he wants to learn. When you put all of these techniques into effect in a systematic and comprehensive way based on your child's individual needs, he will desire to learn from you more than you desire to teach him.

To use any of the procedures in this book, you should first engage the services of a credible ABA/VB provider and/or participate in further study or training.

Most of the children with whom Knospe-ABA works, regardless of severity, pick up their teaching materials and run to their therapists so that the teaching can begin. Additionally, these children follow their parents around the house looking for ways to make the social interaction continue. Should your child fall below your expectations, stop teaching him until he comes to you with a greater determination to learn, and he will! Finally, by assessing your child on the ABLLS-R,™ you can be sure that you are teaching him every skill he needs for the world to make sense. Adding appropriate skills from Teach Me Language and The RDI™ program will enable you to address other social and communication deficits. It is only through the sciences of Applied Behavior Analysis and Verbal Behavior that you will give your child every chance to succeed. Through ABA/VB you can truly turn the table on autism and give your child his best possible outcome and a reasonable shot at recovery.

Although, this book is not intended to walk you through the process of educating your child with autism, it was written to point out the path that is now available and to give you a basis from which to set your goals. To use any of the procedures in this book, you should first engage the services of a credible ABA/VB provider in your area. If you cannot find someone who is under the supervision of a Board Certified Behavior Analyst you should not attempt these techniques at home without further study or training. Finding a behavior analyst to guide your program is important because ABA is the only discipline in the world that teaches people how to make meaningful changes in the skill acquisition and behavior choices of others based solely on what the scientific evidence has shown to be most effective. Behaviorists do not waste time and energy focusing on what the root causes of a behavior might be, but instead determine what is currently maintaining its use and how to increase or decrease its use in the future for the betterment of the person involved. For children with autism, there has been no other approach that has proven nearly as effective as ABA. The reason you should look for a behavior analyst that is board certified is that the Behavior Analyst Certification Board (*www.bacb.com*) is an independent credentialing agency that holds its members to the absolute highest standards of study and experience. Board certification requires a minimum of a Bachelor's degree in fields related to psychology, or education to become a Board Certified Associate Behavior Analyst (BCABA) or a master's degree to become a Board Certified Behavior Analyst (BCBA). In addition to education and experience, all BCABAs and BCBAs must sit for an exhaustive examination process. This examination covers every area important to the field including ethical considerations, definition and characteristics, principles, processes and concepts, behavioral assessment, experimental evaluation of interventions, measurement of behavior, displaying and interpreting behavioral data, selecting intervention outcomes and strategies, behavior change procedures, and systems supports. Additionally, to maintain board certification members must complete 12 continuing education credit hours per year in advanced procedures of the field to remain on the cusp of the latest data and techniques. Any members of the BACB that are found to be lacking in any area of professionalism are up for censure, including having complaints published and their memberships revoked. There are currently approximately 5000 BCBAs in over 20 countries worldwide. BCBAs and BCABAs are mentioned by name as the only certified persons outside of state licenses in Applied Behavior Analysis approved to oversee ABA services given to the members of the American military service insurance carrier TRICARE ECHO program. Echo now covers full benefits for families of qualifying children with autism up to $2,500 per month. The first step in helping your child is finding out what is available to you in the way of information and assistance. The second step involves getting cost reimbursement from the health, education, and government institutions in your hometown. Some school districts in the United States currently fund or staff ABA/VB programs; the American military insurance carrier TRICARE ECHO funds the services provided by qualified BCBAs and

The first step in helping your child is finding out what is available to you in the way of information and assistance. The second involves getting cost reimbursement.

BCABAs while many other government agencies throughout the world now fund services as well. Unfortunately, the work of educating your child toward recovery usually is not enough. You will also need to research and fight for your right to these available funds.

Join the ABA/VB Internet community. Attend workshops and seminars conducted by BCBAs such as Dr. Vince Carbone, Dr. Patrick McGreevey, Dr. James Partington, Dr. Carl Sundberg, Dr. Mark Sundberg, Dr. Bobby Newman, Christina Burk, MA, or myself among others. These seminars and workshops are designed to show you how to use the principles of ABA/VB to become your child's best teacher. Use the list of references at the back of this book to study the science behind the principles and techniques of behaviorism.

At some point you will want to hire additional assistance, but even then, it will be your responsibility to oversee your child's educational program. Even with qualified help, you will have to make sure that all of the people involved stay as consistently motivated to help your child as you are. The best way to motivate others is through the use of ABA/VB. Understanding how to motivate and reinforce goes beyond just working with your child. Becoming your child's best teacher includes becoming your child's best advocate and friend. It means learning all you can about your child and using ABA/VB with him and the people you engage to help you in your fight. It is only you that has been given this responsibility and it is only you that has the incentive, access, and ability to truly turn the tables on autism.

Two Knospe-ABA consultants recently attended a lecture by Axel Brauns. Mr. Brauns is an author who was diagnosed with autism as a child and lived his entire life with autism. He has written two books with a third in the making. The best known is "Buntschatten und Fledermäuse." (currently unavailable in English). He is now working on a movie as a director, writer, and producer while lecturing about his life and experiences. When asked how he overcame autism's challenges to become such an inspirational success, he responded by saying that he was given 2000 gifts of love, understanding, and support. Most typical children, he explained, receive 100 gifts from their parents to whom they return 100 gifts. However, autism acts like a filter. Although parents may give their child 100 gifts, the filter allows only one gift through to the child. Eventually, the child stops giving 100 gifts because he is only receiving one. Fighting against the normal reaction to this phenomenon Axel

Becoming your child's best teacher includes becoming your child's best advocate and friend.

Braun's mother chose to give him 2000 gifts. He credits his mother's ability and willingness to consistently give him 2000 gifts as the reason he was able to grow and learn the way he did. When asked how others can help to teach children with autism to live fuller lives and better understand complex issues like feelings and emotions his answer was simple-- Give them 5000 gifts!

Take the time to observe a child living and learning in the context of a good ABA/VB program. This is all it will take for you to understand how it is possible to consistently give your child as many gifts of love, understanding, and support as he will need to find his true potential, whatever it may be.

Summary of Chapter 17

You can use the reinforcing techniques of Applied Behavior Analysis and the motivational strategies of Verbal Behavior to convert your child's barriers to doorways (page 235).

When it comes to learning functional language, children who are naturally echoic have a head start (page 236).

With many trials of an echo-to-mand procedure in many situations with many different items, a child who can echo mommy or daddy can easily be taught to use those responses to mand (request) for parental attention (page 240).

Thanks to the advances of ABA/VB, self-stimulating behavior is no longer looked at as something to be eliminated. Instead, it is seen as a desire your child has and a tool that can be used to teach (page 240).

By consistently pairing stimming behavior with a less reinforcing item, you can increase the reinforcing value of that item while decreasing the value of the stim. Thus, by using stims to teach your child to do puzzles, look at books, take turns, or ask questions, you will find these new activities filling more of your child's day while the stims become less pervasive and problematic (page 242).

Before you have instructional control, the extinction burst can make teaching difficult. However, once you have turned the table on autism you will embrace the extinction burst as an indispensable teaching tool (page 243).

Always be happy with any progress your child makes. Every skill your child learns is a reason to celebrate (and you should). Just be sure that you are always prepared to help your child address his next challenge. You can do this by consistently pouring on the motivation and offering the reinforcement that he will need to get over increasingly more difficult parts of the sand wall that surrounds him (page 244).

If you want your child to learn everything he can as fast as he can, his desire to learn from you must be greater than your desire to teach him (page 244).

If at any point your child is not holding up his end of an interaction, it is usually best to turn and walk away. Put his unwillingness to participate appropriately on extinction. Then allow the extinction burst that follows to help him find new and more complex ways to gain back your attention and the free flow of reinforcement and pairing that comes with it (page 245).

To truly turn the tables on autism you have to convince your child that you honestly do not care whether or not he participates in learning. That is the only way he will begin to care enough to actively convince you to teach him (page 248).

When you earn and maintain instructional control, use the principles of ABA, and include the procedures of VB, you will have all the ingredients you need to teach your child everything he is capable of learning at the fastest possible rate (page 249).

Although this book is not intended to walk you through the process of educating your child with autism, it was written to point out the path that is now available and to give you a basis from which to set your goals. To use any of the procedures in this book, you should first engage the services of a credible ABA/VB provider in your area. If you cannot find someone who is under the supervision of a Board Certified Behavior Analyst you should not attempt these techniques at home without further study or training (page 250).

Some school districts in the United States currently fund or staff ABA/VB programs; the American military insurance carrier TRICARE ECHO funds the services provided by qualified BCBAs and BCABAs while many other government agencies throughout the world now fund services as well. Unfortunately, the work of educating your child toward recovery usually is not enough. You will also need to research and fight for your right to these available funds (page 251).

Take the time to observe a child living and learning in the context of a good ABA/VB program. This is all it will take for you to understand how it is possible to consistently give your child as many gifts of love, understanding, and support as he will need to find his true potential, whatever it may be (page 253).

Chapter 18

Separate is Never Equal: ABA/VB and the Public School System

Too often, children with disabilities especially those with autism are educated in prisons of kindness that are anything but kind. While growing up, I was always very close to my mother's youngest brother who was born with Down syndrome. My uncle Mickey was an amazing child. He had as big a heart as any person I have ever known. My brothers and I loved being around him. He taught us a great deal about love, respect, understanding, and acceptance. But he also taught me how unkind and unfair the world can be. I remember the paralyzing helplessness I felt when the older children would make a joke out of my uncle. I remember how confusing it was for me as a teenager when I watched my uncle slip away from us into an autistic-like inner world. It is these experiences with my uncle that ingrained in me a concern for the lives of children and adults with disabilities and a passion to help them succeed. I am concerned about people who live unfulfilled lives merely because they are misunderstood. I am concerned for their families who, too frequently, receive little or no support and guidance at a time when the family feels scared and alone.

Mickey was never given a chance to succeed in the way children are sometimes given today. The practice at that time, as it still is in far too many places, was to identify and label children by diagnosis and severity. Once identified, special needs children were grouped into central locations and taught with some form of remediation. The idea was that the children could benefit from the most dedicated and qualified educators and that these educators would return the children to the general population repaired and ready to contribute to society. It is now commonly understood in much of the world that this "separate and remediate" concept is fatally flawed. The primary problem with this concept is its reliance on the notion that children with disabilities need to be fixed. The idea that a child can be in someway broken or in need of repair like a toy or piece of furniture is inherently damaging. It hurts both the self-esteem of the child and the attitude of society about the child's worth and potential. Everyone knows that no child should ever be viewed as unacceptable or broken. Unfortunately there are teachers, therapists, doctors, administrators, and politicians in this world who are unable or unwilling to see these children for who they really are.

It is now commonly understood in much of the world that the "separate and remediate" concept of teaching is fatally flawed.

Children, like adults, are unfinished. Everyone grows and learns from their daily life experiences. All children deserve access to the same social or educational advantages and challenges. Children with disabilities may need more systematic teaching, but excluding a child based simply on an IQ test or a diagnostic label is simply and unequivocally wrong.

Excluding a child based simply on an IQ test or diagnostic label is simply and unequivocally wrong.

The main factors that distinguish one learner from another are processing speed, retention, and generalization of information. At any time in any society it can be estimated with a small margin of error what percentage of the population will be considered gifted, above average, average, below average, and disabled. In a society that prides itself on availability of a free and appropriate education for all, it is inappropriate to exclude any segment of the population based on their religion, race, creed, nationality, or diagnostic label. When did exclusion based on IQ scores or diagnostic labels become acceptable? There exists a common argument that children with disabilities are not excluded but instead given a separate education more specific to their needs. This rationalization is no different from that which supported the segregation of Africa-Americans in schools until it was challenged in 1958 and deemed unconstitutional. In what realm of society is exclusion considered appropriate? One thing society learned through the civil rights movement in the United States is that separate but equal can never truly exist. Many years ago society mistakenly took a wrong turn down a dead-end path. When educational challenges in classrooms that needed special attention were first recognized, society should have addressed teaching methodologies as a whole. It should have looked for a better way to teach all children. It should have begun training every teacher in the most effective strategies and techniques available for the benefit of all students. Instead of accepting our shortcomings as educators, our society chose to blame the children. "This child has a low IQ, and this one can't sit still." "This one makes funny noises and disrupts the other children." "This one is slow." "What is a physical education teacher supposed to do with a kid who can't even walk?" Instead of teaching the teachers how to work through the challenges that come with teaching all children, society hid behind the guise of separate and remediate as an excuse to label and remove. Pulling the most difficult children from the classrooms and schools became the norm. In some cases these children were even removed from society. It started with children with low IQs but quickly spread to children with other disabilities including physical, emotional, and behavioral issues. In some countries like Germany even typical children as young as the age of 10 or 12 are classified and separated based on past educational performance and given different sets of opportunities to succeed. When will our society stop blaming the children and start becoming better teachers?

At the time of its inception the decision to separate and remediate seemed like a win-win proposition. The "troubled" children would go somewhere else for better access to the help required for their special needs. Teachers would be relieved of the stress and responsibility of teaching their most difficult students. The other children in the class would also benefit by having less distraction and more attention from the teacher. The only problem with this thinking was that, in most cases, the children who were identified and removed were not being "fixed" and returned to general education. In reality, society was discarding these children and placing them out of sight in the same way it ignores whatever it deems unpleasant. Most of these children were sent to special classrooms, schools, or institutions where they continued to fall further behind the children in the classes they had once been. Instead of overcoming their disabilities, they, in most cases, continued to lose ground educationally, emotionally, and socially. By being grouped with other children with disabilities, they were robbed of all of the naturally occurring positive role modeling that comes with interaction within the general population. Children removed from real-world encounters and placed in special classrooms have no opportunity to learn from the same positive and negative experiences that are available to all other children in our society. Although the original intentions of special education were undoubtedly good, the cost-cutting decision to force like children into groups in separate settings has been inhibiting at best. In the case of autism, specialized separate education has been disastrous. The truth is, separate and remediate as a philosophy for autism education does not work.

Teaching a child through an exclusionary method that does not include the naturally occurring proportions of society also excludes him from becoming a functioning member of that society. An educational system based on diagnosis lacks diversity. The teachers of specialized classrooms face far more serious challenges on a daily basis than general education teachers do. The children are often forced to endure lower expectations and fewer opportunities. The teachers of these separated classrooms are far more often overworked and overwhelmed. Reportedly, the average burnout rate for a new special education teacher in the United States is between two and three years. This means that on the average, every two and a half years your child will lose the person that has been trusted to help him grow. This leaves your child with new and often inexperienced teachers to once again build that trust.

As a veteran of the public school system in the United States, I know many dedicated and well-intentioned teachers inside and outside of special education. In most cases I feel that teachers are doing a marvelous job in desperately less than ideal circumstances. These teaching heroes are making their mark while being under-paid, under-supported, and in classrooms that are under-funded. Trying to offer your child with autism an appropriate education under the current educational constructs is challenging, if not impossible, for even the best of these teachers. They too are not immune to the same burnout rate as any other teacher. For these reasons, the example I describe here is an all too true reality for far too many children.

What if, instead of labeling and removing, every teacher was taught the best methods for teaching all children? Then every child would have an equal

Teaching a child through an exclusionary method that does not include the naturally occurring proportions of a society also excludes him from becoming a functioning member of that society.

chance of achieving even the loftiest goals. Children with disabilities would have age appropriate role models in their classes from whom to learn. Children without disabilities would be able to learn about diversity and acceptance. Children would not be removed from their home schools to be educated with children whom they will likely never see in their local neighborhoods. Children with social and communication difficulties would no longer have to come home after school, only to look out the window at a group of local children whom they do not know, playing a game they were never taught to play.

In much of the world, segments of society are now beginning to understand the injustices that accompany the philosophy of separate and remediate. Instead of continuing down this ever-narrowing path, these enlightened individuals and institutions are choosing to teach in inclusive settings rather than exclusive ones. They are looking for ways to become better teachers instead of expecting children to be better students and are learning better ways to teach all children, not just the ones that make teaching easy and fun.

This book is not about educational reform. It is about sharing a better teaching method that can help all teachers teach all students in the most productive way.

As a parent of a child with autism, you will undoubtedly be advised at some point or even bullied into allowing your child to be removed and remediated. Understanding why this concept is fundamentally inappropriate and potentially limiting to your child will be your best defense. Grasping the importance of this perspective will help you to stand up and fight for what your child truly deserves: the right to a fair and appropriate education based on your child's needs and not those of a cash-strapped school system.

This book is not about educational reform. It is, however, about sharing with you a better teaching methodology that can help all teachers teach all students in the most productive way. More importantly, it is about helping you to understand how ABA/VB is the best way that you can teach the child with autism in your life all the skills that he has not acquired naturally.

Informed parents of children with autism know that the more their child is in an ABA/VB-rich environment the faster he will be able to learn the skills he needs. These parents also know that every interaction their child engages in is teaching him something. The question then becomes "What is it that he is learning from these interactions?" In many countries educating your child at home is against the law. This law was designed for the protection of your child's right to learn. For parents of children with autism, this law is often accomplishing the opposite. Schools generally have the best interests of a child at heart. School districts are usually willing to make adjustments to a child's education if they think it will help. They will even give your child additional support, if it does not disrupt the other children's education or cost too much. What you will likely find, however, is that they often have not been made aware of the many new and effective techniques available in the field of autism. However, many schools have been lucky enough to meet families who are successfully using ABA/VB with their child at home. But, even with this awareness, lack of funds to attend conferences, as well as the costs of covering classrooms with substitutes, makes it very difficult for teachers to participate in outside training opportunities. The most dedicated teachers will find a way to learn what they need to know. This might include reading books like this one or paying their own way to seminars and workshops about ABA/VB. In Germany, for example, the understanding about autism is at such a low level that even the autism specialists are often unaware of how best to help a family in need. It is hardly reasonable to expect that a local kindergarten teacher will have ever even heard of ABA/VB, let alone be well versed in it enough to help your child through its use. The legal necessity of sending your child to school "no matter what," combined with schools that often do not understand how to help children with autism becomes a Catch 22 of the worst kind. Enlightened parents are often forced to watch as their children are exposed to six hours or more of ineffective or counterproductive experiences each school day. Many of these children begin to develop serious problematic behavior at school that begins to invade the family's home life. For some very sweet and caring children with autism the school environment may create a second child. I cannot tell you the number of times I have visited a child at home and at school and felt that what I was seeing was two completely different children. Often children with autism at home are given the opportunity and security to develop language that they never demonstrate at school. At school, these same children develop disruptive behavior that the parents have never seen at home.

Gene is one such child with autism who began his formalized education in a typical kindergarten, but was removed to a "special" school for the developmentally disabled because of his social and language deficits. Gene's parents originally felt that this placement would answer their prayers for Gene. For the first time, nobody was calling home to complain about Gene's lack of

Once aware of its benefits, the most dedicated teachers will find a way to learn what they need to know about ABA/VB.

motivation, ability, or strange behavior. Additionally, when mom and dad asked how Gene was doing, the answers were always positive. But as the weeks wore on, Gene's behavior started to change at home. Within months of moving to the new school, Gene was losing his temper more quickly and once lost, he was starting to display aggressive behavior such as yelling, growling, and even biting at others.

With the increase in Gene's behavior problems, the family began looking for additional help. Gene's parents invited Knospe-ABA into their home to develop a program. Upon arrival our team found Gene to be a very quiet and sweet child. We were caught completely off guard the first time he attacked us. It took all of our training to be able to protect ourselves. At the insistence of Gene's parents, members of our team were allowed to observe Gene in school. Several glaring problems appeared almost immediately. The first was boredom. Although Gene was not demonstrating his intelligence in typical ways, he was capable of soaking up every piece of information in his environment. Unfortunately, the curriculum Gene was being exposed to progressed so slowly that it was actually quite impressive how long he kept his behavior in check. Eventually, Gene had waited long enough and wanted to engage in something more stimulating. He began by whining, moving around in his seat, and leaning on one of the teachers. He started using simple requests for items such as music, book, or letter blocks. These requests were shushed and Gene was pushed back into a seated position. At that time his stereotypical language began. He started quoting books and movies, repeating phrases his teachers had said to him such as "can't read your book now." Eventually Gene stood up and attempted to turn on some music. When his teacher attempted to stop him, Gene lunged at her trying with all his might to bite her. This attacking behavior led to both teachers engaging Gene in a 10-minute physical struggle for control. Once Gene had stopped his aggression, he was sent into a side classroom to lie on a mattress and read his favorite book. It was reported that this type of interaction repeated itself more than ten times each day. Often with more severity than was witnessed that day.

Gene was given all of the things that parents are told they should want: A classroom with a low student/teacher ratio, specialized and trained teachers, speech and language, occupational and physical therapists, and an autism specialist on staff. However, nearly every interaction Gene experienced in this school was teaching him away from recovery. It was obvious that Gene was being given too little mental stimulation. Additionally, every appropriate attempt by Gene to ask for an increase in his mental stimulation (music, reading, playing with letters, etc.) was being put on extinction. Then when Gene's extinction burst behavior became too difficult to handle, his teachers reinforced this more difficult behavior by allowing him to achieve his original goal of more mental stimulation. Without a firm understanding of the basic principles and procedures of good behavior analysis, Gene's special education classroom was encouraging inappropriate behavior, extinguishing appropriate requests, and reinforcing aggressive behavior. In only a few months this form of behavioral education caused Gene to become a completely different child at school than he was at home.

The normal reaction is that the school starts to believe that the parents are incorrect, in denial, or just plain lying when they talk of their child's abilities.

When this divide in behavior begins, the normal reaction is that the school starts to believe that the parents are incorrect, in denial, or just plain lying when they talk of the skills and behavior that their child demonstrates at home. Then, when parents complain about the school's low expectations or their child's lack of progress or appropriate placement, the school feels that the parents are incapable of offering objective advice and they begin to disregard their suggestions. Luckily the United States government has recognized the problems with this situation and has passed into law the Individuals with Disabilities Education Act (IDEA) that gives parents of children with disabilities a series of rights and procedures they can follow when they feel their children are being denied access to a fair and appropriate education. This is unfortunately not true in many European countries where the schools have the right to force your child to attend but will lead you to believe that they can exact sole decision-making power in how your child will be educated. To parents, it often seems that the school has no legal responsibility to find a better way to teach their child. Then, as their child's behavior problems increase and their deficits continue to grow, so does the rift between the parents and the school. The only clear option for a parent in these situations is to find a way to convince the school to adopt a similar approach to teaching as has been successfully implemented at home.

It becomes imperative that you find a way to keep your child surrounded with adults who understand him and ABA/VB.

If your child is going to spend a majority of his life in school, it becomes imperative that you find a way to keep him surrounded with adults who understand him and ABA/VB. Many times this has to be done at your own expense. Sometimes it can be accomplished by inviting your child's teachers to see your home program. It might include paying for your teachers to attend ABA/VB workshops in the teacher's free time. Other times it will require getting your behavior analyst invited into the school environment to offer advice to the school staff on the best methods of interacting with your child.

The need for consistent motivation and effective reinforcement makes most children with autism reliant on one-to-one teaching in the beginning years of a program. This holds true in a school setting as well as in the home. Even having two or three students to one teacher is often too many to help a child with autism reach or even approximate his true learning potential. If a child needs one-to-one teaching to be successful, then in a two-to-one teaching setting he will be successful no better than one-half of the time. In a three-to-one setting, his success rate drops to 33% or less. When you know that this is the situation, it becomes very difficult to get excited about an integrated classroom ratio of approximately ten-to-one or even a special education classroom where the numbers are usually no better than four or five-to-one. Even in these types of specialized teaching settings, a majority of children with autism will flounder without an additional one-to-one aide trained specifically for them. When your child cannot access the school curriculum without one-to-one help, a school-aide can be trained to observe him in structured and free time activities to make sure that most every interaction becomes a productive learning experience. This integration helper can guide your child's learning, keep him at his most motivated to participate, consequence his behavior choices in productive ways, and act as a social facilitator between your child and the other children.

The need for consistent motivation and reinforcement makes most children with autism reliant on one-to-one teaching in the beginning years of a program.

Compounding the problem is that children with autism who are receiving an intensive one-to-one program tend to move through learning tasks quickly. The slower a curriculum moves the more difficult it becomes to keep the child motivated. The problem with typical small ratio classrooms such as integrated or self-contained classes, is that they usually also come with lessened expectations and remediation. Considering that children with autism often need one-to-one help but also benefit from a more typical rate of instruction and high expectations, only one conclusion can usually be drawn. Ensuring positive learning interactions for your child in school is usually best done with an ABA/VB trained one-to-one school aide in a regular education classroom. For children who have the most severe issues, time in a self-contained special education class or integrated classroom might be a logical preparatory step.

However, regardless of placement, for most children with autism who have more than minor deficits, a well-trained one-to-one aide is essential for even adequate progress.

Finding support from your local school or government agency on the necessity of a one-to-one aide is challenging. Convincing them that a regular classroom holds more benefit for your child can be equally difficult. One argument frequently used to dissuade parents seeking one-to-one support for their child is to equate a one-to-one behavioral education with providing your child with a luxury automobile. The intention is to indicate that the school is only legally bound to offer your child a suitable education and you are unreasonable to expect something above average. Although schools are only responsible for offering appropriate or suitable education to your child, the automobile analogy is false. When confronted with this analogy, your response should indicate that an appropriate educational outcome for your child requires nothing more than dependable transportation. For a child with autism, ABA/VB with a one-to-one aide is both reasonable and appropriate because your child requires additional resources to achieve his potential. Teaching without these important resources is like asking your child with autism to ride down the freeway on a bicycle.

Teaching without ABA/VB is better compared to asking your child with autism to ride down a freeway on a bicycle.

Many schools will help you find the right placement and program for your child. However, since labeling and removing children has historically been the way the system tends to operate, it is often difficult to convince your local school to consider alternatives. Try not to fight for your child's educational rights alone. Bring your Behavior Analyst or other specialists who can speak to the quality of your child's progress in a home program. It helps to have written recommendations from your child's physician and therapists. The bottom line is that when it comes to your child's school placement and program, it will be up to you to do whatever it takes to ensure that your child has access to appropriate education. Optimistically that means having positive and productive meetings with your school staff. However, sometimes that requires changing classrooms, changing schools, or even hiring a lawyer to argue your case in court.

In the United States, affluent parents can financially afford to research available teaching methods, attend conferences, and bring the new information and techniques to their school district. These families who were well educated, knew their rights, and were financially capable of using legal means, began the process of changing the policies and programs that schools were offering to children with autism. This revolution has been occurring classroom-by-classroom and school district-by-school district for the past 10 to 15 years. Based on parental and legal pressure, some school districts in the United States have begun training their teachers in ABA/VB. The Assessment of Basic Language and Learning Skills - Revised™ (ABLLS-R™) written by Verbal Behavior specialists James Partington and Mark Sundberg has quickly become the main curriculum assessment for children with autism in these forward-moving school districts. Even in the U.S. it is still true that the disparity of service from one school district to the next is far too wide to be appropriate from a government-mandated education. It is often the impoverished areas that have the least appropriate services for children with autism. So, even though all parents are forced to send their children to local schools, children with autism who reside in affluent communities often receive a superior education with the latest techniques. This is a problem that can only be addressed by teaching all teachers newer and better methods of teaching, something that the United States has yet to do. In Germany, this classroom-by-classroom revolution is only now beginning to emerge as an increasing number of parents discover that there is something worthwhile that can be done for their children with autism. These parents are becoming their child's experts and are pushing their schools and local government agencies to begin sponsoring their ABA/VB interventions. Unfortunately, the responsibility for pushing the school and government agencies ahead falls to the parents just as it does in the United States. Parents of children with autism must often overcome expensive treatments, social isolation, and much higher than normal divorce rates. Additionally these parents are required to add educating their schools and battling the government system to their list of things to do. For this reason, I marvel at the uncompromising drive I have always witnessed from parents of children with autism. These dedicated parents are the reason I was compelled to write this book to help.

As parents, you should prepare for the fact that your job of educating your child does not end when he begins school. In fact, that is usually when your job of educating your school begins.

As a parent reading this book, prepare for the fact that your job of educating your child with autism does not end when he begins school. In fact, that is often when your job of educating your school begins. Consider reading a book called "How to Compromise with your School District without Compromising your Child" written by Gary Mayerson Esq. for ideas on how to best work with your school staff. This book is available at *www.difflearn.com.*

As a schoolteacher reading this book, you also can work to change the current educational opportunities for children with autism in your classroom, school, and district. The Carbone Clinic (www.drcarbone.com) offers an excellent workshop geared toward applying the principles of ABA/VB in a classroom setting. Additionally, you may request that your administration invite ABA/VB specialists to speak on teacher development days. Learning how to use the ABLLS-R™ assessment will also help you to assess, write goals, and teach to the developmental skills your students with autism will need. Even opening yourself up to new ideas and allowing a one-to-one integration helper to assist you in your teaching can make all the difference in the world for a child in need.

Gene was the boy who had developed a second, aggressive personality after transferring to a special education school. Knospe-ABA's first step with Gene was to find and train a one-to-one aide. The next was to move Gene from his self-contained special education classroom to an integrated classroom with one-to-one help. The more one-to-one support Gene received from his ABA/VB trained integration helper, the more he participated in learning throughout his day. The more he participated the more he learned. Our team did everything possible to make Gene's entire school day work to his benefit. Additionally, a strong behavior plan was developed to help Gene make better choices when he was frustrated. Although the process wasn't easy, Gene was able to move back to his home school in a regular education classroom with one-to-one support in less than two year's time. With the support of his local school administration and teachers, Gene's language skills and tolerance level have improved vastly. For the first time, Gene's school and family are starting to see the extent of Gene's capabilities. Gene now amazes his typically developing classmates by completing his work in less than one-half the time they do. He uses his extra time to study skills from the next grade level. With the help of his school aide, Gene is ever more capable of overcoming his frustrations in appropriate ways, and for the first time in years, Gene's abilities in school are now matching his abilities at home. Although, he still has a long way to go before anyone would consider using the word recovered, Gene is an appreciated and valued member of his class and he loves going to school! Even if recovery from autism remains out of reach for Gene, it was our insistence on always teaching toward recovery that has allowed him to come so far so fast. It is this insistence on continuing to teach toward recovery that will offer the world a glimpse of Gene's ultimate potential. All that Gene ever needed to succeed was a supportive school setting

As a schoolteacher, you can also work to change the current educational opportunities for children with autism in your classroom, school, and district.

designed to look past his peculiarities and to respect him enough to understand him and teach to his needs.

Working through the current school system in Gene's hometown to give Gene the opportunities from which he is now flourishing was not an easy process. It took much time and effort by all parties involved. There is an adage that fits well here, "nothing worthwhile is ever easy." In the case of educating a child with autism, this is certainly true. Changing your child's perception of the world, while changing the world's perception of your child, is a difficult job that takes much time and energy. Having the help of an autism parent support network such as the Internet groups detailed at the end of this book can provide the help and advice that you will need. Once parents realize that they are not alone in their challenges, they usually find the strength they need to succeed. Every new family that joins the battle adds a little something to the collective understanding of how to make each child's education a success. Embracing the help that is available from the online autism community has already begun revolutionizing autism awareness and education in many of the world's classrooms and homes. Be sure to tap into these resources and make the most of them for your child's education as well.

Nothing worthwhile is ever easy. In the case of educating a child with autism, this is certainly true.

Summary of Chapter 18

Children, like adults, are unfinished. Everyone grows and learns from their daily life experiences. All children deserve access to the same social or educational advantages and challenges. Children with disabilities may need more systematic teaching, but excluding a child against the wishes of his parent based simply on an IQ test or a diagnostic label is simply and unequivocally wrong (page 258).

Teaching a child through an exclusionary method that does not include the naturally occurring proportions of society also excludes him from becoming a functioning member of that society (page 260).

As a parent of a child labeled with autism, you will undoubtedly be advised at some point or even bullied into allowing your child to be removed and remediated. Understanding why this concept is fundamentally inappropriate and potentially limiting to your child will be your best defense. Grasping the importance of this perspective will help you to stand up and fight for what your child truly deserves: the right to a fair and appropriate education based on your child's needs and not those of a cash-strapped school system (page 261).

If your child is going to spend a majority of his life in school, it becomes imperative that you find a way to keep him surrounded with adults who understand him and ABA/VB (page 264).

Ensuring positive learning interactions for your child in school is usually best done with an ABA/VB trained one-to-one school aide in a regular education classroom. For children who have the most severe issues, time in a self-contained special education class or integrated classroom might be a logical preparatory step. However, regardless of placement, for most children with autism who have more than minor deficits, a well-trained one-to-one aide is essential for even adequate progress (page 265).

Prepare for the fact that your job of educating your child with autism does not end when he begins school. In fact, that is often when your job of educating your school begins. (page 267).

Chapter 19

The Ethics of ABA/VB

Some have said that the best that can be done for children with disabilities, particularly those with autism, is to simply accept them the way they were created. In my experience, most young children with autism appear to be happy people. However, many of the older children and adults with autism I have met who have not had the benefit of specialized education seem to be troubled and/or lonely. I have never been able to agree that "accepting autism" is a legitimate reason not to educate someone simply because he may be difficult to teach. In developing my philosophy, I asked myself two questions:

Is a lack of understanding that there is a better life available a blessing or a curse?

Is being happy in a tiny fish bowl enough, or is it our responsibility to show the fish in that bowl that there is a better way?

What if the fish in that bowl can be taught to trust enough to let himself be gently scooped up and carefully put into a larger tank with more to see and do? Once he has learned all this new tank has to offer, this fish can be moved into increasingly larger tanks until he is ready to be released into the wild to have a life of true independence and choice.

I have never been able to agree that "accepting autism" is a legitimate reason not to educate someone simply because he may be difficult to teach.

When beginning an ABA/VB program, it is essential that you consult and ideally work under the supervision of a Board Certified Behavior Analyst (BCBA). The reason for this is the sheer power of the principles of behavior. The science of ABA has the strength to make drastic changes in a person's behavior choices over a very short time. As a parent, teacher, or therapist capable of manipulating these principles, you become very important in the life of someone who will benefit from their use.

Humans have shown the capacity to inflict horrible atrocities on each other in the name of politics, religion, progress, and even love. When driving, it is not unheard of for a person to speed down the freeway with complete disregard for the safety or well being of the others on the road. Then immediately after causing an accident that could forever change the life of innocent people, this same individual who caused the accident might turn around and demonstrate heroic acts of bravery to try and save those he has injured. A car is not an inherently ethical or unethical device. How the car is used determines whether driving the car is safe, effective or worthwhile. The same is true with the science of ABA.

Having a detailed evidence based series of behavioral strategies at your disposal comes with a great responsibility.

There is nothing inherently ethical or unethical about applying the principles of behavior to your interactions with other people. Everyone uses these principles in countless ways each day. These principles are the reasons behind the many complex skills and behavior choices all humans make. However, having a detailed and evidence based series of behavioral strategies at your disposal comes with a great responsibility. That responsibility demands you use these principles only for the benefit of your child and only in ways that are meaningful and important to his life or well being.

There is no single approach to addressing an issue or deficit with which your child with autism lives. Ten different ABA consultants could conceivably provide you with ten different strategies. All of these approaches might give you the ability to gain your desired results. Some of the approaches might be based on positive reinforcement, while others might choose to use negative reinforcement, punishment, or extinction procedures. Many could use a combination of all of the above. When deciding how your child should be educated, you should always have these procedures explained to you in their connection to the underlying principles that support their use. When deciding if any one way is appropriate for you and your child, consider if this procedure is not only the most effective but also the most ethical approach available. Sometimes this is a difficult decision. In life, people are often asked to make short-term sacrifices to reach long-term success. Teaching your child to look past his immediate desire to see the greater benefit is an important aspect of his education. The difficulty is in knowing exactly how much sacrifice the end result is worth. Obviously, you will be navigating a tremendous amount of grey area. However, the same is true with any decisions made in the rearing of any child. Is it ethical to stop giving your child without disabilities an allowance based on his performance in school? Is it ethical to pay him for good grades? Is it ethical for a teacher to put a child's name on the board when he has not finished an assignment? Is it ethical to put him in the corner of the room for disruptive talking in class? Should a teacher be allowed to strike a child for any reason? Is it ethical to pick up your three-year-old child and physically put him in the car if he is refusing? At what age should you stop physically forcing an unwilling child into a car? Your answer to these questions will likely be very different from the answers of others reading this book. What is considered ethical in the education of a child is always a difficult question that is open to debate. The current laws that govern the land in which the family resides determine the ethics for a certain child. Even within these laws comes much room for ambiguity that can only be determined by the child's parents.

Teaching your child to look past his immediate desire to see the greater benefit is an important aspect of his education.

The point is that even in a perfect world void of the difficulty of developmental disorders, the individuals in charge often decide what is considered ethical--be it the government, the teacher, or the parent. When you are the parent of a child with autism, the task of negotiating these ethical concerns is often more formidable, especially when all of the usual techniques for teaching have proven unsuccessful. Even if you do not use an approach to ABA with your child, you must address the many ethical questions related to your child's care. Is it ethical to allow your child to stay in diapers at the age of 6 or 12 or 20? Is it ethical to give in to your child's every demand until he can no longer live at home? Is it ethical to allow an environment where one of your children is physically or verbally abusive to your other children or spouse? Is it ethical to sacrifice your family's quality of life for a child who has grown out of control?

The benefit of having the advice and assistance of a Board Certified Behavior Analyst (BCBA) is that you will know that this person has been through a rigorous education and testing process that demonstrates a level of mastery of the science of ABA including its principles, strategies, and techniques. It also means that he or she has studied, demonstrated, and maintained what is considered by an objective credentialing body to be an exemplary level of ethical standards in the field.

A person who uses VB (or any other technique or intervention that you would like to know more about) may not be qualified to help you educate your child toward recovery. Many people claiming to use VB are actually using traditional ABA while incorporating Skinner's behavioral classification of language without concern for EO, errorless learning, three types of teaching and other important VB advancements. An Internet search will help you find independent recommendations about individual's competency. Before you enlist the services of a behavioral consultant, be sure he or she can identify and teach to the needs of your child and knows how effectively to turn the table on autism through a comprehensive manipulation of the environment and not your child.

Remember, you are your child's expert and you are in control. Not every technique is right for you or your child's specific needs. Only you can make this determination. If you ever suspect that someone's approach is less than appropriate, you should be willing to question, and if necessary, refuse him. The numbers of good ABA providers well outnumber the bad, but you must still guard against making an unwise choice. ABA/VB is neither ethical nor unethical. ABA, as well as any other intervention, may be used ethically or not, depending on the decisions made by the person using the techniques.

It is much less likely for someone to cross an ethical boundary line now than it was in the early days of behavior therapy when the science did not have the mass amounts of data-driven positive support strategies and techniques now available. Therapists working without the advancements of modern ABA/VB may have successfully taught children important skills but often the child worked more out of the desire to end teaching than any real desire to learn. Minus the motivational aspects of VB, traditional ABA providers often needed to force a child to participate in order to teach him that participation led to reinforcement. It was this forced submission to instruction that had rightfully made early versions of traditional ABA difficult for many families to consider as a viable option throughout the 1970s and early 1980s. Any discussion about the ethical treatments in behaviorism or warnings you may have heard about ABA from your local autism authorities would have come from these early

You are your child's expert and you are in control. Not every technique is right for your child and only you can make this determination.

ABA is neither ethical nor unethical. ABA, as well as any other intervention, may be used ethically or not, depending on the decisions made by the person using the techniques.

years of development. In fact, anyone who might advise you against using ABA is likely sharing an uninformed opinion from what they have heard about the behavior modification programs of the 1970s without any concept of the progress of the past 25 years.

Luckily as our understanding of how responsibly and ethically to apply the principles of ABA has increased, any warnings of ethical concern dissipated. The widespread use of positive reinforcement procedures such as differential reinforcement of other behaviors (DRO) has replaced the aversive techniques of early ABA. Using extinction instead of positive punishment procedures is now the recommended approach to reducing problem behavior in most programs. Understanding the best ways to manipulate the delivery and type of reinforcement has also made ABA a much more effective and ethical approach to autism education. But it was the addition of the VB approach to ABA that brought us the establishing operation (EO) that has removed the necessity of forcing a child to submit to teaching from the equation completely. With the seven steps to instructional control, it is now possible to teach through manipulation of the environment and not the child. In the hands of caring parents and under the supervision of a BCBA *www.bacb.com* difficult programming decisions can be made without ever approaching the line of what you would consider ethical for your child. For these reasons, when used correctly, the VB approach to ABA may not only be the most effective education possible for autism and its related disorders but the most ethical as well.

When used correctly, the VB approach to ABA may not only be the most effective education possible for autism and its related disorders but the most ethical as well.

Summary of Chapter 19

Having a detailed and evidence based series of behavioral strategies at your disposal comes with a great responsibility. That responsibility demands you use these principles only for the benefit of your child and only in ways that are meaningful and important to his life or well being (page 272).

Teaching your child to look past his immediate desire to see the greater benefit is an important aspect of his education. The difficulty is in knowing exactly how much sacrifice the end result is worth (page 273).

The benefit of having the advice and assistance of a Board Certified Behavior Analyst (BCBA) is that you will know that this person has been through a rigorous education and testing process that demonstrates a level of mastery of the science of ABA including its principles, strategies, and techniques. It also means that he or she has studied, demonstrated, and maintained what is considered by an objective credentialing body to be an exemplary level of ethical standards in the field (page 273).

Remember, you are your child's expert and you are in control. Not every technique is right for you or your child's specific needs. Only you can make this determination. If you ever suspect that someone's approach is less than appropriate, you should be willing to question, and if necessary, refuse him (page 274).

ABA/VB is neither ethical nor unethical. ABA, as well as any other intervention, may be used ethically or not, depending on the decisions made by the person using the techniques (274).

When used correctly, the VB approach to ABA may not only be the most effective education possible for autism and its related disorders but the most ethical as well (page 275).

Chapter 20

ABA/VB and RDI™

Relational Development Intervention (RDI™), developed by Steven E. Gutstein, PhD, is one of the curriculum options that was discussed as part of what to teach your child with autism and related disorders in Chapter 16. Additionally, RDI™ (*www.rdiconnect.com*) includes its own sets of guidelines and procedures designed to answer the question of <u>how</u> to teach your child. RDI™ is designed to enable parents to teach "dynamic intelligence skills" and motivation to their children. Its stated goals include helping children with autism become more flexible thinkers and to adapt more easily to ever-changing environments. It also focuses on helping your child master the interactive skills he needs to form relationships outside the family.

Dr. Gutstein, his wife, and associates originally designed RDI™ in response to concerns about older methods of ABA. For many years in an attempt to be objective, these older forms of ABA recommended a strict impersonal approach to teaching. Because compliance training took precedence, some ABA providers regularly used aversive techniques including physical manipulation or restraint in order to force learning on unwilling learners. Parents were seldom involved in the development or implementation of therapy. Positive relationships between therapist and student were considered unnecessary or disruptive to good teaching. Many prior therapy procedures were designed around teaching in the intensive trial teaching (ITT) environment. Table teaching was rote and repetitive. Because of the inflexible and often counterproductive procedures used in ABA during that time, children were not encouraged to seek or desire social interaction nor did the method foster interaction or experience sharing. Indeed, experience sharing, as defined by Dr. Gutstein, was often inadvertently extinguished. Consequently, many children were inept when it came to forming relationships with others. Although attempts were made to help socialize these children, they were often incapable of adapting to new situations or people and were unable to form meaningful or lasting friendships. Thus, much of the world misunderstood traditional ABA as little more than animal training adapted for human use. Too frequently, this older and less successful form of ABA comes to mind when professionals outside of the ABA world advise parents who are exploring available programs. RDI™ proponents in particular point to the failures of traditional ABA forms to support their contention that their program is a better way.

The VB approach to ABA is diametrically opposed to these antiquated methods of teaching and through the liberal use of pairing procedures had already made extraordinary gains over traditional ABA as a social relationship intervention. However, at the same time that VB was being developed to answer the procedural shortcomings of traditional ABA, Dr. Gutstein and his associates began using a different approach to intervention. He designed his approach specifically to teach to the areas of social experience sharing in which most children with autism were deficient. Dr. Gutstein studied the needs of children who had learned many skills through the teaching procedures of traditional ABA. He concluded that the procedures used to teach these children skills did not foster social experience sharing and in many instances obstructed the development of social goals. Therefore, from a desire to find a better way, he began to develop and then trademarked his recommended compilation of teaching procedures and curriculum called RDI.™

The developers of RDI™ claim that their program addresses the core deficits of autism. This claim to teach to autism's "core deficits" serves the developers purpose of making RDI™ the most important therapy option. However, no one owns ABA/VB and it is not trademarked. There is no opportunity for an individual to make blanket statements about what autism is,

At the same time that VB was being developed to answer the procedural shortcomings of traditional ABA, Dr. Gutstein began using a different approach to intervention.

what information should cost, or what procedures all other followers of the approach are expected to accept. Instead, ABA/VB is guided solely by the scientific data supporting its use. Because of this ABA/VB does not claim a core deficit to autism. In my study and experience, autism is not a thing that has a core deficit. In most cases, autism is a biological predisposition to a combination of several specific behavior deficits that children exhibit. This behavioral predisposition can manifest itself in severe pervasive developmental delays. Therefore, having an intervention that only focuses on a "core deficit" is ineffective because it ignores the other areas of deficit that normally result as a part of autism.

RDI™ proponents believe that teaching without the pressure of consistent S^Ds and artificial reinforcement allows children to begin to invent their own language and desire to interact with others as opposed to being "trained" to do so. ABA proponents point to the fact that ABA is based on the proven principles of behavior and each procedure is developed over time with exacting standards of study and experimentation. These studies are peer reviewed and in many cases independently replicated. As a group, behaviorist's tend to feel that any other options need to have met these same exacting standards before being worthy of consideration. In addition, there is a concern that focusing solely on social relationship development will cause children in RDI™ programs to miss the many other important learning skills they need to become fully functioning independent adults. Although there is anecdotal evidence that RDI™ has helped some advanced and naturally vocal children with autism in meaningful ways, I have seen no independent data supporting the use of RDI.™ I have also heard anecdotal reports that RDI™ is often lacking when attempting to help early learners, especially non-vocal learners and children demonstrating a strong desire for control. The belief in the greater ABA community is that foregoing the proven principles of ABA and focusing exclusively on RDI™ is a potentially dangerous experiment for most families of children with autism with an unattractive risk to reward ratio.

I agree with the assessment of early ABA methods espoused by RDI™ proponents. The procedures used prior to VB were in many ways limiting to a child's ability and desire to participate in relationship development. However, I also feel that the RDI™ program is a case of throwing the baby out with the bathwater. RDI™ used outside of the context of a good ABA/VB program is an

In my study and experience, autism is not a thing that has a core deficit.

The belief in the greater ABA community is that focusing exclusively on RDI™ is a potentially dangerous experiment for most families.

attempt to ignore reinforcement, extinction, EO (motivation), and other proven principles of behavior. Thus, parents using any program that does not teach to these important principles often flounder when things do not go as they are told to expect. In my experience, traditional ABA and RDI™ are polar opposites that have a perfect middle ground. That middle ground is ABA/VB. A good VB program keeps the principles of behavior in the forefront while looking at teaching as more of a fluid process predicated on the desires of the child. However, some of the teaching recommendations of RDI™ deserve a closer look. RDI™ is in many cases an approach and set of goals that can strengthen the social interaction and relationship developments skills of a child in an ABA/VB program.

A parent's choice should not focus on which program is better, but which RDI™ goals and program recommendations can be used to help boost the social development intervention of their ABA/VB program.

A parent's choice should not focus on which program is better, but which RDI™ goals and program recommendations can be used to help boost the social development intervention of their ABA/VB program. Upon closer inspection it becomes clear that RDI™ and ABA/VB are more alike than their respective practitioners would have you believe. RDI™ recommends that about 75% of your interactions be based on the use of non-verbal and declarative language. Declarative language uses words that share thoughts, ideas, and feelings. It does not ask for a response from your child. RDI™ attempts to use this declarative language to teach children a desire to share of themselves through positive modeling and fun. The RDI™ complaint about older ABA and even some ABA/VB is that ABA in general relies too heavily on imperative language. Imperative language requires a response. Most S^Ds (instructions) in ABA are imperative. To some degree, I think Dr Gutstein may be right. When you are taught always to speak to your child in S^Ds, you often lose the ability to share in the joy of your child. When your child is taught to communicate through required response, he also may not learn to share in the joy of you.

In the second step of instructional control detailed in Chapter 5, it is recommended that pairing yourself with reinforcement should be 75% of all of your interactions with your child. Some ABA/VB consultants will recommend that you begin to cheat on this ratio as a child becomes a more willing learner. Some consultants will eventually work their way toward a 50/50 work/pairing relationship. However, whenever one of our therapists or parents forgo the 75% pairing to 25% S^D ratio, teaching becomes more about negative reinforcement and escape extinction procedures rather than positive giving experiences. Negative reinforcement is the process of reinforcing a behavior by removing something from the environment to increase the use of the desired behavior. In most cases, the item you take away will be some form of an aversive. Negative reinforcement is a perfectly valid way to build skills. However, whenever a parent, teacher, or therapist resorts to negative reinforcement, teaching often becomes the process of "If you work hard for me, I will leave you alone." As discussed in Chapter 5, the abundant use of negative reinforcement in any program impedes the concept of teaching toward recovery. Your child will be working because of a motivation to end teaching. Conversely, consistently following the seven steps to instructional control as outlined in Chapters 5 and 6 and taking possible control needs into consideration (Chapter 7), your teaching will be based on positive reinforcement procedures. Positive reinforcement means consistently adding enjoyable items and actions to your child's environment. Doing so will not only lead to skill acquisition but will increase your child's desire to learn as well as his desire to earn and maintain your relationship.

The problem with pairing as a concept in ABA/VB is that it is not well defined. Pairing is a process of playing with your child. Thus, making his daily experience more enjoyable when he is with you than when he is without you. Good pairing does not include the use of S^Ds (instructions). In fact, it only took about one page of this book to explain how best to pair with your child. If you think about it, only one page of what you have read so far discusses what you should be doing with 75% of the time you are with your child. The remainder of this book discusses in extreme detail what you should be doing during the 25% of the time you are not engaged in pairing procedures.

If RDI™ recommends approximately 75% of your interactions to be declarative language and ABA/VB recommends that 75% of your interaction to be without S^Ds (imperative language), then both recommendations are identical. However, rather than pointing to a "core deficit" of autism ABA/VB recognizes that every child with autism is affected in a different way. Consequently, individual children have differing sets of developmental delays in four learning areas. These areas are behavior, general learning skills, communication, and social interaction. In fact, the 1999 Surgeons General report on mental health that recommends ABA interventions for autism identifies these exact deficit areas. Teaching to each of these deficits takes a special consideration. Behavior deals with your child's ability to make decisions that foster positive results. General learning skills include topics such as visual performance, fine and gross motor skills, grooming, toileting, eating, and many of the other important non-communicative functions of daily life. Communication means teaching to all of Skinner's Behavioral Classifications of Language. The final area of deficit is social interaction. Social interaction refers to a child's desire to participate in interactions with others, share himself emotionally and find joy in the individual personalities of others.

If you are to teach toward recovery, you must teach to all of these deficits in any proportion they present themselves in the case of your specific child. Traditional ABA methods used the principles of behavior to address autistic behavior and general learning skills in increasingly better ways over the years. Today these areas are reasonably easy to teach to, even when working with severely affected children with autism. VB has improved the methods of teaching behavior and general learning skills by adding an understanding of EO (motivation) to the equation. VB has also developed an extremely successful way of teaching to the communication deficits where traditional ABA often failed. This development in the teaching of communication skills comes from the analysis of verbal behavior, which includes methods and procedures to teach to Skinner's "Behavioral Classification of Language." However, even the best ABA/VB programs only offer a very general description of how to teach your child to desire participation in learning through pairing. Most attempts at teaching social skills in traditional ABA were developed around instructions, responses, artificial reinforcement, and involved social scripting. However, I feel that the makeup of relationship development comes not from what a child is told or asked to do but from what he chooses to do in order to maintain an interaction with a particular person. It is during the 75% of time spent pairing with a child, that you are purposely not eliciting, prompting, or reinforcing responses. It is only during this pairing time that the child is allowed to make the necessary choices to explore the joy of others and spontaneously share feelings of his own. Similar to the beliefs of RDI,™ I feel that the way to teach social experience sharing and a desire for social relationships is in large part through the 75% of teaching time that we are simply pairing with a child.

Although the scientific research demonstrating the effectiveness of RDI™ procedures is either nonexistent or currently not independently replicated, my opinion is that it is quite possibly a step in the right direction toward finding the missing parts of this final piece to the autism intervention puzzle. What I feel is still missing in even good ABA/VB is the understanding of how to use our pairing time to target the many subtle individual steps involved in building a child's desire to participate in interactions that are purely social in function. This would include the child's desire to socially reinforce others. The RDI™ program uses non-verbal games, social referencing, and declarative statements in large quantities, among other program recommendations to teach to the fourth category of learning deficit that comes with autism. This category is social interaction or more specifically the experience sharing part of social interaction.

Using the principles of ABA in concert with the procedures of VB best prepares you to address all four deficit categories of behavior, general learning skills, communication, and social interaction. However, by more effectively using the time you are not presenting S^Ds (imperative language) through the procedures of RDI,™ you may be able more systematically to address social experience sharing deficits that for some children pairing alone will not overcome.

Every procedure used in RDI™ can be behaviourally defined.

Although many of the techniques have been given different names, every procedure used in RDI™ can be behaviorally defined. The concept of a "master-apprentice relationship" mirrors the modern definition of instructional control. "Productive uncertainty" is a version of the ABA concept of teaching loosely. The RDI™ recommendation of using "temptations" is a non-behavioral way to explain the importance of the Establishing Operation (EO). Additionally, the RDI™ recommendation that parents help their child "give up control in the teaching setting" is another way to explain the importance of restriction of reinforcement. Finally, both RDI™ and ABA/VB recommend that most interventions should be parent instead of therapist driven.

The main difference between ABA/VB and RDI™ is that ABA/VB procedures and principles are experimentally demonstrated effective in detailing exactly what to do with your child during the 25% of time you are using imperative language. While RDI™ is filled with promising but mostly unproven recommendations of how you should use your 75% pairing time to teach to social experience sharing goals.

Rich or poor, all parents have a limit to the amount of time, energy, and money available to them to educate their child toward recovery. So how do you use this yin and yang of ABA/VB and RDI™ to decide where to best allocate your limited resources? This depends on what you have already experienced and to what areas of deficit most significantly affect your child. If you already use the best methods of ABA/VB to help teach your child, you should consider looking into RDI™ so that you have a more definitive set of relationship development goals to more effectively teach to during your pairing time. In many cases the basic books of RDI™ "Relationship Development Intervention with Young Children," and "Relationship Development Intervention with Children, Adolescents and Adults" along with "The RDI™ Program Progress Tracking System," and the most recent version of the RDI™ video is sufficient to achieve this goal. Conversely, if you have already begun teaching yourself how to use RDI,™ consider studying ABA/VB. Go to a few of the major workshops and consider employing a BCBA. Try to become competent at using the seven steps to instructional control to give you a complete and systematic path to developing the important Master/Apprentice relationship you must have for RDI™ success. According to his book "Relational Development Intervention for Young Children" Dr. Gutstein also believes that a good ABA/VB program might be a prerequisite to RDI.™

> *"We are often asked if there are any precursors to beginning RDI. While our activities in Stage 1 are geared towards a very basic level, they cannot be successful with a Novice who is unwilling to comply with instructions, or one who is highly defiant. These Novices are candidates for initial behavioral approaches that emphasize compliance and acceptance of direction and instruction, hopefully using positive reinforcement approaches." (page 33)*

By embracing ABA/VB you also will benefit from understanding the other principles and procedures of this book, including the concept of turning the tables on autism. These ABA/VB principles and procedures will allow you to take full advantage of the 25% percent imperative language you are allowed to use in RDI™ to best teach to your child's deficits in behavior, communication, and general learning skills.

If you are currently not familiar with either approach, the decision comes down to your child. Regardless of his social deficits, if your child is at all delayed in his behavior, communication, or general learning skills, you are best advised to focus your time and energy on the evidence based teaching techniques of ABA/VB. The ABA/VB program has an ever-growing record of accomplishment. Since ABA/VB works directly to all of your child's deficits, you may not need a detailed approach to use your pairing time more effectively for social relationship development. This was the case with Dennis, the little boy pictured on the cover that Knospe-ABA helped in February of 2005 to recover from the effects of autism. However, if your child has mastered all the skills of the ABLLS-R™ (Assessment of Basic Language and Learning Skills - Revised™) and is only showing difficulty in the area of social interaction and relationship development, it might be worth your while to look into the recommendations and goals presented by RDI.™

Because of the outstanding record of success and ever growing body of evidence supporting its use, it is strongly recommended that you make ABA/VB the main focus of your child's intervention plan. However, if you have the resources, it might be beneficial to consider RDI™ as a supplementary social relationship development approach.

If your child is at all delayed in his behavior, communication, or general learning skills, you are best advised to focus your time and energy on the evidence based teaching techniques of ABA/VB.

Summary of Chapter 20

A parent's choice should not focus on which program is better, but which RDI goals and program recommendations can be used to help boost the social development intervention of their ABA/VB program (page 280).

Similar to the beliefs of RDI™ I feel that the way to teach social experience sharing and a desire for social relationships is in large part through the 75% of teaching time that we are simply pairing with a child (page 282).

Using the principles of ABA in concert with the procedures of VB best prepares you to address all four deficit categories of behavior, general learning skills, communication, and social interaction. However, by more effectively using the time you are not presenting S^Ds (imperative language) through the procedures of RDI,™ you may be able more systematically to address social experience sharing deficits that for some children pairing alone will not overcome (page 283).

The main difference between ABA/VB and RDI™ is that ABA/VB procedures and principles are experimentally demonstrated effective in detailing exactly what to do with your child during the 25% of time you are using imperative language. While RDI™ is filled with promising but mostly unproven recommendations of how you should use your 75% pairing time to teach to social experience sharing goals (page 283).

Because of the outstanding record of success and ever growing body of evidence supporting its use, it is strongly recommended that you make ABA/VB the main focus of your child's intervention plan. However, if you have the resources, it might be beneficial to consider RDI™ as a supplementary social relationship development approach (page 285).

Chapter 21

Become Your Child's Expert and

Teach Toward Recovery

If you only gain one thing from this book, let it be this: The parent is the only person qualified to become an expert on a child.

No specialist, no author, no teacher, no physician will ever understand a child better than his parents can. As a teacher and child advocate, I see autism as a descriptive label for one segment of the typical population that for whatever reason has not learned some of the essential basic developmental skills the way that others do. A child with autism is merely an individual who has proven extremely difficult to teach. Studying the major evidence-based teaching methodologies and becoming a better teacher by applying the principles of ABA/VB has allowed me to assist in the education of many children. It is what has allowed Knospe-ABA to assist in Dennis' recovery from autism's negative effects. However, every child with or without autism is an individual. Each individual has different educational needs. It is unwise for you to believe that someone who has never met your child is more qualified than you to make therapeutic or educational decisions for him based solely on the existence of a diagnosis.

If you are a parent with a child diagnosed with autism, you will be exposed to well-intentioned naysayers who tell you that your child will never become an independent being. Once you have found the strength to reject this no hope prognostication, you will find yourself in the company of many "experts." The behavior analyst, occupational therapist, physical therapist, inclusion specialist, psychologist, pediatrician, schoolteacher and your child's family members should all become various specialists in your child's life. However, each of these specialists can give you insight only about that part of your child that they know best. The most useful specialists are generally those who have refused to specialize. Finding a Board Certified Behavior Analyst who has studied and used ABA, VB, speech, PECS, sign language, RDI™ and TEACCH methods would be a great start. Finding someone who can discuss with you the benefits of biomedicine and someone who is familiar with the pros and cons of special education will also help. It is these people who have the capacity to compare and contrast the proven options and help you apply the right tools to your child's individual needs. However, not one of these experts will ever be qualified enough to make therapy decisions without you. Regardless of how much a professional knows about his subject or subjects of specialization, it is nearly impossible for him to see your child in his totality. It is only you who has this perspective. It is only you that can make decisions based purely on your child's best interests that fall safely within your ethical boundaries. Regardless of a professional's area of specialization, even the most dedicated specialist cannot always put your child before everything else when making decisions in his care. However, you can. You are the one who will experience the proper mix of motivation and reinforcement necessary to do whatever it takes. If you can base your decisions on your informed analysis of the advice of many well-rounded professionals applied to a good understanding of your child, you will be the expert that your child needs. Becoming your child's expert requires a better understanding of your child not his medical label. You can then use this better understanding to caringly apply the proven teaching methodologies of ABA/VB to your every interaction.

To most effectively teach with ABA/VB, you must not only become your child's expert but as that expert you need to always consider yourself and your child on a long journey toward recovery. Every step you take along the way needs to be taken with the objective that it will eventually lead your child to adult independence. Regardless of how old your child is, regardless of how

The most useful specialists are generally those who have refused to specialize.

Becoming your child's expert requires a better understanding of your child not his medical label.

he is affected by the behaviors considered autistic, and regardless of his current levels of performance, the goal of ultimate independence is always your best choice. Teaching to any goal with a lesser expectation than full recovery leaves your child with a learning ceiling--a level of ability that he is not being taught to achieve. Expectations are too often limitations for a child with autism. Your child will have enough potential limitations in his life. Do not allow low expectations to limit his potential as well. What is the harm done if your child learns everything he possibly can in his lifetime but still falls short of recovery? Now compare that to a child who has lived a life of little or no expectation resulting in a life of little or no social interest or joy.

Expectations are too often limitations for a child with autism.

The best I can offer you is this: Always educate <u>toward</u> recovery. Not doing so is like starting a 5,000 piece puzzle without ever expecting to complete it. What would be the point? The pieces are there and you have the time. Plan to someday have a beautiful complete picture looking back at you. Begin with the pieces of the puzzle that are the simplest to work with and put them together one by one. Be grateful for every piece you find a place for, but always remember that each connection is only one small triumph in a long and important process. Regardless of how long it takes, there is no reason ever to stop until every piece is in place and your child can fully experience the joy of living an independent and socially fulfilling life. It is quite possible that even with the best teaching and most attentive parenting, a single lifetime might not be long enough to finish the puzzle you have been given. But you will never know this is the case unless you make the commitment lovingly to teach toward recovery and share in every success and setback along the way.

Teaching toward recovery is a better way to help your child fulfil his learning potential and become ever more successful in life.

If your teaching goals are designed to help you manage your child's behavior so that you can get through the day, you will find yourself working on that same never-ending goal twenty years down the road. Teaching toward recovery with ABA/VB is a better way. Only then will you be able systematically to help your child overcome his learning barriers without limitation. This is the best way to help your child fulfill his learning potential and become ever more successful in life.

As you begin the process of becoming your child's expert, try to keep things in perspective. Rome wasn't built in a day and neither are the world's best teachers. Give yourself time to learn the skills you will need. Do not be too hard on yourself, for you will make mistakes. We all do. Nobody is telling you that this is going to be easy. However, it is possible and you can do it. Do not allow anyone to convince you otherwise. Just do your best to get better each day and never let your teaching get in the way of the relationship you have with your child. The best way to build and maintain a positive relationship with your child is to keep yourself well paired with reinforcement. Pairing is the process of establishing yourself as a generalized reinforcer. Pairing yourself with reinforcement can be looked at as social relationship intervention. Teaching should be fun for everyone involved and your relationship should always take precedence over learning goals. Without a positive instructional relationship you cannot teach. My final piece of advice to you is this: Regardless of what you are trying to teach, whenever you are not sure what to do with your child, try more pairing. It is impossible for you to develop too good of a relationship with your child.

Much of the information contained within these pages is based on my experiences helping children with and without autism lead happier more successful lives. Applied Behavior Analysis and Verbal Behavior are sciences that rely on peer-reviewed research to determine the value of its principles and procedures. In an attempt to keep this book readable for parents, teachers, or therapists, I have specifically chosen not to present any of this kind of research or data.

It is important that you proceed with helping your child based not on what I have written, but on what you have decided is best for your child's future. This determination should come only from your analysis of the techniques, philosophies, and research available to you. With the exception of the newer developments that we have been spearheading at Knospe-ABA (Teaching Arc and Mini-consequences discussed in Chapter 14 and the conceptual discussion of control as a reinforcer for socially mediated behavior in Chapter 7), there is proven evidence available for most, if not all, of the techniques and strategies I have presented. This research can be found in the "Journal of Applied Behavior Analysis" and "The Analysis of Verbal Behavior" among others. This evidence can be found in the studies of the Lovaas Institute, The Wisconsin Early Autism Project, and many others. More evidence can be found in the workshop materials given by Dr. Partington, Dr. Sundberg, Dr. Carbone and their associates. This evidence can also be found in the Catherine Maurice book "Behavioral Interventions for Children with Autism" as well as

Whenever you are not sure what to do with your child, always try more pairing.

It is important that you proceed with helping your child based not on what I have written, but what you have decided is best for your child's future.

from many other sources including those listed in the references section at the end of this book.

Though I understand the scientific principles and techniques of ABA/VB and I use them every day to help children with autism and other related disorders to live happier more independent lives, I am not a scientist or researcher. I am a child advocate, practitioner, and teacher. I do not have the desire to ever look past the child for whom I am currently responsible. I can afford to do this only because there are researchers out there who are making the burden of proof. These unsung heroes of education are conducting the studies and publishing the results. I recommend that you critique their data and findings just as I have. Before deciding on basing your child's education on ABA/VB you should reconcile the research and evidence for yourself. Before allowing anyone else to convince you they have a better way, you should ask to see their scientific evidence as well.

There is absolutely nothing that a parent can do to cause a child to develop autism. The strong motivations and pervasive deficits that come with autism are more than any parent and most teachers would be able to overcome without specialized training and support. Remember, part of becoming your child's expert means forgiving yourself. Unwarranted feelings of guilt over past choices offer no benefit to you or your child. If you have always done the best you could for your child with the information that was available to you at the time, your job has been appropriately done. If the information of this book offers you new insights to begin making different decisions, consider this just another step along your journey toward finding a better way.

Summary of Chapter 21

The parent is the only person qualified to become an expert on a child (page 287).

Becoming your child's expert requires a better understanding of your child not his medical label. You can then use this better understanding to caringly apply the proven teaching methodologies of ABA/VB to your every interaction (page 288).

Expectations are often limitations for a child with autism. Your child will have enough potential limitations in his life. Do not allow low expectations to limit his potential as well (page 289).

If your teaching goals are designed to help you manage your child's behavior so that you can get through the day, you will find yourself working on that same never-ending goal 20 years down the road. Teaching toward recovery with ABA/VB is a better way. Only then will you be able systematically to help your child overcome his learning barriers without limitation. This is the best way to help your child fulfill his learning potential and become ever more successful in life (page 289).

Regardless of what you are trying to teach, whenever you are not sure what to do with your child, try more pairing. It is impossible for you to develop too good of a relationship with your child (page 290).

Before deciding on basing your child's education on ABA/VB you should reconcile the research and evidence for yourself. Before allowing anyone else to convince you they have a better way, you should ask to see their scientific evidence as well (page 291).

Resources

One of the main purposes of this book was to give people involved in helping educate a child diagnosed with autism spectrum disorder a place to go for useful and practical advice in how to handle daily situations. To be truly successful in this endeavor, the book must also point you in the right direction for further help. In the field of autism education, information and support comes from many sources. The following is a list of resources that will benefit you on your search for a better way to educate the child or children with autism in your life.

<u>Books</u>

Barbara, M. L.(2007). *The Verbal Behavior Approach: How to Teach Children with Autism and Related Disorders.* London: Jessica Kinglsey Publishers

Fovel, T. J. (2002). *The ABA Program Companion: Organizing Quality Programs for Children with Autism and PDD.* New York: DRL Books, Inc.

Freeman, S., & Dake, L. (1997). *Teach Me Language.* Langley, B.C. Canada: SKF Books.

Gutstein, S. E. & Sheely, R. K. (2002). *Relationship Development Intervention with Young Children: Emotional Development Activities for Asperger Syndrome, Autism, PDD and NLD.* London & Philidelphia: Jessica Kingsley Publishers.

Leaf, R., & McEachin, J. (Eds.). (1999). *A Work in Progress.* New York: DRL Books Inc.

Lovaas I. O. (2003). *Teaching Individuals with Developmental Delays: Basic Intervention Techniques,* Austin, Texas: PRO-ED, Inc.

Luckevich, D. (2004). *Language Targets to Teach a Child to Communicate.* Mercer Island, WA: Talkingwords, Inc.

Maurice C., Greene G., Luce, S. (1996). *Behavioral Intervention for Young Children with Autism: A manual for parents and professionals.* Austin, Texas: PRO-ED, Inc.

Mayerson, G. (2004). *How to Compromise with your School District without Compromising your Child: A Field Guide for Getting Effective Services for Children with Special Needs.* New York: DRL Books Inc.

Michael, J. (1993). *Concepts and principles of behavior analysis.* Kalamazoo, MI: Society for the Advancement of Behavior Analysis.

Skinner, B.F. (1991). *Verbal Behavior.* (B.F. skinner Reprint Series). Action, MA: Copley Publishing Group (Oringinal work published 1957).

Sundberg, M. L., & Partington, J.W. (1998). *Teaching Language to Children with Autism or Other Developmental Disabilities.* Pleasant Hill, CA: Behavior Analysts, Inc.

Sundberg, M. L., & Partington, J.W. (2006). *The Assessment of Basic Language and Learning Skills- Revised.* Pleasant Hill, CA: Behavior Analysts, Inc.

Parent Groups/listserv

ABAplusRDI@yahoogroups.com (http://groups.yahoo.com/group/abaplusrdi/)
Autismus-ABA@yahoogroups.de (http://groups.yahoo.de/group/aba-autismus/)
DTT-NET@yahoogroups.com (http://groups.yahoo.com/group/DTT-NET)
Verbalbehavior@yahoogroups.com(http://groups.yahoo.com/group/VerbalBehavior/)
ME-LIST@LISTSERV.IUPUI.EDU (listserv@indycms.iupui.edu - subscribe me-list)

Workshops

Bobby Newman, Ph.D. BCBA (www.room2grow.org).
Christina Burk, MA, BCBA (www.christinaburkaba.com).
Holly Kibbe, MS, BCABA, Cherish Twigg, MS, BCBA, (establishingoperationsinc.com).
James Partington, Ph.D., BCBA (www.behavioranalysts.com).
Mark Sundberg, Ph.D., BCBA (search Mark Sundberg).
Patrick McGreevy, Ph.D., P.A., BCBA (www.behaviorchange.com).
Robert Schramm, MA, BCBA (www.knospe-aba.com).
Vince Carbone Ed.D., BCBA and associates (www.drcarbone.com).

Video and DVD

Information Evening on ABA/VB from Knospe-ABA, Robert Schramm, MA, BCBA,
    (pro-aba.com).

Intensive Teaching Series: Holly Kibbe, MS, BCBA and Cherish Twigg, MS, BCBA
    (establishingoperationsinc.com).

Teaching Verbal Behavior: An Introduction to Parents Teaching Language, James Partington,
    Ph.D., BCBA, (behavioranalysts.com).

The Early Learner at Home, Juliet Burk, (Autismteachingtools.com).

The Verbal Behavior Approach to Teaching Children with Autism. Vince Carbone, Ed.D., BCBA,
    (ABAtoolchest.com).

Internet Sites

www.abainternational.org
www.abaconnections.com
www.abaresources.com
www.autismteachingtools.com
www.autismusaba.de
www.autismweb.com
www.behavioranalysts.com
www.christinaburkaba.com
www.cureautismnow.com
www.difflearn.com
www.drcarbone.com
www.establishingoperationsinc.com
www.feat.org

www.janpalmer.ca
www.knospe-aba.de
www.mariposaschool.org
www.nlconcepts.com
www.pro-aba.com
www.rdiconnect.com
www.simplifiedsigns.org
www.talkingwords.com
www.vbcommunity.org.uk
www.vbteachingtools.com
www.verbalbehavior.pbwiki.com
www.verbalbehaviornetwork.com

Journals

American Journal of Mental Retardation
Analysis of Verbal Behavior
Behavior Analyst Today
European Journal of Behavior Analysis
Experimental Analysis of Behavior
International Journal of Behavior Consultation and Therapy
Journal of Applied Behavior Analysis
Journal of Early and Intensive Behavior Intervention
Speech and Language Pathology and Applied Behavior Analysis

Verbal Behavior Schools

Janus Academy	Calgary, Alberta	www.janusacademy.com
The Bay School	Santa Cruz, CA	www.thebayschool.org
STARS School	Walnut Creek, CA	www.behavioranalysts.com
ABC Schoolhouse	Sanford, FL	www.abcschoolhouse.net
Jericho School	Jacksonville, FL	www.thejerichoschool.org
Victory School	Miami, FL	www.victoryschool.org
R.A.C.E. School	Lake Zurich, IL	www.theRACEschool.org
Applied Behavior Center	Indianapolis, IN	www.abaservicesinc.com
Little Star School	Carmel, IN	www.littlestarschool.com
VBCA	Fishers, IN	www.vbca.org
Margaret Murphy School	Freeport, ME	www.jfmhomes.org/MMCC.htm
ACT Network	Bingham, MI	www.actnetwork.org
Holland Center	Excelsior MN	www.hollandcenter.com
Special School District	St.Louis County, MO	
Rivendale Institute	Springfield, MO.	(417) 864-7921
ABC School	Winston-Salem, NC	
Garr Christian Academy	Charlotte, NC	www.garrchristianacademy.org
Mariposa School	Cary, NC	www.MariposaSchool.org
Allegro	Morristown,NJ	
Above and Beyond	Hawthorne, NJ	www.aboveandbeyondlearninggroup.com
Center for Developmental Excellence	Voorhees, NJ	www.cdeinfo.com
Interactive Kids LLC	Marlton, NJ	www.interactivekidsllc.com
NJ public schools	New Jersey	www.poac.net
Princeton Child Development Institute	Princeton, NJ	www.pcdi.org
Capital Region BOCES	Albany NY area	http://www.capregboces.org/
Carbone Clinic	Valley Cottage, NY	www.carboneclinic.com
Mohanason Schools	Schenectady County, NY	
Primetime	Rockland County, NY	
The Nexus School	Huntington Valley, PA	
PA Public School Units	Pennsylvania	www.pattan.k12.pa.us.org
		www.pavbsafe.org
Vista School	Middletown, PA	www.thevistaschool.org
Central TX Autism Center	Austin, TX	http://www.ctac1.com
Treehouse Day Center	San Antonio, TX	www.treehousepediatrics.com
Wayman Learning Center	Plano, TX	www.waymanlearningcenter.com
Aurora School	Purcellville, VA	TheAuroraSchool@aol.com

Selected Studies Supporting ABA/VB

Anderson, S. R., Avery, D. L., DiPietro, E. K., Edwards, G. L., and Christian, W. P. (1987). Intensive home-based early intervention with autistic children. Education and Treatment of Children, 10 (4), 352-366.

Baer, D. M. (1993). Commentaries on McEachin, Smith and Lovaas: Quasi-random assignment can be as convincing as random assignment. American Journal on Mental Retardation, 97 (4), 373-380.

Baer, D. M. & Sherman, J. (1964). Reinforcement of generalized imitation in young children. Journal of Experimental Child Psychology, 1, 37-39.

Bennett, F. C. & Guralnick, M.J. (1991). Effectiveness of developmental intervention in the first five years of life. Pediatric Clinics of North America, 38 (6), 1513-1528.

Bryson, S. E., Clark, B. S. and Smith, I. (1988). First report of a Canadian epidemiological study of autistic syndromes. Journal of Child Psychology and Psychiatry, 29 (4), 433-445.

Cattell-Gordon, D & Cattell-Gordon, D. (1998). The development of an effective applied behavior analysis program for a young child with autism. Infants and Young Children, 10 (3), 79-85.

Dawson, G. & Osterling, J. (1997). Early intervention in autism. In M.J. Guralnick (Ed.), The Effectiveness of Early Behavioral Intervention (pp.307-326). Baltimore: Paul H. Brookes Publishing

Fenske, E. C., Zalenski, S., Krantz, P. J. and McClannahan, L. E.(1985). Age at intervention and treatment outcome for autistic children in a comprehensive intervention program. Analysis and Intervention on Developmental Disabilities, 5 (1), 49-58.

Ferster, C. B. (1961). Positive reinforcement and behavioral deficits of autistic children. Child Development, 32, 437-456.

Ferster, C. B. & DeMyer, M. A. (1962). A method for the experimental analysis of the behavior of autistic children. American Journal of Orthopsychiatry, 32, 89-98.

Ford, L., Riggs, K. S., Nissenbaum, M. and LaRaia, J. (1994). Facilitating desired behavior in the preschool child with autism: A case study. Contemporary Education, 65 (3), 148-151.

Fotheringham, J. B. (1991). Autism: Its primary psychological and neurological deficit. Canadian Journal of Psychiatry, 36, 686-692.

Foxx, R. M. (1993). Rapid effects awaiting independent replication. American Journal on Mental Retardation, 97 (4), 375-376.

Goodman, J. F. (1992). When Slow is Fast Enough: Educating the Delayed Preschool Child. New York, New York: The Guilford Press.

Green, G. (1996). Early behavioral intervention for autism: What does research tell us? In C. Maurice (Ed.), Green, G. (Ed.), and Luce, S. C. (Ed.) Behavioral Intervention for Young Children With Autism: A Manual for Parents and Professionals (pp. 29-44). Austin, Texas: Pro-ed.

Gresham, F. M. & MacMillan, D. L. (1997). Autistic Recovery? An analysis and critique of the empirical evidence on the Early Intervention Project. Behavioral Disorders, 22 (4), 185-201.

Gresham, F. M. & MacMillan, D. L. (1997). Denial and defensiveness in the place of fact and reason: Rejoinder to Smith and Lovaas. Behavioral Disorders, 22 (4), 219-230.

Gresham, F. M. & MacMillan, D. L. (1998). Early intervention Project: Can its claims be substantiated and its effects replicated? Journal of Autism and Developmental Disorders, 28 (1), 5-13.

Guralnick, M. J. (1997). (Ed.) The Effectiveness of Early Intervention, Toronto: Paul H. Brookes Publishing.

Harris, S. L., Handleman, J.S., Gordon, R., Kristoff, B. and Fuentes, F. (1991). Changes in cognitive and language functioning of preschool children with autism. Journal of Autism and Developmental Disorders, 21 (3), 281-290.

Hewett, J. M. (1965). Teaching speech to an autistic child through operant conditioning. American Journal of Orthopsychiatry, 35, 927-936.

Howlin, P. & Rutter, M. (1987). Treatment of Autistic Children, Toronto: John Wiley and Sons

Kanner, L. (1943). Autistic disturbances of affective contact. Nervous Child, 2, 217-251.

Kazdin, A. E. (1993). Replication and extension of behavioral treatment of autistic disorder. American Journal on Mental Retardation, 97 (4), 377-380.

Koegel, R. L. & Koegel, L. K. (1995). (Ed.) Teaching Children with Autism: Strategies for Initiating Positive Interactions and Improving Opportunities, Toronto: Paul H. Brookes Publishing.

Kohler, F. W. , Strain and Shearer (1996). Examining levels of social inclusion within an integrated preschool for children with autism. In L. K. Koegel (Eds.), R.L. Koegel (Eds.) and G. Dunlap (Eds.), Positive Behavioral Supports: Including People with Difficult Behavior in the Community, (pp.305-322), Toronto: Paul H. Brookes Publishing.

Lovaas, O. I. (1987). Behavioral treatment and normal educational and intellectual functioning in young autistic children. Journal of Consulting and Clinical Psychology, 55, 3-9.

Lovaas, O. I., Berberich, J. P., Perloff, B. F. and Schaeffer, B. (1966). Acquisition of imitative speech by schizophrenic children. Science, 151, 705-707.

Luce, S. C., Christian, W. P., Anderson, S. R., Troy, P. J. and Larsson, E. V. (1992). Development of a continuum of services for children and adults with autism and other severe behavior disorders. Research in Developmental Disorders, 13 (1), 9-25.

McCain, M. N. & Mustard, J. F. (1999). Reversing the Real Brain Drain: Early Years Study Final Report. Toronto: Publications Ontario.

McClannahan, L. E. & Krantz, P. J. (1997). Princeton Child Development Institute. Behavior and Social Issues, 7 (1) 65-68.

McEachin, J. J., Smith, T. and Lovaas, O. I. (1993). Long-term outcome for children with autism who received early intensive behavioral treatment. American Journal on Mental Retardation, 97 (4), 359-372.

Maurer, R. G. & Damasio, A. R. (1982). Childhood autism from the point of view of behavioral neurology. Journal of Autism and Developmental Disorders, 12 (2), 195-205.

Maurice, C. (Ed.), Green, G., (Ed.), and Luce, S. C. (Ed.), (1996). Behavior Intervention for Young Children with Autism: A Manual for Parents and Professionals, Austin, Texas: Pro-ed.

Menolascino, F. J. & Eyde, D. R. (1979). Biophysical basis of autism. Journal of Council for Children with Behavioral Disorders, 5 (1), 41-47.

Metz, J. R. (1965). Conditioning generalized imitation in autistic children. Journal of Experimental Child Psychology, 2, 389-399.

Meyer, R. G. & Hardaway Osborne, Y. (1987). Case Studies in Abnormal Behavior, Toronto: Allyn and Baron.

Mulick, J. A. (1999). Making a difference: Comments on Weiss. Behavior Interventions, 14 (1), 29-34.

Ornitz, E. M. & Ritvo, E. R. (1976). The syndrome of autism: A critical review. The American Journal of Psychiatry, 133 (6), 609-623.

Ozonoff, S. & Cathcart, K. (1998). Effectiveness of a home program intervention for young children with autism. Journal of Autism and Developmental Disorders, 28 (1), 25-32.

Ritvo, E. R. & Freeman, B. J. (1978). Current research on the syndrome of autism: The National Society for Autistic Children's definition of the syndrome of autism. American Academy of Child Psychiatry, 565-575.

Romanczyk, R. G. (1999). Comments on Weiss. Behavioral Interventions, 14 (1), 35-36.

Rosenberger-Dibiesse, J. & Coleman, M. (1986). Brief report: Preliminary evidence for multiple etiologies in autism. Journal of Autism and Developmental Disorders, 16 (3), 385-392.

Sheinkopf, S. J. & Siegel, B. (1998). Home-based behavioral treatment of young children with autism. Journal of Autism and Developmental Disorders, 28 (1), 15-23.

Schopler, E. (1989). Principles for directing both educational treatment and research. In C. Gillberg (Ed.) Diagnosis and Treatment of Autism, 167-183, New York: Plenum Press.

Sigman, M. & Capps, L. (1997). Children with Autism: A Developmental Perspective, London: Harvard University Press.

Smith, T. & Lovaas, O. I. (1997). The UCLA Young Autism Project: A reply to Gresham and MacMillan. Behavioral Disorders, 22 (4), 202-218.

Smith, T. & Lovaas, O. I. (1998). Intensive and early behavioral intervention with autism: The UCLA Young Autism Project. Infants and Young Children, 10 (3), 67-78.

Smith, T. (1999). Outcome of early intervention for children with autism. Clinical Psychology: Science and Practice, 6 (1), 33-49.

Waters, L. (1990). Reinforcing the empty fortress: An examination of recent research into the treatment of autism. Educational Studies, 16 (1), 3-16.

Weiss, M. J. (1999). Differential rates of skill acquisition and outcomes of early intensive behavioral intervention for autism. Behavior Interventions, 14 (1), 3-22.

Wing, L. (1979). Autistic Children: A Guide for Parents and Professionals. Seraucus, New Jersey: The Citadel Press.

Wolf, L. & Goldberg, B. (1986). Autistic children grow up: An eight to twenty-four year follow-up study. Canadian Journal of Psychiatry, 31, 550-556.

Wolf, M. M., Risely, T. and Mees, H. (1964). Application of operant conditioning procedures to the behavior problems of an autistic child. Behavior Research and Therapy, 1, 305-312.

Breinigsville, PA USA
26 August 2009
223027BV00004B/2/A